Queen Victoria
& The French Royal Families

Christina Croft

Contents

Prologue

Throughout the six decades of Queen Victoria's reign, France underwent immense political changes, fluctuating between monarchies, empires and republics. Relations between Britain and France were equally variable, as the shadow of Napoleon Bonaparte still hung over the collective memory, and it was widely believed on both sides of the Channel, that one day his successors would attempt to avenge the defeat of Waterloo.

Against this background, Queen Victoria was forced to navigate the tumultuous waters of international relations, balancing her personal feelings with her role as a constitutional monarch. Despite the mistrust between Britain and France, and the animosity between the Orléans and Bonaparte families, she succeeded in forming firm friendships with both King Louis Philippe d'Orléans, and Napoleon's nephew, Emperor Napoleon III, without compromising her position as Queen.

As disparate in their political outlook as they were in character, each, at different times, impressed and disappointed the Queen.

"If we compare [Napoleon III] with poor King Louis Philippe," she wrote, "I should say that the latter was possessed of vast knowledge upon all and every subject, of immense experience in public affairs, and of great activity of mind; whereas the Emperor possesses greater judgment and much greater firmness of purpose, but no experience of public affairs, nor mental application; he is endowed, as was the late King, with much fertility of imagination."

Although they would both betray her trust, she remained a faithful friend in times of crisis, and, when revolutions deprived them of their crowns, they turned to her to provide them a safe haven in England.

Part I – The Orléans Family

Chapter 1 – Deserving of the Highest Praise

On the day of her accession in June 1837, eighteen-year-old Queen Victoria was deeply touched to receive a letter from King Louis Philippe of France, offering his condolences on the death of her uncle and predecessor, William IV. After expressing his confidence in her ability to adapt to her new role, he went on to remind her of his friendship with her late father, the Duke of Kent, and concluded with an assurance of his 'attachment' to her.

It was not the first time that the King had corresponded with the young Queen. Soon after his own accession in 1830, he had sent her two hundred pounds in repayment of a loan from the late Duke; and, throughout her lonely childhood, he had regularly sent her gifts from himself and his wife, Queen Amélie.

While Queen Victoria happily returned his affection, she soon discovered that few of her associates shared her sentiments, as ministers and members of her extended family viewed him with suspicion and disdain. The Foreign Secretary, Lord Palmerston, thought him a cunning man 'in whom no solid trust can be reposed'[1]; and King William IV had openly described him as 'a puppet in the mob's hands.'

> "Kings ought not to allow themselves to talk publicly on such subjects," wrote Earl Grey. "But I am afraid discretion is not the most prominent amongst the good qualities of William IV. This language alarms me the more, as I am afraid it may proceed from the discussion of these matters with his Ministers."[2]

King William was, though, merely voicing the opinion of most of his countrymen, and his ministers, who recalled that Louis Philippe had actually welcomed the French Revolution, and his father had been a signatory to the death sentence of King Louis XVI. Queen Victoria's half-sister, Feodore, was equally contemptuous of him, calling him a usurper, and accusing him of having shamelessly used his friends to further his own ambition as he plotted his ascent to the throne.

Whether or not Feodore's accusations were justified, prior to the French Revolution of 1789, no one could have foreseen that Louis Philippe would one day be King. At the time of his birth on 6th October 1773, he appeared rather to be destined for a life of luxury and leisure as the eldest son of the Duke of Orléans[a] – and his immensely wealth wife, Louise of Bourbon-Penthièvre. It was true that the family moved in the highest circles, and Louis Philippe numbered Louis XVI and Marie Antoinette among his godparents, but a deep-rooted antipathy existed between the ruling House of Bourbon, and the House of Orléans. Notwithstanding his wealth and position as one of the most prominent men in France, the Duke espoused the republican beliefs of Jean-Jacques Rousseau and was a member of the radical Jacobin club, which promoted the benefits of a revolution. He frequently criticised the Bourbon court, and, as a result, Louis XVI mistrusted him, and Marie Antoinette despised him.

An indolent but kind-hearted boy, Louis Philippe was blind to the faults of his 'gay and even-tempered' father, whom the rest of the world viewed as an irascible libertine; and he was equally attached to his mother, a pious and long-suffering woman, who, hurt by her husband's constant philandering, 'bore the stamp of an incurable melancholy.'[3] Unlike her husband, she was always:

> "…very guarded in her conduct; good and indulgent to others, she never allowed herself to commit the slightest indiscretion. She loved her

---

[a] At the time of Louis Philippe's birth, his father was Duke of Chartres, but in 1775, he succeeded as Duke of Orléans, and Louis Philippe became Duke of Chartres.

husband with an affection that nothing could shake, an affection that cost her many a bitter pang."[4]

In spite of his parents' disparities and his father's infidelities, Louis Philippe enjoyed a carefree early childhood. In the company of his younger brothers, Montpensier and Beaujolais, and his sister and closest confidante, Adelaide, he ran cheerfully through the sumptuous Palais Royal in the heart of Paris, or the Chateau d'Eu in Normandy, untaxed by his solitary tutor: a singing master whose services were somewhat superfluous since his royal pupil 'had neither voice nor ear.'[5]

Not until Louis Philippe was nine years old did his father decide that he and his brothers required a more formal education, but, instead of entrusting them to the care of a clergyman or academic, he appointed as tutor his wife's lady-in-waiting and his own former mistress, Mme Stephanie de Genlis. While the Bourbon court gasped in horror at this 'ridiculous' decision, the beautiful Mme de Genlis diligently set about preparing a broad curriculum. She immediately replaced the singing master with an Italian valet and a German gardener, both of whom were ordered to speak to the boys only in their native languages; and created a detailed timetable, beginning at seven o'clock every morning and continuing until late in the evening. Between studies in mathematics, sciences, history and geography, there were periods of strenuous physical activity, and various practical lessons. The princes worked alongside gardeners, botanists, apothecaries, cabinet-makers, book-binders and various other craftsmen, who were instructed to teach them the necessary skills to earn their keep in the event of a dramatic change of fortune.

With uncanny foresight, Mme de Genlis was determined to strengthen their characters to deal with any eventuality, and, to that end, each evening she posed a series of questions concerning their behaviour, the answers to which they wrote in notebooks alongside a firm intention to improve the following day. Often, she dictated lengthy passages and platitudes, concerning their manners, relationships and the attributes of a gentleman.

"You will," she told them, for example, "know your friends if they never flatter you; if they give you salutary advice at the risk of displeasing you for the moment…You ought not to suffer any one of your friends to be accused of any offence against yourself without proofs, especially to your private ear. Distrust everyone who attempts to give you a bad opinion of your friends; envy is almost always the motive of these informations, and when they are not supported by positive proofs you ought to despise them, and impose silence by an air of coldness and of complete incredulity upon those who are the informers."[6]

Building her pupils' physical stamina was as important to Mme de Genlis as was strengthening their moral calibre. She had them sleep on simple wooden beds covered only by rough mats; and Louis Philippe was encouraged to walk up to fifteen miles a day with leaden soles on his shoes. The strict regime left him little time for leisure, and, as the poet and statesman, Lamartine, recorded:

"Education suppressed [childhood]…in the pupils of Madame de Genlis. Reflection, study, premeditation of every thought and act, replaced nature by study, and instinct by will. At seventeen years of age, the young prince had the maturity of advanced years."[7]

Rather than repelling him, Mme de Genlis' harsh methods so enraptured Louis Philippe that he became utterly infatuated by her, hanging on her every word like 'some half-witted boy that cannot exist away from his mentor.'[8] If the governess were flattered by such devotion, she took pains to conceal it from her pupil, warning him that it was:

"...childish and unmanly to be ever listening to, or fixing your eyes on me, and appearing so melancholy when you cannot sit by my side. You cannot imagine how ridiculous it makes you appear to others."[9]

The rebuke served only to increase the boy's infatuation with her; and even years later, after his marriage, he tactlessly told to his wife that Mme de Genlis was the only woman whom he had ever truly loved.

In spite of her harsh words, Mme de Genlis was delighted by her pupils, and was particularly gratified by Louis Philippe's progress. He was not, she wrote, caught up in frivolities as were many young men of rank, but rather he applied himself diligently to his studies. What was more, had 'an excellent heart, which is common to his brothers and sister, and which, joined to reflection, is capable of producing all other good qualities.'[10]

When, at the age of thirteen, he began a period of military training, his commanding officers were equally impressed by his commitment to his studies, and the ease with which he mixed with ordinary soldiers. There was no doubt, they concluded, that Mme de Genlis' methods were most beneficial in training him to carry out his duties with mature conscientiousness and sound judgement.

Not everyone, though, viewed the governess in such a favourable light. Louis Philippe's mother was envious of the affection that she inspired in her sons; and many society ladies thought her quite manly, having discarded her femininity for 'the culottes of a pedagogue'. Others described her as arrogant, self-promoting and attention-seeking, and they laughed that she took her harp with her on all of her travels and insisted on playing it at every opportunity.

"I did not like her," wrote Baroness d'Oberkirch, "in spite of her accomplishments and the charm of her conversation...nothing about her is natural. She is constantly in an attitude, as it were, thinking that her portrait, moral or physical, is being taken."[11]

More seriously, courtiers and ministers were disturbed that she spoke openly of the flaws of the Bourbon dynasty and impressed their father's radical views on her susceptible pupils. Like the Duke, Mme de Genlis supported calls for a revolution, and when, in July 1789, she heard that the Parisians were storming the Bastille, she hurried her pupils to the garden of the Beaumarchais, to witness the spectacle. Many years later, having seen the excesses of the revolution, she realised that it had been 'imprudent' to have taken the princes to such an event, but she still recalled the pleasure she had felt in seeing the rapid destruction of a fortress 'in which had been confined, and wherein had perished, without even a form of justice, so many innocent victims!'[12]

Swayed by his beloved governess's enthusiasm, Louis Philippe welcomed the revolution, and was so exuberant to hear that the right of primogeniture had been abolished that he threw his arms around his younger brother, Montpensier, rejoicing that they were now equals. His father was even more delighted by the downfall of Louis XVI, and was rumoured to have been at the front of the mob that marched into Marie Antoinette's bedroom at Versailles, demanding the head of the King. Whether or not the story were true, the Duke committed himself to the new regime, changing his name to Philippe Egalité and putting himself forward as a candidate for the National Convention, which would eventually enable him to vote in favour of the King's execution.

In spite of his initial burst of excitement, the revolution had little immediate impact on Louis Philippe. As his father retained his wealth and palaces, he quietly continued his education under the supervision of Mme de Genlis, until his seventeenth birthday when the Duke decided that he was old enough to serve his country. At that time, war had broken out between France and the combined forces of Prussia and Austria, and so Louis

Philippe dutifully joined his regiment on the Austrian front, taking Montpensier with him as his aide-de-camp. Both princes acquitted themselves well in battle, demonstrating such courage that their commanding officer reported to Convention in Paris:

> "Where all were brave, it is invidious to pick out any for special comment, yet I must name the Duc de Chartres and his brother, the Duc de Montpensier, since their extreme youth makes the courage and self-control shown by them in the midst of firing so prolonged a matter deserving of the highest praise."[13]

By then, though, as the full horror of the revolution began to unfold, Louis Philippe's initial enthusiasm was turning into disgust. The guillotine was never idle, and the streets of Paris were so drenched in blood that it became clear that the revolutionaries would not rest until every member of the extended Royal Family had been executed. The threat was so great that the Duke ordered Mme de Genlis to take his daughter, Adelaide, to the safety of England, from where the governess, appalled by the excess of violence, sent a petition to Paris, vainly pleading for mercy for the imprisoned King and Queen.

Egalité, meanwhile, discovered to his horror that the Convention was compiling lists of emigres in order to condemn them as traitors. He hurriedly wrote to Mme de Genlis, telling her return his daughter to France as quickly as possible, but no sooner had he sent the letter than he discovered that Adelaide's name had already been included on the list.

> "If you have not crossed the sea, " he wrote at once to the governess, "remain in England till further orders; if my courier meet you on the road after entering France, remain at the place where this note may reach you, and come not to Paris. Another messenger will let you know what is necessary to be done."[14]

By the time that the second letter reached them, Mme de Genlis and Adelaide had reached Dover, and, failing to grasp the seriousness of the situation, the governess decided to ignore the warning and continue on to Paris. When they arrived in the city, Egalité exploded with rage and, berating Mme de Genlis for ignoring his orders, before hastily arranging for her to take Adelaide to Switzerland.

From the battlefield, Louis Philippe was unaware of all that had happened but his disillusionment with the revolution intensified when he discovered that his father had voted to execute the King. Under the influence of his commanding officer, General Charles François Dumouriez, who was suspected of helping aristocrats to escape the guillotine, he wrote to his father, explaining his disenchantment and asking his permission to leave the army and the country. Egalité replied that he had a duty of allegiance to his regiment and to France, and so, for several weeks he struggled to continue with his duties, until Dumouriez told him that he was convinced he would have the support of the army if he were to begin peace negotiations with Austria before leading the troops back to Paris to restore the Bourbon dynasty in the person of the young Dauphin. Louis Philippe was agreed with his plan but Dumouriez had seriously misjudged the mood of the army, and when the anticipated support failed to materialise, he and Louis Philippe fled to Austria.

In Vienna they were welcomed by Archduke Karl, a younger brother of the Holy Roman Emperor, Francis II, who offered Louis Philippe a commission in the Austrian army, but, reluctant to take up arms against his own people, he declined the proposition, and asked instead for a passport to Switzerland so that he might visit his sister and Mme de Genlis.

Back in France, word of his desertion and Adelaide's escape, had dire consequences for the rest of their family. The Duke and Duchess of Orléans were arrested and imprisoned together with seventeen-year-old

Montpensier and thirteen-year-old Beaujolais. A few months later, in November 1793, the Duke was tried for treason and was sent to the guillotine, leaving his young sons to anticipate a similar fate for themselves.

Fearing for his own life, Louis Philippe knew that he could neither return to France nor remain in Switzerland, where republican spies were operating. To raise money to travel, he adopted a disguise and, under the pseudonym, Mr Corby, found work teaching mathematics at a local college until he was dismissed for disrupting the smooth running of the kitchens after getting the cook pregnant!

For the next three years, he endured a nomadic existence, travelling across the continent with few financial resources, and little news of what had happened to his family. Eventually, he made contact with the Duke of Kent, who was serving as a Major-General in Halifax, Nova Scotia, and who loaned him the two hundred pounds to enable him to visit Canada and the United States. In the autumn of 1796, he departed from Hamburg aboard the appropriately named *America,* and arrived in Pennsylvania in time to witness George Washington's farewell address to Congress, and the inauguration of his successor, John Adams.

Chapter 2 – The March of a Man Who Makes No Step

While Louis Philippe was settling comfortably into the basement of a cleric's house in Philadelphia, his mother had been freed from prison and was living in dire financial circumstances in Spain, but his brothers remained incarcerated in separate cells in a filthy gaol in Marseilles. Initially they had been thrown into 'a dark hole, about nine feet square, intolerably dirty and stinking,'[15] but, after four days they were removed to slightly larger rooms, which were still so dark and damp that Beaujolais' health began to fail.

His gaolers, taking pity on the young man, allowed to walk outside for a few minutes each day, which enabled him to make contact with Montpensier, who was convinced that escape was the only alternative to dying in captivity. Throughout their brief meetings, the brothers began to draw up a plan, with the help of Montpensier's faith valet, who had followed the brothers to Marseilles and was allow to make regular visits to his master. Beaujolais' escape was effected with remarkable ease as, while taking his daily exercise, he simply walked through the gates and on to the harbour where the valet had arranged for a boat to be waiting. When, though, Montpensier attempted to follow him by climbing out of a window, he lost his footing and fell thirty feet to the ground, breaking his leg in the process. Refusing to abandon his brother, Beaujolais returned to the prison and voluntarily handed himself over to his gaolers.

Week after week, their mother pleaded for their release but not until the violence of the revolution had begun to subside was it agreed that they would be freed on condition that they left Europe. A reputable officer, General Amédée Willot, arrived at the prison and informed them that a ship was waiting to take them to their brother in Philadelphia.

"The prisoners at first could scarcely credit their senses," the General recorded. "They looked steadfastly at each other; then, throwing themselves into each other's arms, they began to cry, laugh, leap about the room, and for several minutes continued to manifest a temporary derangement."[16]

Montpensier wrote later:

"It is impossible to describe the sensation I experienced on crossing the drawbridge, and contrasting with the present moment, the frightful periods when I crossed it before — the first time on my entrance into that odious fort, where I remained two years and a half, and the second, on my unfortunate attempt to escape from it. The delightful idea that I was crossing it for the last time, could with difficulty impress itself on my mind, and I really could not help fancying myself in a dream, from which I was in dread every moment of being awoke."[17]

Louis Philippe, delighted at the prospect of a reunion, left the cleric's basement and rented a larger house from the Spanish Consul in which his brothers could recuperate from the stormy ninety-nine day voyage, and their years in prison. Throughout the winter, Montpensier and Beaujolais regained their strength, and with the first glimmer of spring, all three embark on an extended tour of the Americas. All that they saw so fascinated them that they would have ventured further had a lack of money not compelled them to return to Philadelphia. By unfortunate chance, the city had been struck by a yellow fever epidemic, similar to an outbreak which had killed over five thousand people in the city two years earlier. The majority of the wealthy citizens led to the country, but unable to afford that luxury, brothers had no option but to remain as, within two months, almost three hundred people died. 'The terror of the citizens for a while was very great,' the prominent physician, Benjamin

19

Rush, reported and it was computed that about two-thirds of the inhabitants left the city.'[18] Just as the heavy rains of autumn threatened to exacerbate the epidemic, the brothers were blessed by a stroke of good fortune. The French authorities had returned a part of her fortune to their mother, who sent them a substantial sum to continue their travels.

Again, they covered vast distances, visiting cities, camping in forests and plains, and enjoying spending time with the Native American Indians. Much to the bemusement of the natives, Louis Philippe, ever conscious of his health, always carried a lancet in his luggage so that he could bleed himself at the first sign of a fever. The people of one particular tribe observed that the procedure always seemed to achieve the desired result and so, when their Chief fell ill, they asked Louis Philippe to bleed him. Other members of the tribe were far more sceptical, and, fearing that he was some form of magic, insisted on taking his brothers hostage until they saw a positive outcome. Fortunately, the Chief quickly recovered and Louis Philippe was rewarded with the highest honour of being permitted to sleep between his patient's aunt and his mother.

Eventually, their travels took the princes to Cuba, where they received such harsh treatment from the Spanish authorities that decided to return to Europe. During their absence, a relatively unknown Corsican upstart, Napoleon Bonaparte, had seized power in France, and, unsure of how he would receive them, they decided that it would be better to settle in England. In February 1800, they arrived in Falmouth and, before disembarking, requested King George III's permission to enter his country. As the King sent a warm reply, the brothers journeyed to London where they soon gained possession of High Shot House on Crown Road in Twickenham. Their presence provoked a good deal of interest among the British aristocracy and it was not long before they were receiving invitations to the most fashionable events in the capital; and as Louis Philippe renewed his friendship with the Duke of Kent, he was regularly entertained by the Royal Family.

The years of incarceration had taken their toll on Montpensier's health, and within a few years of arriving in England, he was diagnosed with tuberculosis. By the spring of 1807, his condition had become so alarming that Louis Philippe decided to take him to Devon in the hope that the sea air might alleviate his symptoms. They had only travelled a few miles when Montpensier's became so breathless that they were forced to retire to an inn at Salt Hill near Windsor, where, a few days later, on 13th May, the thirty-two-year-old prince passed away. Louis Philippe accompanied his body back to London for a Requiem Mass in the Roman Catholic church in Portman Square, after which, thanks largely to the influence of the Duke of Kent, he was laid to rest in Westminster Abbey.

Louis Philippe returned with his younger brother to Twickenham where he devoted much of his time to studying the British political system and institutions. He maintained his friendship with the Royal Family, and by 1808 he had become so confident of the King's affection that he requested permission to marry his eighteen-year-old daughter, Princess Elizabeth. Affronted by the suggestion, the King declined his request on the grounds of Louis Philippe's Roman Catholicism, his impecuniousness, and the precariousness of his position.

His plan thwarted, Louis Philippe realised he had little hope of gaining an important position in England, and decided that he must seek his fortune elsewhere. By chance, at that time, the diminutive Beaujolais had begun to manifest symptoms of tuberculosis, which provided his elder brother with a perfect excuse to move him to warmer climes.

"I feel that my life is soon to terminate as Montpensier's did," Beaujolais objected. "What is the use of going so far to seek a tomb, and lose the consolation of dying in this retreat, where we have

21

at last found repose? Rather let us remain in this hospitable land; here, at least, I shall be permitted to die in a brother's arms, and share a brother's tomb."[19]

Disregarding his wishes, Louis Philippe insisted on taking him to Malta, but, as the change of air did nothing to alleviate his condition, he wrote to King Ferdinand of the Two Sicilies[b] to ask if he might take him to Palermo. While it appeared that he had made the request solely out of consideration for Beaujolais, it could hardly have escaped Louis Philippe's notice that King Ferdinand had several available daughters, marriage to any one of whom would improve his prospects and position. The King replied affirmatively but, before the letter reached Valletta, twenty-eight-year-old Beaujolais died.

King Ferdinand sent his condolences and invited Louis Philippe to continue with his plans to visit the island, in spite of much opposition from his wife, Queen Maria Carolina. As a younger sister of Marie Antoinette, Maria Carolina despised the Orléans family, and was so disgusted by the way that the French had treated her sister, that she vowed she would never speak the language again. Unsurprisingly, Louis Philippe anticipated a stormy first meeting, but it turned out to be more cordial than either he or the Queen had expected. After staring at him curiously for several seconds, she told him that she ought to hate him but, for some reason, she did not. She then summoned two of her daughters, Cristina and Amélie, who observed that Louis Philippe was:

> "...of middle height, inclined to be stout; he is neither handsome nor ugly. He has the features of the House of Bourbon and is very polite and well-educated."[20]

---

[b] The Kingdom of the Two Sicilies was the largest of the Italian states prior to unification. It comprised the Kingdom of Sicily and the Kingdom of Naples.

For all their differences, Louis Philippe and Maria Carolina soon found they had a common enemy – Napoleon Bonaparte, whose rise to power prevented the former from returning to France to claim his family's estates; and whose conquest of Naples had forced the latter and her husband to abandon the greater part of their Kingdom and retreat to the island of Sicily. Their shared dislike of Napoleon provided a modicum of rapport between Louis Philippe and the Queen, and, in the days that followed, he succeeded in ingratiating himself with the rest of the family, particularly twenty-five-year-old Amélie. When the King and Queen realised that their daughter had become so enamoured of their guest that she was openly speaking of marriage, they desperately tried to quash the idea by reminding her that Louis Philippe had no money and was harbouring unrealistic ambitions of returning to France to seize the throne.

In the meantime, however, Louis Philippe had invited his sister, Adelaide, to the island, and, as she struck up a warm friendship with Amélie, she encouraged her to believe that, with continued persuasion, her father would relent. This time the King said that he had insufficient money to provide her with a dowry, but, even when Louis Philippe countered that a dowry was of no consequence to him, he still refused to give the couple his blessing, until Amélie threatened to run away to a convent, and he finally yielded.

A few days before the wedding, the King Ferdinand fell downstairs and broke his leg, and so, on 19th November 1809, a preliminary service was held in his bedroom. This was followed by a longer ceremony in the Chapel Royal, where Amélie was so nervous that, 'my limbs tottered under me' until her bridegroom 'pronounced his 'Yes' in such a resolute voice that it gave me courage.'[21]

It was clear to everyone that Amélie was deeply in love with her new husband, but it was equally clear to his critics that to Louis Philippe the marriage was chiefly a

23

means of furthering his ambition. His wife's greatest asset, he explained, was her resemblance to his mother; and in a letter to a friend he expressed greater delight in the advantageousness of the match than in any genuine feeling for his bride:

> "What a benefit it will be to me! What a slap at prejudice! What a means of reconciliation with the elder branch of my family, and of entering into close relations with the royal family of Austria! What an advantage for me to marry a Bourbon!"[22]

As a wedding gift, King Ferdinand gave the couple the magnificent eighteenth-century Palazza Santa Teresa, renamed the Palazza d'Orléans where they were soon joined by Louis Philippe's beloved sister, Adelaide. For six months the two women lived happily together, while Louis Philippe became increasingly restless, feeling that his talents were being stifled. In the spring of 1810, he travelled to Cadiz to offer advice to the Spanish military as to how to repel Napoleon's armies, and he was still in Spain six month later, when Amélie gave birth to the first of their ten children – a son named Ferdinand.

When he eventually returned to the island, Louis Philippe's relationship with his mother-in-law rapidly deteriorated. Convinced that the success of the French Revolution was due to Louis XVI's vacillations, she had come to the conclusion that the only means of securing stability in Sicily was to ignore any popular demands which could weaken the King's authority. To Louis Philippe's dismay, she persuaded her husband to behave with autocratic intransigence, dismissing all calls for justifiable reforms, without discussion. The regime became so tyrannical that the British, on whom the King depended, threatened to withdraw their support; and matters came to a head when, despite objections from the aristocracy, she insisted on raising exorbitant taxes to cover the costs of the army. When the British Ambassador warned her that, unless she modified her behaviour, his government would no longer provide financial and military assistance, she flew into such a rage that, for several days, she was confined to bed allegedly suffering from apoplexy[c].

When Louis Philippe defended the Ambassador, her antipathy towards him became so intense that she wrote to her daughter:

> "Since I committed the folly of taking him for my son-in-law, I must put up with him as your husband and the father of your child. But he ought to realise that legitimate authority is always successful, and that to it one must remain attached."[23]

By then, King Ferdinand realised that the only way to calm a volatile situation was to persuade the Queen to leave the country, while he unofficially abdicated in favour of his two-year-old grandson. Louis Philippe briefly entertained the hope that he would be named as regent, but, in the event the role was given to his brother-in-law, the Duke of Calabria. In 1813, sixty-one-year-old Maria Carolina returned to her native Vienna, where, a year later, she suffered a stroke and was found dead in bed on the morning of the 8th September.

While the Queen's departure eased the tension in Louis Philippe's household, it did little to reduce his anxiety about the constant political intrigues that plagued the island. He was so concerned about the threat of revolution that he kept a horse permanently saddled so he could flee at a moment's notice; and his habitual lack of money only added to his frustration. As his fortieth birthday came and went, it seemed that all hope of ever returning to France had come to an end, when, suddenly, on 14th April 1814, an English ship appeared in the harbour, bringing news that the Emperor Napoleon had been forced to abdicate and the Bourbon monarchy had been restored under Louis XVIII – a younger brother of

---

[c] Her behaviour was probably affected by the daily doses of opium which she took to relieve neuralgia.

the executed Louis XVI. Scarcely able to believe the news, Louis Philippe hurried to the hotel where the British Envoy was staying to discover whether or not it were true. On hearing that it was, he immediately contacted King Louis, seeking permission to return to France, and was overjoyed to receive a positive reply, which included an assurance that his ancestral estates would be restored to him.

A month later, he returned to the palace that he had not entered for over twenty years, to find much of it damaged or wrecked by revolutionaries and Napoleon's troops. Falling to his knees in tears, he kissed the marble floor, and vowed that he would restore it to its former glory. Over the next few years, he would spend more than eleven million francs on the restoration, turning his home into a centre for the most fashionable, intellectual and artistic members of Parisian society.

The day after his return to France, the King invited him to the Tuileries where he restored to him his military rank and position, but left him no doubt that the part that his family had played during the revolution was not forgotten. As the King greeted Louis Philippe's wife and mother with affection, he pointedly turned his back on Louis Philippe and Adelaide, refusing to acknowledge them. This snub made Louis Philippe more determined than ever to prove his allegiance to the crown, and an opportunity arose sooner than expected when, within weeks of the Bourbon restoration, Napoleon escaped from exile and marched towards Paris with an army of followers. As they approached Fontainebleau, the King hurried to Lille, where Louis Philippe persuaded him to leave the country without delay. As the King departed for Ghent, Louis Philippe arranged the safe passage of his own family to England, before journeying to Lyon to monitor the situation. Within days, it became clear that support for Napoleon was growing, and Louis Philippe followed the fugitives across the Channel.

Ironically, Napoleon's return to France coincided with an international conference in Vienna, designed to discuss the best means of establishing peace in the wake of the havoc caused by the Napoleon wars. It was widely agreed that, during his brief restoration, Louis XVIII had done little to secure his country's stability, and several delegates concurred with the Tsar of Russia that it would be better to replace him with Louis Philippe. Not everyone supported this proposition – the Duke of Wellington mocked the idea, stating that Louis Philippe would be 'merely a well-bred usurper'; and Louis XVIII was so affronted that, following Napoleon's ultimate defeat at Waterloo, he refused to allow the Orléans family back into the country.

For two more years, Louis Philippe remained with his wife and ever-increasing number of children at Twickenham, until his mother finally persuaded the King to allow him to return to France. From then onwards, the two men outwardly enjoyed a harmonious relationship, but, beneath the surface, mistrust and resentment festered.

> "The Duke of Orléans is the chief of a party without seeming to be," the King told a confidante. "His name is a threatening flag, his palace a rallying-place. He makes no stir, but I can see that he makes progress. This activity without movement is disquieting. How can you undertake to check the march of a man who makes no step?"[24]

To Louis Philippe's intense annoyance, the King refused to restore to him the title of *Royal* Highness, which his father had forfeited, and denied him any meaningful position. Once again, his ambitions appeared to have been thwarted, as he complained that the King viewed him as nothing more than 'a part of a procession, or as a hanging for a wall!'[25]

Louis XVIII, however, did not have long to enjoy the dubious pleasures of Kingship, and his final years were plagued by paranoia and illness. He lived in constant fear that Orléans family was planning to usurp him; and he was racked with anxiety about what would happen to France when his ultra-conservative brother, Charles, succeeded to the throne. To add to his woes, he contracted an excruciating gangrene in his legs and spine, which ultimately led to his agonising death in September 1824.

Louis VIII's concerns about his successor's ability to maintain the monarchy appeared to be unfounded when Charles X ascended the throne. At sixty-seven years old, Charles retained a youthful appearance, and his kindly manner endeared him to his people. His thick white hair accentuated the benevolence of his face, which was, according to Count d'Haussonville, 'always animated by an easy, perhaps a slightly commonplace smile, that of a man conscious that he was irresistible, and that he could, with a few amiable words, overcome all obstacles.'[26]

'An honest man,' in the opinion of the King of the Belgians, he was, 'a kind friend and honourable master, sincere in his opinions, anxious to do everything that was right.'[27] A week after his accession, he won universal acclaim for abolishing censorship and restoring the freedom of the press.

> "Happy is the Council of His Majesty to greet the new King with an act so worthy of him," reported a leading Parisian newspaper. "It is the banquet of this joyous accession; for to give liberty to the press is to give free course to the benedictions merited by Charles X."[28]

Unfortunately, his initial popularity led Charles to two erroneous conclusions. He became convinced that his people would accept all his decisions without question, and that the majority of them wanted a return to the way of life before the revolution. He, therefore, restored to Louis Philippe the title of Royal Highness with all the privileges and honours which had formerly belonged to the House of Orléans; and he insisted on compensating all those whose lands had been lost in the revolution, regardless of the burden this placed on the bourgeoisie tax payers.

While his coteries of advisors encourage him to believe that his popularity was increasing, he failed to recognise that unrest still stirred beneath a surface of calm, and, in the words of one of his earliest biographers, 'he believed the Revolution finished, and it had but begun.'[29]

Ignoring calls for a more liberal government, he clung to his reactionary advisors, and, in 1829, appointed as Prime Minister, the unpopular Jules de Polignac – a son of the much-maligned Duchess of Polignac, whose relationship with Marie Antoinette had been the subject of much malicious slander. Comparisons were immediately made between Marie Antoinette's attachment to her favourites, and Charles' insistence on appointing his cronies to positions of power. Consequently, even before Polignac had begun his premiership, he was viewed with mistrust and widely condemned.

Within twelve months, the first rumblings of revolution echoed through the country, and Charles was urged to dismiss Polignac in order to save the throne. He replied firmly that Louis XVI had yielded to such demands and had thereby been the author of his own downfalls, whereas, 'I had rather be led to execution on horseback than in a cart.'[30]

In the summer of 1830, in an effort to subdue his critics, he signed a series of edicts – the 'July Ordinances' – limiting the freedom of the press, dissolving the Chamber of Deputies, and preventing the middle classes from participating in elections. The decrees served only to intensify public anger, and, when riots erupted in Paris, he ordered troops into the city to restore order. The soldiers were easily outnumbered, and, by 27th July, crowds were swarming through the Louvre and the Tuileries, looting and calling for the downfall of the monarchy. At the height of the disturbances, advisors urged Charles and his son, the Dauphin, to abdicate in favour of his ten-year-old grandson, the Duke of Bordeaux, or even to hand the throne to Louis Philippe. Instead, he fled to the Petit Trianon at Versailles where, in desperation, he withdrew the July Ordinances and dismissed the unfortunate Polignac. Sadly for him, the concessions came too late, and, no sooner had the Dauphin arrived in Versailles to discuss the situation with him, than an alarmed officer rushed into the room warning that an angry mob was marching towards the palace. In a panic the King and the Dauphin fled to the Château de Rambouillet[d], and, by the beginning of August, it was clear that Charles' only hope of saving the dynasty was to abdicate in favour of his grandson. He, therefore, appointed Louis Philippe Lieutenant-General of the Kingdom and ordered him to serve as the boy's regent.

> "You will," he wrote, "therefore have, in your quality of lieutenant-general of the kingdom, to cause to be proclaimed the accession of Henry V to the crown. You will, furthermore, take all measures that befit you to regulate the forms of the Government during the minority of the new king."[31]

The appointment provoked a great deal of disagreement in Louis Philippe's household into turmoil, as his sister, who despised the Bourbons, urged him to seize the crown himself. His wife, Amélie, on the other hand, reminded him of his oath of allegiance to the King, and urged him to carry out Charles' orders.

Louis Philippe was still undecided when a group of bankers arrived at his estate in Neuilly to warn him that, unless he accepted the crown, the monarchy would collapse and the country would return to a state of anarchy. The Chamber of Deputies, they explained, had already reached the same conclusion and wished to appoint him as a constitutional monarch, not by hereditary right, but by the agreement of the people.

---

[d] A royal hunting lodge about thirty miles south-west of Paris

As soon as Louis Philippe accepted the proposal, Amélie burst into tears, sobbing that he would always be seen as a usurper. Her prediction was to prove accurate, for, although his sons later claimed that he had acted solely for the good of the country, his many critics asserted that his decision was based only on self-interest.

"He had neither courage enough to seize the crown which was offered to him, nor virtue enough to refuse it," wrote one of his detractors. "He would gladly have declined the crown if he had been sure of retaining his estates. The most powerful argument for accepting it was, that by so doing he could save his property."[32]

Whatever his true motives, on 9th August 1830, at the age of fifty-six Louis Philippe, eschewing a coronation to avoid unnecessary expense, was proclaimed the King of the French – the Citizen King.

Chapter 3 - All My Sons Are Brave; My Daughters Virtuous and Beautiful

Whatever accusations his critics might have levelled against him, all agreed that his domestic life was exemplary. By the time of his accession, he was the father of ten legitimate children, two of whom had died in infancy, and all of whom had been raised in relative simplicity in Twickenham. On returning to France, the family settled happily into the Chateau of Neuilly – a 'fine domain' surrounded by an enormous park, west of Paris – which was, according to one of the children:

> "…the favourite residence of my mother and father who created it, and year by year embellished it, and who delighted in their life there surrounded by their numerous children, whom they loved so tenderly, and who returned their love so warmly; it was also our favourite home."[33]

In keeping with his bourgeois image, Louis Philippe encouraged his sons to associate with people of different backgrounds, and, rather than following the traditional course of educating them at home, he arranged for them to attend a public school – the Lycée Henri IV in Paris. All five princes acquitted themselves well, earning praise for their studiousness and the ease with which they associated with their classmates.

> "The whole family," wrote Mme de Genlis, "…is truly the most interesting I ever knew. The members of it are charming by their personal attractions, their natural qualities and education, and by the reciprocal attachment of parents and children."[34]

The eldest son, Ferdinand, who succeeded his father as Duke of Orléans, was a particularly attractive, outgoing boy who had inherited his intellect from his mother, whose own youthful brilliance was attributed to her having been blessed by the pious bishop and future saint, Alphonsus Ligouri. Orléans' possessed a unique combination of self-confidence and sensitivity, which won him many devoted friends and admirers. 'That amiable child,' gushed Mme de Genlis, 'has such a feeling heart'[35]; and, a few years later, she returned to the same theme:

> "To a very handsome person, [he]...joins a very precocious judgment, and a demeanour extremely interesting by its softness and modesty."[36]

As he grew older, his patronage of the arts and genuine concern for the poor made won him popularity with the masses; and, in the words of one of his brothers, he was 'a charmer...of soldiers, of artists, of women.' His virtues, though, were offset by a fiery temper which, combined with his extreme loyalty to his father, alienated several politicians, who viewed him as intransigent and unapproachable.

Overshadowed by his elder brother, the second son, Louis, Duke of Nemours, quietly pursued his own eclectic interests, allowing Orléans to remain the centre of attention. Well-read and blessed with a virtually photographic memory, Nemours' sincerity led one wag to comment that 'he never took the trouble to tell a lie,' but his natural reticence gave him an air of aloofness which was often mistaken for arrogance. In reality, his reserve concealed a deeply spiritual nature, which created a strong bond between him and his mother, while one of his friends described him as 'simply a saint.'

> "The Duc de Nemours was a believer," wrote his confessor, "and acted up to his belief. He loved the ancient liturgy, the tradition and ritual of his church. He spoke little of his profoundest feelings, but he lived them."[37]

As was the custom, Nemours was commissioned as a colonel in a cavalry regiment when he was thirteen years old and, as he progressed through the ranks, he proved himself to be an able and courageous commander.

In spite of his aloof air, he endeared himself to the ordinary soldiers by his concern for their welfare; and stories abounded of his spontaneous generosity. On one occasion, for example, on being approached by a young officer in desperate need of money, he immediately opened his purse to give him all that had, humbly apologising that there was so little in it.

The third son, François, Prince of Joinville – known to his family as Hadji – had neither Orléans' outgoing personality nor Nemours' reserve but he soon earned a reputation for his intelligence and artistic ability. At the age of two, he impressed visitors by the clarity and extent of his vocabulary, and, according to a close acquaintance, he was:

> "…gentle, sometimes melancholy [and] had the air of a good young man who had few illusions about the future, and whose natural integrity did not allow him to deceive himself with the pettinesses of the present."[38]

Following his formal education, he opted for a naval career, which enabled him to use his artistic talents by publishing illustrated accounts of his extensive travels. An English commentator seeing his work, remarked that he was:

> "…a clever draughtsman and capital caricaturist; but if the first of these talents proved an unfailing source of delight to his parents, the second frequently inspired them with terror, especially his father, who never knew which of his ministers might become the next butt for his third son's pencil."[39]

Like Nemours, he showed himself to be courageous in battle, as when he was dining at Veracruz and his plate was shot from the table. Taking off his hat, he stood up and saluted his Mexican opponents, before leading his own regiment towards the enemy. In his capacity as commander, he was responsible for the arrest of one of the Mexican's leading generals, and, on his return to France, he was rewarded with a promotion and entry to the order of the Legion d'Honneur. During his life at sea, he enjoyed the camaraderie of his shipmates, with whom he shared a sailor's sense of humour. When his sister, Clementine, asked him to send her the complete costume of an American Indian Chief's wife, he returned from his travels and handed her a string of glass beads. Why, Clementine asked, had he not brought her the entire outfit, to which he responded, smiling, 'This is the complete dress. She never wore any other.'

When Louis Philippe's fourth son, Henri, Duke of Aumale, was only eight years old, his godfather, the immensely wealthy Prince of Condé, died, leaving him a vast fortune and numerous properties including the magnificent Chateau de Chantilly. This legacy came as a mixed blessing for it was impossible to discern whether or not his many admirers surrounded him for his personal attraction or for the lure of his riches. In the words of Princess Catherine Radziwill, he:

> "...made himself popular, with a low kind of popularity of which he never succeeded in getting rid during the whole course of his life; but still he was popular in his way...He was always considered to be the clever man of his family...There was much of chivalry in [his] nature, more so, perhaps, than in the character of his brothers, who were less princely in their manners and ways."[40]

During his schooldays, he won several prestigious prizes for rhetoric and history, before embarking on his military training with the Light Infantry at Fontainebleau. Like Nemours, he idolised his eldest brother, who promised that, as soon as his training was complete, he would take him on his first campaign.

True to his word, in 1840, when Aumale was eighteen years old, Orléan invited him to participate in an African expedition but, unprepared for the hardships of active service, he fell ill and was unable to serve in a planned battle. At his own request, Orléans arranged for him to watch the proceedings from the safety of an ambulance, but this did not prevent an admirer from telling the King that he had shown such courage in the field that the entire army hoped he would be rewarded with the Légion d'Honneur.

The youngest son, Antoine, Duke of Montpensier, bore an uncanny resemblance to his father in both character and appearance, and was widely believed to be his favourite child. As soon as he had completed his early education, he began his military training with the artillery, where he perfected his swordsmanship and shooting skills, and would go on to become one of the King's chief advisors.

While Louis Philippe encouraged his sons to associate with as many people as possible, Amélie insisted on keeping his daughters Louise, Marie and Clementine, cloistered to the point of suffocation, instilling in them a belief in the virtues of obedience and adherence to duty. Their sheltered upbringing could not, though, completely suppress their unique personalities, as Louise became known for her gentleness; Marie for her enthusiasm, artistic ability and high spirits; and Clementine for her beauty and intelligence.

'All my sons are brave; my daughters virtuous and beautiful,'[41] Louis Philippe declared proudly, but this did not prevent him from using them to sure up his own position and that of his country.

Within months of his accession, he saw an opportunity of extending his influence when the people of the Southern Netherlands rose up against their Dutch overlords and demanded independence. Following a conference in London, the new Kingdom of Belgium was established and Louis Philippe immediately recommended his son, Nemours, as a candidate from the throne. Due to British opposition, he was soon forced to withdraw Nemours' name, but was greatly irked to discover that the British had promoted their own candidate – Prince

Leopold of Saxe-Coburg-Saalfeld[e], the widowed son-in-law of King George IV. Suspecting that Leopold was nothing more than a British puppet, Louis Philippe vehemently objected to the suggestion and refused to consider a compromise of allowing Leopold to marry his eldest daughter, Louise. Although he had no doubt, he said, that Leopold was a perfect gentleman, there were 'family objections, prejudices perhaps, which are in the way of the projected union.'[42].

Regardless of Louis Philippe complaints, Leopold was chosen as King, and soon after his coronation, realising that he needed to secure a dynasty, he earnestly considered the many advantages of marrying Louise. Her Catholicism would appeal to his predominantly Roman Catholic subjects; and her presence in Brussels would win him French support in the event of a Dutch invasion. He therefore arranged a meeting with Louis Philippe at Compiègne and, using all his legendary charm, succeeded in persuading him that the union would be in the best interest of all parties.

For Leopold, this was to be purely a marriage of convenience; and for twenty-year-old Louise, the prospect of a philandering husband, who was twice her age, was anything but appealing. Nonetheless, she had been raised to do her duty, and, knowing that this was her father's will, she meekly complied with his wishes.

The wedding took place in Compiègne in August 1832, after which the couple made a solemn entrance into Brussels to be greeted by ecstatic crowds.

"The nation," wrote an observer, "was literally transported with joy at seeing their Queen, who was introducing the Catholic religion into the dynasty. Her complexion was white and rosy, and

---

[e] Leopold was the brother of Queen Victoria's mother, Victoire of Saxe-Coburg-Saalfeld. He had married George IV's daughter and heir, Charlotte of Wales in 1816. Charlotte died in childbirth eighteen months later.

her figure bore a family likeness to the two houses of which she was the issue. She had the features of the Bourbons, whilst her blonde hair and her general deportment reminded me of the Archduchesses."[43]

The wily Leopold then began trying to arrange matches between other members of his own and Louis Philippe's families. Seven years later, he was instrumental in bringing about the marriage of Louise's sister, Marie, and his nephew – Queen Victoria's cousin – Alexander of Württemberg.

Fortunately, this was a love match, and Marie's only regret was that the husband, whom she adored, did not share her Catholic faith. The wedding took place in autumn 1837, and, nine months later, Marie gave birth to a son. Her joy, however, was short-lived, as, a few weeks later she was diagnosed with tuberculosis and set out for the warmer climes of Pisa. When her brother, Nemours, heard of her illness, he hurried to Italy, arriving shortly before Christmas 1838, and was initially delighted to discover that she appeared far better than he had expected. Her cheerfulness and youth, he said, would surely lead to a full recovery, but he was soon disillusioned when her doctors informed him that there was no hope of a cure. Believing he had a spiritual duty to tell her that she was dying, he broke the news to Marie who responded with resignation. On 2nd January 1839, she received the sacraments, before pleading with her husband to convert to Catholicism and to adhere to his promise to raise their son in that faith. As her pain intensified throughout the rest of the day, she asked her brother to tell their mother how deeply she loved her, and added that she was glad she was not there to witness her suffering.

"She showed admirable courage, strength, resignation, true piety, holiness," wrote Nemours. "Her words were inspired, heavenly….Towards seven-thirty, although her sufferings were increasing, she removed the chain that she wore around her neck and told Alexander to wear it always. At five-past eight, her breathing stopped...Thus died this angel who set us all a great example. Nothing in the world can give an idea of this scene, which was an inspiration from Heaven. I am broken."[44]

Much to the surprise of Marie's friends, her distraught parents made no official announcement of her death, nor was the French court ordered into mourning. The King merely asked Nemours to bring her body back to France, where she was interred with due ceremony in the Chapel Royal at Dreux.

While the arranged marriages of Louis Philippe's daughters might be useful in cementing alliances, the marriage of his eldest son was vital to secure the succession. Unlike his eldest sister, however, Orléans was unwilling to accept his father's selection of his bride, and, by the time of his thirty-fifth birthday he had already rejected several eligible princesses. A year later, while visiting Germany, he met an ardent Francophile, Hélène, the younger daughter of the late Hereditary Grand Duke of Mecklenburg-Schwerin. A cousin of King Leopold of the Belgians, and niece of the Prussia King Friedrich Wilhelm III, Hélène was so fascinated by France that she had avidly studied its history and mastered the language fluently. Intelligent, attractive and benevolent, she had won the hearts of her own people, one of whom gushed to a visiting journalist:

"Oh, our Helena!...I have seen her pass our house so often as a little child! My wife and children also know her well, and could tell you how she is beloved."[45]

Orléans was instantly smitten by her many charms and it was obvious that she reciprocated his feelings. When, however, he returned to Schwerin a year later to ask for her hand in marriage, her brother, the new Grand Duke refused to sanction the match on the grounds that the French throne was so unstable. The French were equally reluctant to accept Orléans choice of bride, as questions were raised about the wisdom of his marrying a Protestant. Refusing to be deterred, Orléans firmly told the objectors:

> "I see inscribed in our fundamental code, in the first line, religious liberty as the most precious of all the liberties granted to the French; I do not understand why the Royal Family alone should be excluded from this benefit, which is perfectly in harmony with the reigning sentiments of French society."[46]

Critics were grudgingly forced to accept the logic of his argument, and, after much persuasion, the Grand Duke allowed the betrothal to take place on 5th April 1837. Ten days later Héléne and her step-mother set out for France, only to discover that the Archbishop of Paris had refused to allow the wedding to take place at Notre Dame Cathedral because the bride was not a Roman Catholic. Arrangements were quickly made for the ceremony to be conducted instead at Fontainbleau, where the bride charmed the congregation and silenced the objectors.

> "The young princess has truly a royal bearing;" wrote one witness, "though so youthful and even childlike in her appearance, she seems to govern all around her. Her countenance admirably accords with her intellect and character; it is an index of her soul; her eyes are radiant with intelligence and animation; it would be impossible to conceive of more dignity and ease of manner, void of boldness…She never lost self-possession for a moment, and I believe that God reigns in the very depths of her heart. She impresses the imagination like those princesses in fairy tales led by good genii into brilliant palaces."[47]

Sadly, the fairy tale was short lived, for, in the midst of the subsequent celebrations, several revellers were crushed to death on the Champs de Mars. The event was widely viewed as an ill-omen and Hélène became convinced that, much as she loved her husband, their marriage was doomed to disaster.

Five happy years went by and her fears appeared to be groundless as her love for Orléans deepened, and the birth of two sons – the Comte de Paris and the Duke of Chartres – added to her joy. Her journals and letters were filled with expressions of a profound contentment, despite Orléans frequent absences as he carried out his duties. He was, she wrote, 'my protector, my friend, my life' and when, following a trip to Africa, he was seriously ill for some weeks, she barely left his side. The only cloud in her otherwise sunny existence was Queen Amélie's constant attempts to control her, and her refusal to accept her Protestant faith.

In July 1842, Orléans set out to review the troops at Saint Omer, and Hélène, who was used to being apart from him for weeks at a time, commented brightly that this time, 'our separation will happily not be long.' Tragically, she spoke too soon, for, he had only travelled a short distance, when one of his horses bolted and he was hurled from the carriage. As he landed headfirst on the road, it soon became clear that his skull was fractured, and word was sent at once to his family, who hurried to the scene, but, by the time that they arrived, he had died without having regained consciousness.

Queen Amélie was so broken by his death that her hair reputedly turned completely white; while her daughter, the Queen of the Belgians bewailed the loss of 'the head, heart, soul of our family.'

"My poor dearest Louise, how my heart bleeds for her," Queen Victoria wrote to the King of the Belgians. "I know how she loved poor [Orléans] – and deservedly, for he was so noble and good. All our anxiety now is to hear how dear frail Hélène has borne this too dreadful loss. She loved him so, and he was so devoted to her. We can hardly think of anything but this terrible misfortune, and of all of you."[48]

Hélène, in fact, was bearing her grief with remarkable courage, sighing resignedly that, 'I was too proud of him so God has taken him from me as a punishment'[49]; but the tragedy had awoken in Louis Philippe an awareness of his own mortality and the necessity of preparing for the succession after his demise. Orléans' elder son, the Comte de Paris, was now the heir to the throne but there was every possibility that he would succeed before he reached his majority. It was vital, therefore, to prepare for a regency, and, as neither the King nor the Queen believed that Protestant Hélène was suited to the role, they chose instead their second son, Nemours.

This decision was so unpopular with a large section of the public that the press printed numerous articles stating that the Duke was disliked and was consequently unfit to act as regent. Swayed by such stories, a faction developed in favour of Hélène, which caused intense friction in the family, despite her protestations that she had done nothing to encourage the stories and wanted only to devote herself to her children's education. Nemours' supporters, meanwhile, rushed to his defence, publishing letters and articles asking what he had done to merit such disapproval.

> "L'air distingué, élégant, rêveur et patricien du prince, est peut-être le principal grief qu'on a contre lui. L'extérieur du Duc d'Orléans était noble; celui du Duc de Nemours est nobiliaire."[50]

Even his staunchest allies understood that he had accepted the role solely out of duty to his father and love for his late brother, but they feared that he was making little effort to endear himself to the public, and one his associates felt obliged to upbraid him for his natural reticence, reminding him that, 'he was now placed in a new position, which would require a very different line of conduct.'

Nemours agreed to try to present a more sociable face in public, but his situation was not helped by the fact that his wife, Queen Victoria's cousin, Victoire of Saxe-Coburg-Kohary, was equally unpopular. Both were viewed as having too great a sense of their own importance, and were mocked for adhering to ridiculous and obsolete Bourbon traditions. In their defence, the Duke and Duchess believed that the King's waning popularity was the result of his failure to give the Parisians the pomp and ceremony that they craved, and so, in their own way, they clung to outdated shows of etiquette, believing that this was the best means of maintaining the support of the people.

If, however, Victoire had failed to win the affection of the public, her piousness and docility had endeared her to Queen Amélie. The Queen had become so attached to her daughter-in-law that she controlled every aspect of her existence, refusing to allow her to leave the house without telling her exactly where she was going and when she would return. They attended Mass together each morning, and, at the Queen's insistence, spent the greater part of each day in each other's company. Unlike Héléne, Victoire appeared to be perfectly happy with this arrangement, wanting nothing more than to be a good wife, and mother to her three children.

The King of the Belgians was so delighted that his niece, Victoire, had married Nemours that he tried to strengthen his influence over the French Royal Family still further by encouraging his nephew Ernest of Saxe-Coburg-Gotha[f], to propose to Nemours' younger sister Clementine. When Ernest refused to be persuaded, King Leopold found an alternative nephew – Victoire's brother, August ('Gusti') of Saxe-Coburg Kohary. As a lowly lieutenant in the Austrian Hussars, the 'odd and inanimate' Gusti seemed entirely unsuited to the pretty and vivacious Clementine, but, to the surprise of the

---

[f] The elder brother of Queen Victoria's consort, Prince Albert.

43

extended family, she accepted his proposal, claiming that she was in love with him and was eagerly anticipating their life together in Vienna.

This, too, had been Gusti's plan, as he had assumed that, once they were married, the Austrian Emperor would offer him an immediate promotion and raise him to the status of Royal Highness. Both he and Clementine were much put out when the Emperor failed to do so, and, in a fit of pique, Gusti resigned his commission and announced that he was leaving the country to live with his new wife in France.

The wedding took place in Saint Cloud in April 1843, and, over the next five years Clementine gave birth to four children; a fifth – the future King Ferdinand of Bulgaria – being born thirteen years later in 1861. The family occupied a 'pleasant house' in Paris where Clementine excelled as a hostess, and was, according to one of her guests, 'amiable and intelligent, like all the members of her family whom I have ever known.'[51]

A month after his sister's wedding, Hadji, the Prince of Joinville, made a more advantageous match when he married Francisca di Braganza, a daughter of the Portuguese Emperor Pedro I of Brazil. The couple had first met when Hadji arrived in Rio di Janeiro as a naval officer in 1837. At the time, Francisca ('Chica') was only twelve years old, but when he returned to Brazil in early 1843, she had blossomed into an attractive young woman, whom Queen Victoria would later describe as 'a charming, sprightly, lively creature, with immense brown eyes'[52]. Their romance developed so quickly that just a few months later, on 1st May, they were married in Rio, where they remained for the rest of the year.

A great welcome party assembled to greet the prince and his wife on their return to France, but the ladies of the court were shocked when the Brazilian princess immediately requested parrot broth to ease her seasick stomach. In the months that followed, Chica continued to disconcert the stately ladies by her cheerful unconventionality, but they all agreed that she and Joinville were ideally suited, and rejoiced with them at the birth of a son and a daughter.

Five months after Joinville's wedding, his brother, Aumale, arrived in Naples to propose to his maternal cousin, Marie Carolina ('Lina') of the Two-Sicilies, whom he had never even seen before. The marriage was the Queen's idea and, while she made the wedding arrangements, Aumale merely complied with her wishes, and, with a feeling of excited anticipation, he prepared to meet his bride. The first meeting did not go entirely to plan, as Aumale confessed that he was a little disappointed by her appearance, but this did not prevent him from going through with the wedding, which took place in Naples in November 1844. A few days later, the couple returned to France where Queen Amélie was so delighted to welcome Lina, that it was widely remarked that she loved her as though she were her own daughter.

In spite of the inauspicious beginnings, sensible and docile Lina so adored her husband that one commentator noted that she saw the world through his eyes, adopted all his ideas, and supported him in all his undertakings. All in all, wrote Aumale's early biographer:

> "La duchessse était l'épouse idéale, la compagne fidèle des bons et des mauvais jours, celle dont la raison conseille, dont le courage réconforte et dont la tendresse console. Initiée aux pensées de son mari, associée parfois à ses travaux, lui servant tour à tour de lecteur et de secrétaire, elle ne le quittait que rarement.[g]"[53]

Aumale soon overcame his initial disappointment as he began to appreciate his wife's many qualities, and, what began as merely a marriage of convenience, soon

---

[g] 'The Duchess was an ideal spouse, a faithful companion in good and bad days, one whose reason counsels, whose courage comforts and whose tenderness consoles. Initiated into her husband's ideas and sometimes his work, she served as his reader and secretary and rarely left him.'

developed into a mutually loving relationship, blessed by the birth of a son, Louis Philippe, in September 1845. Sadly, over the next two decades six more children were born, none of whom survived beyond infancy.

Chapter 4 – The Queen's Earnest and Only Wish

When Louis Philippe accepted the crown, the Austrian Chancellor, Prince Metternich, gloomily predicted that:

> "...The Duke of Orléans, who, having been called to the throne neither by right of succession nor by the distinct and legitimate expression of the national will, can only maintain himself in power by flattering every party in turn, and yielding to the one that offers him the greatest chance of success, at the cost of whatever means."[54]

It did not take long for Louis Philippe to realise the accuracy of this prediction or to see that his reign would be filled with as many challenges as had beset his predecessors. From the start, the country was so divided that, although he had many supporters, he also had many opponents, who viewed him as a usurper. 'Legitimists' claimed that the Bourbons should have retained the throne; while the Bonapartists wanted Napoleon's heir to seize power; and republicans continued to demand the complete abolition of the monarchy. With adversaries on all sides, it was hardly surprising that as soon as Louis Philippe was proclaimed King, disturbances broke out in Paris. Although he quickly restored order by calming riding through the streets with his son, Nemours, the next decade was plagued by further strikes and riots.

> "What a bad state a country must be in," sighed Earl Grey. "...It is impossible to know who to rely on in France, and who is really master. How poor Louis Philippe must regret being no longer Duke of Orléans! and what a poor business it is being a King."[55]

To the great disappointment of many of his erstwhile supporters, the Citizen King surrounded himself with bourgeoisie bankers and wealthy industrialists, who failed to warn him of the depths of dissatisfaction among the working classes. Relying solely on the counsel of his trusted advisors, he high-handedly refused to extend the franchise to anyone who did not own their own property; and, in an effort to restore unity and order, he became increasingly autocratic.

His authoritarian stance increased the number of his enemies, and he soon became the target of several assassination attempts, the most bizarre of which occurred in 1835 during the celebrations of the July Revolution.

A Corsican named Giuseppe Fieschi had begun life as humble shepherd before enlisting in the army and serving in several campaigns in Tuscany and Naples. He soon came to the conclusion that stealing was more lucrative than soldiering, and, after making a reasonable living as a thief, he travelled to Paris, where he made the acquaintance of an ardent republican, Pierre Moray. Fieschi was so impressed by Moray that decided that he had a duty to kill the King, and for several months the two men worked together to create a suitable weapon for that purpose. With the financial support of a grocer named Pepin, they eventually came up with 'the infernal machine' – a frame to which twenty muskets were attached and arranged to fire simultaneously. The machine was placed in an upstairs window of a house on the Boulevard du Temple, overlooking to route that the royal party would take to the celebrations.

On 25th July, as the King and his sons approached, the confident conspirators discharged the guns, killing eighteen people including several bystanders, but the King escaped with nothing more than a graze on his forehead from a passing bullet. The conspirators were immediately arrested and sent to the guillotine.

A year later, Louis Philippe had a second lucky escape when a disabled former soldier, Louis Alibaud, fired into his carriage as it approached the Pont Royale. Amazingly, as the very moment that the gun was discharged, the King lowered his head to salute the

National Guard, and the bullet passed over him into the roof of the carriage. At his trial, Alibaud attempted to justify his actions by claiming that:

> "Since the king first put Paris into a state of siege; since he chose to govern instead of reigning; since he caused citizens to be massacred in the streets of Lyons, and in the cloisters of Saint-Merry; his reign is a reign of infamy; I wished to kill the King."[56]

Over the next decade, at least six more unsuccessful attempts were made on Louis Philippe's life, all of which served as constant reminders of the precariousness of his position and the growing dissatisfaction with his domestic policies. He could, though, take some comfort from his achievement overseas, when, building on the efforts of his predecessor, Charles X, he succeeded in establishing a prosperous colony in North Africa.

A month before he was deposed, Charles had attempted to distract from the unrest at home by sending an army to seize Algeria from the Turks. In June 1830, thirty-seven-thousand Frenchmen, under the command of General de Bourmant, landed at Sidi-Ferruch and, although four hundred Frenchmen were lost in the subsequent invasion, Turkish casualties numbered over ten thousand. On July 5th Bourmant led the victorious troops into the capital, Algiers, but the outbreak of the July Revolution prevented him from completing the annexation.

Over the next four years, the charismatic Algerian ruler, Abd el-Kader, fought to repel the invaders until February 1834, when he and a French General, Louis Alexis Desmichels, reached an agreement whereby part of the country was annexed by France, and the remaining territories were left under the control of 'the sovereign of believers,' el-Kader. Within a matter of months, the French began to break the terms of the agreement, by repeatedly marching into el-Kadir's provinces before launching a full invasion.

Three of Louis Philippe's sons – Orléans, Nemours and Aumale – saw active service in the ensuing war, all claiming that their aim was to bring civilisation and Christianity to the country, but as the conflict dragged on for over two years with heavy losses on both sides, the French resorted to underhand means to achieve their objective. After calling for peace negotiations, they succeeded in arranging a second treaty with Abd el-Khadir, while making secret preparations for the seizure of the strategic city of Constantine. A few months later, Nemours ordered his troops to besiege the city and after only three days of constant bombardment, the citizens were forced to surrender.

News of the capture of Constantine sparked spontaneous rejoicing throughout Paris, where church bells rang and crowds attended services of Thanksgiving. In Constantine itself, the soldiers were rewarded for their success with a series of celebrations; and Louis Philippe was hailed as the King who had succeeded in evangelising the heathen Algerians.

> "All hostilities have, now ceased," reported the Journal of the London Statistical Society in 1839, "and France is occupied in securing her sway by the extension of civilization, the establishment of the means of internal communication, and the active promotion of commerce and national industry."[57]

Beneath the triumphant overtures, all was not quite as it seemed, for the fighting would continue for a further four decades, and a third of the entire French army was required to maintain control of the region.

Distant conquests could not compensate for a lack of good relations with other European nations, and, although, through the marriage of his daughter and King Leopold, Louis Philippe had forged strong links with Belgium, other nations and their rulers continued to view him with disdain. Tsar Nicholas I of Russia stated openly that Louis Philippe's method of seizing the throne undermined the sacred 'principle of legitimacy', and he was so concerned that the French would seek to expand their territories that he sent an emissary to Prussia to assure King Friedrich Wilhelm that, should he find himself at war with France, Russia would willingly support him. The Austrians were equally suspicious of Louis Philippe's personal ambitions, and two months after his accession, Prince Metternich informed a French diplomat that:

> "The Emperor [of Austria] abhors what has recently taken place in France; in doing so, he is not indulging a preference for any particular form of Government, or for any particular system...The Emperor's deep, irresistible feeling is that the present order of things in France cannot last."[58]

In response, Louis Philippe wrote to Emperor Francis, explaining his reasons for accepting the throne, and assuring him that ties of kinship, fellow-feeling and a love of peace inspired in him a strong desire to maintain goodwill between their two nations. At the Emperor's insistence, the Austrian ministers finally acknowledged Louis Philippe's legitimacy, but, in spite of this outward show of amity, they continued to mistrust him. Prince Metternich openly described him as incredibly arrogant; and, when the Duke of Reichstadt[h] was invited to meet the French Ambassador, he replied that he had willingly met Ambassadors from all over the world, 'but as for Louis Philippe's representative, he would certainly not go near him since the former had less right to the throne of France than he had himself, and he saw no reason why he should pay any deference to a usurper.'[59]

---

[h] The Duke of Reichstadt, also known as Napoleon II, was the son of Napoleon Bonaparte and had spent most of his life in Austria, serving in the Emperor's army.

Through his friendship with the late Duke of Kent, and the years he had spent in England, Louis Philippe might well have expected support from King William IV and his government. King William, though, deeply mistrusted him, telling an aide that:

> "I must say that whether at peace or at war with that country, I shall always consider her as our natural enemy, and whoever may be her King, I shall keep a watchful eye for the purpose of repressing her ambitions."[60]

From the moment of his accession, Louis Philippe did nothing to assuage the King's suspicions, but rather gave rise to even greater mistrust by his efforts to extend his influence beyond his own borders. Soon after being proclaimed King, he let it be known that he was trying to arrange a 'happy event' – the marriage of his son, Nemours, to the young Queen of Portugal, Maria II de la Gloria, in the hope that soon afterwards Spain and Portugal would be 'united under the same sceptre.' When the other European powers refused to accept this arrangement, Louis Philippe suggested that instead the Portuguese Queen should marry his nephew, Prince Charles of Naples[i]. Although his plans came to nothing, they demonstrated his ambitions, and relations between Britain and France deteriorated further when he recommended Nemours for the throne of Belgium. The Foreign Secretary, Palmerston, was so incensed that he warned that if the proposal were accepted, Britain would have no option but to declare war.

> "I must say," he added, "that if the choice falls on Nemours, and the King of the French accepts, it will be a proof that the policy of France is like an infection clinging to the walls of the dwelling, and breaking out in every successive occupant."[61]

---

[i] In the event, Maria II de la Gloria married Queen Victoria's uncle, Prince Ferdinand of Saxe-Coburg-Kohary,

The British Ambassador to Spain was equally sceptical about Louis Philippe's interference in the Iberian Peninsula, and, when civil war erupted, a British minister in Madrid reported that the conflict was due 'more to the conduct of Louis Philippe than anything else, who…is playing false diabolically.'[62]

The slightly biased Princess Dorothea Lieven claimed to be unable to comprehend the extent of the animosity towards Louis Philippe, but even she added that he was:

> '…one of those persons whose capacity will be found to bear the character of cunning rather than wisdom, and that in the end, in seeking selfishly his own advantage, he will lose the confidence and support of those in whom, by a straightforward course, he might have found supporters.'[63]

In view of William IV's antipathy towards him, it was unsurprising that Louis Philippe sought to ingratiate himself with Queen Victoria the moment that her predecessor died. Fortunately for him, Victoria was devoted to his daughter, Louise, Queen of the Belgians, whom she considered, 'quite delightful and charming…gay and merry'. 'Belgium,' she wrote to her uncle, King Leopold '– which was in former times the cause of discord between England and France – becomes now a mutual tie to keep them together.'[64] When Louise's brothers visited England, they went out of their way to charm the impressionable young Queen, who was instantly drawn to Orléans' amusing conversation and handsome appearance, and flattered when, one evening at the theatre, he made his way to her box and sat down beside her. She was only slightly less enchanted by Nemours, who was, she wrote, 'good-looking but not so much so as his brother the Duke of Orleans. [He] is extremely pleasing but rather timid' and 'has such a good kind expression in his face.'[65]

It did not take long, though, for the Queen to realise that her personal affection for the French Royal

Family was not sufficient to maintain good relations between the two countries. Only three years after her accession, a volatile situation in Egypt, again brought France and Britain to the brink of war.

In 1840, the Egyptian Khedive, Mohammed Ali Pasha, attempted to establish his own kingdom within the Ottoman Empire – a move supported by the French Prime Minister, Adolphe Thiers, who hoped that in return Ali Pasha would to promote French interests in Africa. The British, Prussians and Austrians, however, formed an alliance to protect the Ottoman Sultan, and the threat of war was so great that when Louis Philippe's son, Joinville, was sent to St Helena to retrieve Napoleon's ashes, he remarked that if he were attacked by the British, he would blow up his own ship to ensure that 'the ashes of Napoleon shall never fall into the hands of the English.'[66]

Queen Victoria found herself in a serious dilemma, for while Palmerston and most of her countrymen were condemning the French and their King, her uncle, the King of the Belgians was bombarding her with letters, warning that war would 'set Europe ablaze' and suggesting that Palmerston was prejudiced and over-reacting.

> "I cannot understand," he wrote, "what has rendered Palmerston so extremely hostile to the King and Government of France. A little civility would have gone a great way with the French."[67]

Even in Britain, there were some who considered Palmerston's language extreme. The Whig politician, Earl Grey, felt that he had exposed his country to the danger of war 'for an object that was not worth the expense of preparing a single ship,' although he agreed that it was wise to be wary of French ambitions, and warned the government to tread carefully for fear of leaving Louis Philippe 'powerless to resist the storm of bad passions, which, if uncontrolled, must precipitate France into a new revolutionary war, and open another Iliad of calamity to all Europe.'[68]

In September 1840, the allies sent a combined force to the region, and the French, realising that they were outnumbered, promptly withdrew their support for the Khedive. The King of the Belgians used the situation to Louis Philippe's advantage by writing to Queen Victoria that he was responsible for the peaceful outcome having pressurised the more bellicose Thiers into finding a pacific solution. As Queen Victoria willingly accepted this explanation, Palmerston was so incensed that he sent her a strongly-worded letter, claiming it was his duty to inform her that:

> "...the appeals made to your Majesty's good feelings by the King of the French...have no foundation in truth, and are only exertions of skilful diplomacy."[69]

Affronted by the tone of his letter, the Queen dismissed his suggestion, telling him that she:

> "...cannot believe that the appeals made to her by the King of the French are only exertions of skilful diplomacy. The Queen's earnest and only wish is peace, and a maintenance of friendly relations with her allies, consistent with the honour and dignity of her country."[70]

Although the immediate crisis had passed, relations between Britain and France remained tense; and other European monarchs became so suspicious of Louis Philippe's ambition that, as he complained to Prince Albert, he felt that all his family had been 'placed under a ban, as though they were lepers, by all Europe, and by every Court, and expelled from the society of reigning Houses.'[71]

Sympathising with his plight, Queen Victoria decided to demonstrate her support for the King by arranging to visit him at the Chateau d'Eu. Although their meeting would be brief and unofficial, it was of major significance being the Queen's first journey abroad, and the first time that a reigning British monarch had visited France since the famous meeting of Henry VIII and Francois I on the Field of the Cloth of Gold. Consequently, Louis Philippe rated 'very highly the visit of the most powerful Sovereign in Europe,'[72] and was determined to make the event a memorable occasion.

A few days before his guests were due to arrive, a near catastrophe threatened to jeopardise the visit. As the King and Queen were travelling with their grandson, the Comte de Paris, along the banks of a canal, one of their horses, startled by the sound of a lock gate, bolted and fell into the water, almost dragging the carriage down with him. The Queen, recalling Orléans' fatal accident, instantly burst into tears, but the driver had the presence of mind to turn the other horses away from the bank, and succeeded in rescuing the passengers from danger.

Although he was badly shaken, the King insisted on continuing his preparations for Queen Victoria's visit, and, on the day of her arrival, he set out on a barge with two of his sons to meet Royal Yacht *Victoria & Albert* as it drew into the harbour. With obvious delight, he boarded the yacht to greet his guests before accompanying them to the chateau where Queen Amélie and Queen Louise of the Belgians were waiting. British journalists, lining the route, watched the procession with a combination of fascination and trepidation, half-expecting the Queen to be given a hostile reception. To their relief and surprise, however, enthusiastic crowds cheered and applauded as they jostled and vied with one another to gain a glimpse of the 'legendary' Queen.

Over the next three days, Louis Philippe went out of his way to ensure that his guests enjoyed their visit, and his efforts were not in vain:

> "…We are in the midst of this admirable and truly amiable family…where we feel quite at home, and as if we were one of them," Queen Victoria wrote to the King of the Belgians. "Our reception by the

dear King and Queen has been most kind, and by the people really gratifying."[73]

On returning home, she enthused so effusively about the French Royal Family that Lord Melbourne felt it necessary to remind her it had been a private visit and was of no political significance. He urged her to ensure that it did not lead to any treaties between the two countries, or give the impression that she was involving herself in international affairs.

The Duke of Wellington was equally anxious, writing to a friend that visit:

"...will of course create a great sensation on the Continent, and I am not surprised that King Louis Philippe should be gratified beyond measure by that paid to him at the Chateau d'Eu! But excepting the personal compliment...those would be in error who should imagine that there was any motive for the visit; or that it can be followed by any political or other consequence whatever!"[74]

Louis Philippe was indeed 'gratified beyond measure', and was so determined to strengthen the bond that he had established with the Queen that, she had barely left France before he began preparations for an official State Visit to England the following year. Queen Amélie, though equally eager to continue the friendship, was far less enthusiastic about the proposed visit due to her husband's increasing frailty and the fear that the journey might prove too much for him. Through her daughter, the Queen of the Belgians, she approached Queen Victoria, explaining her worries and describing his needs.

"He is naturally so imprudent," she wrote, "and thinks so little about himself, that he requires to be watched to prevent his doing what is injurious to himself. Though my father has sent over his horses, my mother begs you, if possible, to prevent his riding at all. He is one of the most easy beings to please, and his eventful life has used him to everything. A hard bed and a large table for papers are all that he requires in his room."[75]

A couple of months before he was due to depart, the resurgence of a long-standing dispute between Britain and France cast a shadow over the proposed visit. For over two decades, British Protestant and French Catholic missionaries had been active on the island of Tahiti, vying with one another to gain the upper-hand. The French repeatedly accused the British of turning the people against them; and the London Missionary Society claimed that the French priests thought it 'more acceptable to Him they professed to serve to enter into and destroy other men's labours than to seek to bring the light of truth to isles yet dwelling in darkness.'[76]

When the British Consul, a Protestant missionary named George Pritchard, expelled two French priests from the island, the French responded by sending Admiral Dupetit-Thouars to demand reparation. In 1843, the Admiral expelled two British missionaries and declared Tahiti a French protectorate. The Prime Minister, Robert Peel, protested vehemently in the House of Commons, in response to which the French Government and Louis Philippe himself denounced Dupetit-Thouars, stating that he had no authority for his actions. Although Peel doubted this explanation, he had no evidence to accuse the King directly and so, as the matter was temporarily laid to rest, it was agreed that the visit would go ahead as planned.

Again journalists' fears of a hostile reception were unfounded, as enthusiastic crowds turned out to welcome the King to Portsmouth, where Prince Albert and the Duke of Wellington were waiting to accompany him to Windsor. The crowds became even more animated when he paused to make an address, thanking the British people for their hospitality during his exile in England.

At Windsor the Queen and her children gathered to receive him, while members of the household watched the proceedings with fascination.

"At two o clock he arrived," wrote the royal governess, Lady Lyttelton, "this curious King; worth seeing if ever a body was!...His hand rather shook as he alighted; his hat quite off, and grey hair seen. His countenance is striking, much better than the portraits, and his embrace of the Queen was very parental and nice...It was a striking piece of real history made one feel and think much."[77]

Thanks to the Queen's hospitality, the King enjoyed every minute of his visit, the highlight of which was his investiture in the Order of the Garter – a confirmation that he was accepted as a legal sovereign. While the Queen and the King talked freely, their ministers engaged in more significant discussions. A writer for *Punch* observed that, when Peel and the French Foreign Minister, Guizot, took a long walk, their conversation appeared to be convivial, and, the ease with which they passed over a stile together 'would do more towards enabling them to get over Tahiti and other questions, than all the diplomacy that could ever pass between them.'[78]

Before he left, the King invited the Queen and Prince Albert to return to France the following year – an invitation which the Queen accepted on condition that it should remain a private visit in which she would not be required to make any speeches or official appearances. The visit took place in the autumn of 1845, and, although Queen Victoria enjoyed the brief stay, she was somewhat disconcerted by her host's insistence on speaking of a potential marriage between his son, Montpensier, and the Spanish Infanta – a subject which, within twelve months, would again bring their countries to the brink of war.

Chapter 5 – In the Centre of a Battlefield

In 1838, Louis Philippe's arch-detractor, Palmerston, commented that the French King was 'as ambitious as Louis XIV, and wants to put one of his sons on the throne of Spain as husband to the young Queen.'[79] At the time, the 'young Queen' – Isabella II – was only five years old, but, over the next seven years, the question of whom she would marry was frequently discussed in the courts of Europe.

In the early 1840s, Palmerston proposed Queen Victoria's cousin, Prince Leopold of Saxe-Coburg Koharyj, but Louis Philippe, who had already decided that his son, Montpensier, should marry Isabella, objected on the grounds that the Coburgs were becoming too powerful and were too closely connected to the British Royal Family. In order to maintain good Anglo-French relations, Queen Victoria assured Louis Philippe that she would do nothing to promote her cousin's candidacy; and, in return, he withdrew Montpensier's name from the list. He would not, though, rule out the possibility of Montpensier marrying Isabella's younger sister, Infanta Luisa Fernanda.

Palmerston immediately saw through the seemingly innocuous suggestion, for if Isabella should die childless, Luisa Fernanda would succeed her, and Montpensier would, in effect, become King. In order to allay these suspicions, Louis Philippe told Queen Victoria during her visit to Eu that he 'never would hear of Montpensier's marriage with the Infanta of Spain (which they are in a great fright about in England), until it was no longer a political question, which would be, when the Queen is married, and has children.'[80]

---

j A brother of Victoire, Duchess of Nemours

Queen Victoria concluded that this was a 'very satisfactory' resolution, but when Louis Philippe then began recommending husbands for the Spanish Queen, she feared that his interference was becoming excessive and told him that this was a matter for Isabella and her people to decide.

In the meantime, unbeknown to Queen Victoria, Isabella's mother, Queen Maria Christina, had entered into a clandestine correspondence with Prince Albert's brother, Ernest, in which she claimed that his Leopold of Saxe-Coburg was the most appropriate candidate to 'reconcile my daughter's happiness with that of the Spanish nation.'[81]

Relishing the role of mediator, Ernest forwarded the letter to a horrified Prince Albert, who feared that he was being dragged into an intrigue which would cast doubt on his and Queen Victoria's sincerity in their dealings with Louis Philippe.

> "This gives us the appearance of faithlessness, intrigue, perfidiousness, etc., etc.," he wrote angrily to Ernest, "and affords France just reason to complain. We have seen ourselves forced to wash our hands of the matter, and to explain to France that we are no parties to this step."[82]

Desperate to remain transparent, Queen Victoria immediately forwarded the letter to Louis Philippe, assuring him that neither she nor her husband had played any part in the plot, nor were they or her ministers doing anything to promote Leopold's candidacy.

Palmerston and several other ministers were convinced that Maria Christina was secretly in league with Louis Philippe, and had deliberately drawn the gullible Ernest into a scheme to embarrass Queen Victoria, and provide him with an excuse to implement a plan which he had been hatching.

> "I met...yesterday," wrote the diarist, Thomas Raikes, "a very clever and well-informed Spaniard, who is just arrived from Madrid, and

who, among many other things, said we might rely upon it that she never meant this Coburg match at all, and that the proposal was only meant as a snare to us; and if we had listened to it, France would have taken advantage of our doing so, and laid to our charge the intrigues of which we now accuse her."[83]

It was a view shared by Prince Albert's erstwhile mentor, Baron Stockmar, who recorded that:

> "The reports from Paris make out that the overtures of Queen Christina to the Duke of Coburg, were a step devised by her with Louis Philippe, and a trap for…the English Government. Had the latter fallen into it, they would have given Louis Philippe a pretext for saying, with an appearance of justice: 'As you have swerved from your part of the agreement, I am justified in trying to effect the marriage with one of my sons.'"[84]

These suspicions were well-founded, for, no sooner had Louis Philippe received the letter from Queen Victoria than he pressurised Isabella into marrying without delay. The groom whom he had chosen for her – her double first-cousin, the effete, homosexual and probably impotent Francis, Duke of Cadiz – was clearly the most unsuitable candidate, being 'a little bit of a man, almost a dwarf, with a squeaky voice and a spiteful character.'[85] Queen Victoria was horrified that the young girl had been all but compelled to marry 'such a wretch of a husband' and was even more aghast when she received a friendly letter from Queen Amélie, casually mentioning that, despite Louis Philippe's promises, Montpensier would marry Isabella's younger sister on the same day. The change of plan, she unconvincingly explained, was due to Isabella herself, as she had insisted on arranging the date for Luisa Fernanda's wedding. Unconvinced by this explanation, Queen Victoria responded coolly, telling Queen Amélie that Montpensier's marriage was a political matter, on which, as a constitutional monarch, she could not comment. She made no attempt, though, to conceal her anger when, on the day before the wedding, she wrote to the King of the Belgians:

> "The settlement of the Queen of Spain's marriage, coupled with Montpensier's is infamous and we must remonstrate…This is too bad, for we were so honest as almost to prevent Leo's marriage…and the return is this unfair coupling of the two marriages…The King should know that we are extremely indignant, and that this conduct is not the way to keep up the entente which he wishes."[86]

Her reaction came as a blow to Louis Philippe, who had been counting on their friendship to secure her support. That, having failed, he turned to his daughter, the Queen of the Belgians, in the hope that she might persuade Victoria to express in public her satisfaction at the marriage.

Queen Victoria replied curtly that 'the King had forfeited the word he had given her,' which so incensed Louis Philippe that for two years he made no further contact with her. Neither the Queen nor Prince Albert had any desire to heal the rift, for both believed they had been betrayed personally and politically; and, what was more, they felt genuine sympathy for the Spanish sisters, and for Montpensier, who never even met his rather unattractive fourteen-year-old bride. As Queen Victoria anticipated, neither marriage was happy, for although Isabella thwarted Louis Philippe's plans by giving birth to nine children, few people believed that her husband was their father. As stories of her numerous affairs became the talk of every court in Europe, Prince Albert gallantly defended her renowned promiscuity by stating that she could hardly be blamed for her behaviour when she had been so ill-used at such a young age. The Infanta's marriage began on equally miserable footing, as Montpensier frequently plotted against Queen Isabella and was rumoured to be cruel to Luisa Fernanda when she failed to conspire with him to discredit her sister.

"Louis Philippe's ambiguous reputation as a master of the arts of statesmanship has been most unequivocally mined by the Spanish intrigue," wrote Baron Stockmar. "If he lives long enough, he can hardly fail to suffer some portion of the punishment, which, according to the laws of nature, he has incurred."[87]

The predicted 'punishment' came sooner than expected, and his duplicitous behaviour had so damaged his relationship with Queen Victoria that he had lost a powerful friend who might have offered the support he needed at a time of great political and social upheavals.

Throughout his sixteen years on the throne, Louis Philippe had not only failed to heal the deep divisions within French society, but had also alienated many of his erstwhile supporters. The more liberal-minded ministers who had expected a constitutional monarch soon discovered that the Citizen King had no intention of sharing power, for, according to the British statesman, Henry Brougham, he had 'the failings of most kings of great capacity, and of consequent self-reliance.'[88] Those who had trusted him were shocked to learn that 'in their constitutional King they had got a master, not a servant,' and consequently 'their rage was intense in proportion to the degree to which they had duped themselves.'[89]

Louis Philippe had not deliberately set out to dupe his ministers but rather had failed to understand the immensity of the task which he had undertaken. Naively, he convinced himself that he could please all parties by shows of magnanimity but, more often than not, his efforts backfired. When, for example, he attempted to ingratiate himself with the Imperialists by having Napoleon's ashes returned to France, he succeeded only in highlighting the vast difference between himself – an aging and mediocre man – and the Emperor who, in the minds of his supporters, appeared to be little less than a god.

Equally, his efforts to endear himself to the ordinary people by regularly walking or riding among them failed when he simultaneously demanded over eighteen-million francs to cover the expenses of his growing family. Even his sons realised that his expectations were excessive, and when Nemours married, he declined the customary increase in the stipend which was awarded to princes on their wedding day. Nonetheless, with his eleven palaces, collection of Bourbon jewels, and the revenue obtained from the extensive Crown Forests, Louis Philippe was glaringly out of touch with the majority of his subjects, many of whom were struggling to survive.

A series of unfortunate events further diminished his reputation, as he seemed incapable of dealing with disasters or comprehending their effects on his people. Twelve months after his accession, nineteen-thousand French citizens died in a cholera epidemic; and, when subsequent years were plagued by a series of bad harvests, leading to a substantial rise in the price of bread, the King did nothing to alleviate the consequent suffering, and was generally viewed as ineffectual, or worse, indifferent to the cries of his people.

More damagingly still, he continued to rely solely on his coterie of advisers; and, as Henry Brougham observed, 'He wished to have Ministers of sufficient ability to perform their official duties, but not of sufficient weight to have a will of their own.'[90] Becoming increasingly autocratic, he insisted on maintaining personal control of all ministerial departments, hampering his appointees by his constant interference in their decisions. On one occasion, the Prime Minister, Adolphe Thiers, was so irked by his frequent interruptions that he threw down his portfolio, walked out of the chamber and refused to return for three days.

"The great error of his life," said Thiers, "was that he never would submit to be a constitutional King. To work a constitutional Government the different powers should be in equilibrium. The King and the Chambers should resemble the passengers in a wherry…If either party destroys its balance it oversets. Now he never would submit to sit still; he was always getting up to seize the rudder. I warned him that one day he would be capsized in a [ministerial crisis]."[91]

When Thiers eventually resigned in frustration, he became one of Louis Philippe's most vocal opponents. Subsequent Prime Ministers were equally frustrated, and by the time that François Guizot was appointed to the position in 1847, the government's reputation had reached its nadir. Corruption was rife; votes were bought and sold; and the King had refused to remedy the situation by extending the franchise to allow for the election of worthier representatives. Guizot – 'a little man, with a thin face, good features and very dark complexion'[92] – confidently averred that the people were happy with the status quo, unaware of, or unwilling to accept, that resentment was turning to anger, until a domestic tragedy brought the country to the point of revolution.

Shortly before dawn on Monday 18th August 1847, blood-curdling screams shattered the silence of the Hôtel Sébastiani – the Parisian residence of the Duke and Duchess de Praslin. Startled into action, servants scrambled along the corridors to the rooms of the thirty-year-old Duchess, only to find the doors bolted from the inside. As they struggled to force the locks, the screams gradually faded until, at last, the Duke appeared in the doorway. Behind him, amid overturned furniture, the Duchess, soaked in blood, lay gasping her last. Her throat had been slit, her hands slashed and her head bludgeoned by the candlestick that lay beside her on the floor. The Duke, feigning shock, insisted that this was the work of an intruder but, within minutes of the arrival of the Sureté Nationale, there appeared to be little doubt that he was the killer. Not only were his blood-stained clothes and hunting knife found in an adjoining room, but the whole of Paris knew that he had a motive for murder.

Behind of their façade of domestic harmony, the Duke and Duchess de Praslin had, for more than five years, endured a strained co-existence. Amid rumours and hints of child abuse, the Duke had forbidden his volatile wife from playing any part in their children's upbringing, handing over all authority for their welfare and education to their English-trained governess, Henriette Deluzy. While the hysterical Duchess ranted and raved, newspapers reported sordid details of an affair between the governess and her master until, at last, under pressure from his father-in-law, the Duke was compelled to send Henriette away. Far from easing the situation, her departure served only to increase the tension in the household, culminating in the frenzied attack on the 18th August.

'What a mess!' sighed Louis Philippe as the Duke, still protesting his innocence, was brought before a Court of Peers and found guilty of murder. To appease the public's demand for justice, he was condemned to death but, before the sentence could be carried out, he poisoned himself with arsenic and died in agony six days later.

There, the domestic tragedy might have ended, but these were unsettling times, and a scandal involving a well-known aristocrat was enough to destroy public confidence in an already teetering monarchy and government.

> "This horrid Praslin tragedy is a subject one cannot get out of one's head," wrote Queen Victoria. "The Government can in no way be accused of these murders, but there is no doubt that the standard of morality is very low indeed in France, and that the higher classes are extremely unprincipled. This must shake the security and prosperity of a nation."[93]

As the year drew to a close, the repercussions of the Praslin affair continued to reverberate across the capital, reinforcing the perception of France as a country with 'neither religion nor morality' where, according to Baron Stockmar, 'everything...is in a state of hopeless rottenness, as was the case with the Romans before the fall of the Empire.'[94]

The New Year brought further bad tidings to Louis Philippe as his beloved sister and confidante, Adelaide, died on the 1st January. News of her death so touched Queen Victoria that, in spite of the acrimonious dispute about the Spanish marriages, her first instinct was to write to the King to offer her condolences. On reflection, though, she thought it might be better to contact him via his daughter, Clementine, but, before doing so, she sought the advice of the Prime Minister, Lord Russell.

> "There may be people," she told him, "who will construe this into a political act, but the Queen thinks that this risk should rather be run than that she should appear unfeeling and forgetful of former kindness and intimacy."[95]

The Prime Minister agreed and saw no harm in her writing directly to the King, and so, to the delight of Queen Amélie, she constructed a carefully-worded letter, avoiding any suggestion that former disputes were forgotten.

Louis Philippe was still in mourning a month later when a group of reformers arranged a mass meeting – or 'banquet' – in Paris to discuss their hopes of extending the franchise. Rather than recognising the dangers, Guizot high-handedly placed a ban on public gatherings, provoking such anger that, on the evening of 22nd February, virtually every shop and café in the city was closed for fear of a riot. One British diplomat, residing in Paris, reported that:

> "...The quarter of the town in which I reside was warlike in its appearance. All was still save the tramp of patrols and heavy detachments of the military. Along the Rue de Rivoli, which skirts the

gardens of the Tuileries, along the quai, on the Place de la Concorde and Place du Carrousel, the soldiers of the King were bivouacked by huge camp fires...The effect of this scene was most striking. It was the monarchy guarded by a cordon of cannon and bayonets against the people for whom all Governments are instituted...and Louis Philippe and his family went to rest, as it were, in the centre of a battle-field."[96]

The following morning, Nemours rode through the streets and was able to report that everything seemed calm, but when the former Prime Minister, Thiers, walked through Paris, he was cheered by the crowds who were rapidly erecting barricades. Nemours and Guizot advised the King to summon the popular Thiers to Tuileries, and, for the sake of the country, he accepted the summons. On arriving, he found Louis Philippe in a state of such utter despair that he agreed to return to his former post as Prime Minister. That afternoon, Louis Philippe naively attempted to placate the crowds by dismissing the hated Guizot, but, as Thiers had feared, his efforts proved to be too little, too late.

A large crowd had already gathered outside the Ministry of Foreign Affairs, demanding immediate reform and a new constitution; and the National Guard let it be known that, if riots should ensue, they were not prepared to protect the monarchy at the expense of the people. In view of the rising tension, the officers guarding the Ministry were ordered to fix bayonets, and, in the process, one accidentally discharged his rifle, which the others took as a signal that an order to fire had been given. As the soldiers began shooting indiscriminately into the crowd, fifty-one civilians were killed, provoking such outrage that thousands of protestors stormed towards the Tuileries in search of the Royal Family.

Queen Marie Amélie urged her husband to step out at the head of the National Guard to appeal for calm, while she and the rest of the family would appear on the balcony, but, as the King donned his uniform, Nemours received word that the mob demanded Louis Philippe's abdication in favour of his ten-year-old grandson, the Comte de Paris.

Louis Philippe was still hesitating when the cries of the angry crowds echoed through the windows, prompting the distraught Queen Amélie to call loudly, "You do not deserve so good a king!"

As urgent message was sent to the Duchess of Orléans, telling her to bring her children to the Tuileries, but, when she heard that the King intended to hand the throne to her elder son, she threw herself at his feet and begged him not to abdicate. Much to the astonishment of his ministers, however, he ignored her pleas and ordered carriages to be brought so that he and his family could evacuate the palace. As he waited for his order to be obeyed, he discarded his wig and shaved off his beard to disguise his appearance.

Soon afterwards, followed by the rest of his family, he hurried across the courtyard only to discover that, in the chaos, no carriages could be found. Queen Amélie fainted in terror, and panic swept through the household until Nemours, who remained sufficiently calm to take charge of situation, went in search of alternative transport. He returned with three small broughams, each capable of carrying only three passengers. Louis Philippe pushed his fainting wife into the first, and ungallantly climbed in beside her, followed by several of his grandchildren, some of whom were passed through the window onto his lap. The rest of the party found what spaces they could, except for Clementine and Gusti who donned disguises in the hope of passing unrecognised through the crowds.

As the broughams were about to depart, the desperate Duchess of Orléans asked her father-in-law what was to become of her and her sons, the elder of whom was now ostensibly King. Louis Philippe replied that she had a duty to defend his position and must remain in the city to preserve his crown, before cravenly speeding away into the darkness. Nemours rallied the few remaining loyal troops to defend the Tuileries to give the fugitives time to escape, and then, taking charge of the little Comte de Paris, led him and his mother to the Chamber of Deputies to seek official recognition of her regency.

The Deputies assured him that no harm would come to the family, but, following a vote, announced that there was no need for a regency since the country no longer wanted a King. While Nemours was trying to come to terms with the announcement, an angry mob stormed into the room and pointed their muskets towards the Duchess and her sons. Several of the Deputies fled in terror, but others bravely formed a protective wall around the family to allow them to escape unharmed. One led them out of the building, and, calling on the National Guard for protection, guided them in the direction of the President of the Chamber's home. As they made their way through the crowded streets, the Comte de Paris tripped and fell into the arms of a workman, who, struggling to protect him carried him in to the nearest house. Others, seeing what had happened, gathered beneath the window, and, when the boy had been lowered into their arms, they passed him between them all the way to the President's house where his mother and brother were waiting.

That evening the Duchess and her children remained with the President but, the following morning, he persuaded her to take them out of the country. She agreed to go to her late mother's home, Eisenach in Thuringia but, before departing she assured him that at the first opportunity she would return to France so that her son could take up his rightful position as King.

For a while, Nemours remained in Paris, in the hope of rousing sufficient support to retain the monarchy, but when it became clear that his efforts were in vain, he donned a disguise and boarded a passenger steamer bound for England.

Chapter 6 – The Misfortunes of that Family

Although word of Louis Philippe's downfall reached England within hours of his abdication, several days passed before Queen Victoria obtained any information regarding the family's whereabouts. Even then, the news was scanty and vague, as Prince Albert observed, 'Victoire, Alexander, the King, the Queen, are still tossing upon the waves, or have drifted to other shores; we know nothing of them.'[97]

Louis Philippe's eldest daughter, the Queen of the Belgians, was utterly distraught.

"We have been thirty-six hours without any news," she wrote desperately to Queen Victoria, "not knowing even if my parents and the family were still alive or not, and what had been their fate. Death is not worse than what we endured during these horrible hours. We don't know yet what to think, what to believe, I would almost say, what to wish; we are stunned and crushed by the awful blow. What has happened is unaccountable, incomprehensible; it appears to us like a fearful dream."[98]

All past disputes forgotten, Queen Victoria urgently sought to discover their whereabouts, and when, after various perilous journeys, a bedraggled band of refugees began to arrive on the south coast of England, she sent food, clothes and the assurance of a safe haven.

Under the pseudonyms Mr and Mrs Smith, Louis Philippe and Amélie endured a rough sea-crossing before reaching Newhaven, where the proprietor of the Bridge Inn took care of them until the Queen was informed of their arrival and arranged for them to be brought to London. When their daughter, Clementine, appeared, she was dressed in 'real rags, her only clothes torn half off, and she was very nearly crushed to death in the mob.'[99] Victoire, Duchess of Nemours remained missing for some time, until eventually she sent word that she was in

73

Jersey; and when Montpensier's wife, the Infanta, reached London, Queen Victoria wrote sorrowfully to Baron Stockmar:

> "You know my love for the family; you know how I longed to get on better terms with them again…Little did I dream that this would be the way we should meet again, and see each other all in the most friendly way. That the Duchess de Montpensier, about whom we have been quarrelling for the last year and a half, should be here as a fugitive, and dressed in the clothes I sent her, and should come to thank me for my kindness, is a reverse of fortune which no novelist would devise, and upon which one could moralise for ever."[100]

Louis Philippe's grandchildren were initially housed with Queen Victoria's children in the royal nurseries but their unruly and sometimes violent behaviour disrupted the entire household. They were, wrote the royal governess, 'naughty, riotous, disobedient and unmanageable,' and they bit and kicked the dressmaker who was sent to measure them for new clothes. Their attendants were equally difficult, and one maid was caught was caught in Queen Victoria's dressing-room, trying to steal her dresses.

Fortunately, their stay was brief as the Queen obtained permission from her uncle, the King of the Belgians, to house the refugees in his former home – Claremont House in Esher, which he had received as a wedding present on his marriage to the late Princess Charlotte. To make their stay more comfortable, she sent crates of food, clothing and luxury items, but, much to Prince Albert's annoyance, Louis Philippe was so absorbed in self-pity that, even months later, he had not bothered to have them opened.

The King's misery was compounded by the realisation that he had been virtually forgotten in France, where he was not viewed as a tyrant but rather as a nonentity.

"Well might have Louis Philippe spared himself the trouble of overhasty flight and the humiliating annoyance of a disguise," wrote the British Ambassador, "as neither the people nor their chosen rulers took the slightest notice of him. His name was not even mentioned in the first deliberations of the Provisional Government."[101]

While the French politicians ignored him, many of their British counterparts were more openly hostile and questioned the wisdom of providing him with a home in England. Unable to forget his duplicitousness in the affair of the Spanish marriages, they believed that he was the author of his own misfortune and had forfeited the Queen's affection and the respect of her people. Most indignant of all was Palmerston, who took it upon himself to travel to Claremont to inform the ex-King that he could not remain there indefinitely, in response to which Louise Philippe 'complained of this to all the people he saw (talking very loosely and foolishly), and it got wind and made a noise.'[102]

To the surprise of Louis Philippe's critics, however, Queen Victoria sent the Duke of Wellington to Claremont to tell him that she did not share Palmerston's opinion; and she asked her uncle, the King of the Belgians, to write to assure him that he was welcome to stay at Claremont for as long as he wished.

"I learn to my great astonishment," wrote Charles Greville, "that all the Queen's former attachment to Louis Philippe and the French Royal Family has revived in greater force than ever; she says the marriages are not to be thought of any more. Nothing but the extraordinary good sense of Prince Albert and the boundless influence he has over her keeps her affectionate feelings under due restraint; but for him she would have made all her household go to Claremont, and when the French

75

Royal Family have come to visit her she has received them as King and Queen, and one day one of the children went up to Louis Philippe and called him 'Your Majesty,' which had no doubt been done by the Queen's commands."[103]

Other monarchs and ministers, who had initially sympathised with his plight, were gradually coming to the conclusion that he deserved all that happened to him. Many believed he had abdicated too easily, and were aghast that he still failed to accept responsibility for his actions.

'Who would not recognise the avenging hand of the King of Kings in all this?' wrote the King of Prussia; while journalists across the continent accused him of having left France in greater chaos than he had found it when he ascended the throne.

Louis Philippe, adamantly refusing to shoulder the blame, complained that he had been unjustly vilified. 'The world,' he moaned, 'will not do me justice till I am dead,'[104] but, even in this, he was so be mistaken.

Death, it seemed, was very much on his mind from the time that he arrived in England. The shock of the revolution had left him so depressed and broken that it seemed he had nothing left to live for. His health rapidly deteriorated, and, although a holiday in St Leonards temporarily revived him, by mid-August 1850 it was clear that he was dying. When Queen Amélie, mindful of his eternal salvation, asked his doctors to tell him the truth so that he might prepare his soul, he replied cheerfully,

"Oh! yes, I understand quite well! You have come to tell me it is time to pack up."[105]

As the priest administered the Last Rites, his family gathered around his bed, and he allegedly told his sons that henceforth they must view the Comte de Chambord – a grandson of Charles X – as the head of the family. He died peacefully at eight o'clock in the evening of 26th August 1850, six weeks before his seventy-seventh birthday, and was interred with due ceremony at the

Roman Catholic church of St Charles Borromeo in Weybridge.

Death did nothing to improve his rather sorry reputation, nor did it result in his hoped-for reassessment of his successes.

'The death of Louis Philippe delivers me from my most artful and inveterate enemy, whose position gave him in many ways the power to injure me,'[106] wrote Lord Palmerston; while journalists were even more condemnatory. *The Times* reported that he was merely a man who possessed 'a singular combination of the lower qualities of human nature'; *The Sun*[k] accused him of having betrayed the trust of his people; and the *Daily News* stated that throughout his entire reign 'not one single great or generous idea germinated in his soul.'[107]

"The poor old King has been buried quite unostentatiously," wrote Prince Albert, "and yet after his death the papers have assailed him with remorseless severity."[108]

Although few in Britain or France mourned his passing, his eldest daughter, the Queen of the Belgians was so devastated by his death that she survived him by only two months, dying of tuberculosis on 11th October 1850.

After the King's death, Queen Victoria maintained her friendship with members of his family, particularly those who continued to reside in England. Queen Amélie remained at Claremont with her son and daughter-in-law, the Duke and Duchess of Nemours; the Aumales lived in Twickenham; and the Duchess of Orléans and her sons often stayed in Richmond and Devon.

As the widowed Duchess had fled with few funds and even fewer possessions, she had taken her sons to Thuringia, where, despite offers of help from her extended

---

[k] *The Sun* was a 19th century newspaper with a relatively small circulation, not to be confused with the modern *Sun*.

family, she had insisted on living frugally and accepting their charity only when it was absolutely necessary. Devoting herself to her children's education, she continued to believe that they would eventually be called to France where her older boy, the Comte de Paris would take his place as the rightful King.

When she heard that Louis Philippe was unwell, she visited him at St Leonards and, moved by his frailty, returned soon afterwards to Richmond in order to be closer to him and Queen Amélie. Unfortunately, the British climate depressed her, and, soon after the King's death, she told a friend that 'the heavy and enervating atmosphere' was so oppressive that she longed 'for a more bracing climate.' She and her sons duly returned to Germany before travelling on to Switzerland where an incident occurred that so shattered her nerves that she never fully recovered.

While she and her children were being driven across a swollen river, their carriage overturned and fell into the fast-flowing water. The boys managed to scramble to the bank, but the Duchess fainted in fear and lay face down beneath the surface. A quick-thinking coachman managed to pull her to safety where it was discovered that she had fractured her collar bone and dislocated her shoulder. Queen Amélie visited her as she was recuperating and persuaded her to return again to England, where she rented Kitley House in Devon – a very damp and not very relaxing place in Queen Victoria's opinion – before returning to Cranbourne House in Richmond to continue her children's education.

"It is an indescribable joy to me," she wrote at that time, "to see my sons developing after my own heart, to see them growing in goodness...I think that the present age of my eldest son is the most delightful time in a man's life. He has all the candour of youth, with its freshness of impressions, and its uprightness of principle untarnished, and to these is added an increasing strength of mind, a power of thought which takes the place of experience, and a constant striving after and longing for perfection. Robert, though younger, is also beginning to combine more mature qualities with his childish innocence, and his quick, impulsive nature is held in check by a daily increasing good sense."[109]

Nevertheless, the shock of her husband's early death, the revolution and the accident in Switzerland left her prone to long periods of agitation and psychosomatic illnesses. She was deeply distressed to hear that her brother-in-law, the Duke of Nemours, was so desperate to restore the monarchy that he was willing to accept Comte de Chambord, as the rightful French King[l]; and she balked at his suggestion that the childless Chambord could adopt the Comte de Paris and name him as his heir. Although their dispute was acrimonious, their arguments were immaterial, for, by then, a more unlikely candidate had declared himself Emperor of the Second French Empire[m].

In spite of the disagreement Hélène remained on affectionate terms with Nemours' wife, Victoire, who also maintained a firm friendship with her cousin, Queen Victoria. In October 1857, Victoire gave birth to a daughter, but when the doctor congratulated her on bringing forth a healthy child, she replied ominously, 'Don't sing of victory too soon.' Queen Victoria, who had recently given birth to her own youngest child, visited Claremont soon afterwards, and was shocked to see that her cousin looked 'aged and drawn, and not like a patient who was making a rapid recovery.'[110] A few days later, as the maid was combing her hair, the Duchess suddenly gasped, 'Oh mon Dieu!' and instantly died.

---

[l] As the grandson of Charles X, Chambord had long been the favourite candidate of the Legitimists, who had never accepted Louis Philippe's right to the throne.
[m] See Chapter 7

Saddened, Prince Albert hurried at once to Claremont, where he found:

> "Nemours quite crushed and stunned; the body of good dear Victoire pale and rigid, but like an angel of beauty, her glorious hair falling in waves over her bosom, and in the adjoining room the baby in rosy unconscious slumber. I was deeply moved."[111]

The next day he returned with Queen Victoria, who was equally struck by the tragic scene:

> "There was the broken-hearted, almost distracted widower – and her son – and lastly, there was in one room the lifeless, but oh! even in its ghostliness, most beautiful form of his young, lovely, and angelic wife, lying in her bed with her splendid hair covering her shoulders, and a heavenly expression of peace; and in the next room, the dear little pink infant sleeping in its cradle."[112]

For Hélène, the death of yet another close relation came as a severe blow and, just five months later, she contracted cold, which developed into influenza. On May 17th, Queen Victoria, who had insisted on being kept informed of her progress, was shocked to hear from the apothecary that his patient was sinking, and her younger son, Robert, and Queen Amélie had also contracted the illness[n]. Unbeknown to either Queen Victoria or the apothecary, at the moment they were speaking, Héléne had asked her doctor and ladies to leave her to sleep, and, when they returned they found she had died. Prince Albert set out at once for Richmond and found an almost identical scene to that which he had witnessed at Claremont a few months earlier.

> "The misfortunes of that family are unparalleled!" Queen Victoria sighed to the King of the Belgians, before turning her thoughts to, "The poor sons! What is to become of them at a moment when a

---

[n] Robert and Queen Amélie later recovered.

mother is so important, and when a mother's roof is of such essential use to young men?"[113]

Queen Victoria ordered a month of mourning and was most put out that her eldest daughter, the Crown Princess of Prussia, failed to show similar respect 'for her memory…and our very near and numerous relationships with the Orléans family who are in this country.'[114]

Queen Amélie, who had already lived through so many bereavements, found comfort in her faith, impressing Queen Victoria by her 'pious resignation to the Will of God' and her readiness 'to devote her remaining years and strength to her grandchildren.'[115] Over the next few years, she regularly travelled to warmer climes for the good of her health, but by January 1866, her frailty was apparent to all who met her. Within three months she was confined to her bedroom, and on 24th March she sank into a coma from which she never awoke. Immediately after her death, Nemours told his son that he was relieved that her sorrows and trials were over, and that she had passed away gently and without pain. Queen Victoria arrived at Claremont two days later to pay her respects, and, as was her custom, insisted that the room in which the former Queen had died should remain exactly as it was at the time of her death.

"I sincerely mourn for the dear Queen," wrote Queen Victoria's daughter, Princess Alice, "and she was so kind to me always."[116]

After a quiet funeral, she was buried beside her husband in the Church of St. Charles Borromeo in Weybridge°.

° In 1876, she and Louis Philippe were re-interred in the Chapel Royal, Dreux.

Part II – The Bonapartes

Chapter 7 – He Really Believes He Will Yet Be Emperor

In 1802, the future Emperor Napoleon Bonaparte ordered his brother, Louis, to marry Hortense Beauharnais, a daughter of his wife, Josephine, by her first husband. Intelligent, beautiful and charming, eighteen-year-old Hortense might have appeared as an ideal bride for the twenty-three-year-old Captain of the Artillery, but Louis, who was prone to depression, resented his brother's ability to control every aspect of his life. Grudgingly, the unenthusiastic groom muttered his vows in an almost inaudible whisper, and sighed that his miserable wedding day was a portent of the unhappiness that would follow.

It was a self-fulfilling prophecy for, although, within two years, Hortense had borne him two sons, by 1806, the couple were living virtually separate lives in separate apartments. That summer, Napoleon – now Emperor – again took charge of Louis' life, by creating him King of Holland, where he was to serve as his brother's viceroy. This time, Louis took a firmer stand and, before leaving France, told Napoleon:

"Let me act freely or let me remain here. I will not go to govern a country, where I shall be known only by disaster."[117]

Disregarding his elder brother's orders, he adopted the Dutch language and customs, while Hortense, adhering to the Emperor's wishes, insisted on speaking French and attempted to create a court that resembled that of Napoleon. The disparate couple grew further and further apart, and when, a year later, their elder son, Napoleon Charles, died of croup, Hortense was so broken-hearted that she abandoned her husband and returned to Paris. There, a few months later, she gave birth to a third son, Louis Napoleon on 20th April 1808.

The Emperor, who, at that time, was at the height of his power, developed such a deep affection for his little nephew that he alone, out of all the family, was permitted to join him for breakfast. Little Louis was so entranced by tales of his powerful uncle's political and military victories, that, from his earliest years, he formed an idealistic desire to emulate his successes. At the same time, the cultured and well-educated Hortense encouraged Louis' philosophical and romantic leanings, and frequently reminded him that, as princes and kings are easily deposed, he must be ready to support himself in all eventualities.

> "It is generally the misfortune of princes," she stated, "to imagine that they are made of a different material from other men, and therefore have no obligations towards them. They rarely know anything about human sufferings and want, and think it almost impossible that these should ever assail them. As soon, therefore, as adversity befalls them, they are so surprised and disconcerted that they cannot find the strength to resist, but are crushed. From such a fate I will preserve my sons."[118]

Her foresight was astute, for, when Louis was only two years old, the Emperor lost patience with his brother and forced him to abdicate as King of Holland. Just five years later, Napoleon himself was defeated at Waterloo, and the entire Bonaparte family was banished from France.

Derided and humiliated, Hortense took her sons to Geneva, but they had barely settled in the town when the French Ambassador pressurised the Swiss into ordering them to leave. They moved on to rent a shabby and gloomy house in Aix and, a few months later, Louis' father insisted that his elder son should join him in exile in Italy. Louis was distraught at being separated from his closest companion, and worse was to follow when, once again, the French authorities arranged for him and his mother to be   unceremoniously driven from their home. Not knowing where else to go, Hortense wrote to her cousin, the Grand Duchess of Baden, asking her for permission to settle in the Grand Duchy. With great reluctance, the Grand Duke eventually granted the request on condition that the Bonapartes never visited him nor attempted to enter the capital city of Karlsruhe.

For a few happy months they resided peacefully in Konstantz, where Hortense focussed all her attention on Louis, frequently reminding him of Napoleon's heroic exploits, and fostering in him the burning ambition to follow in his footsteps. Soon, though, the peaceful interlude came to an end when the Grand Duke suddenly ordered them to leave Baden, forcing them to return to Switzerland where Hortense purchased a sixteenth century chateau, Schloss Arenberg, which she aimed to restyle on the model of her childhood home, Malmaison. By then, since Louis was old enough to begin a military education, Hortense arranged for him to be enrolled in the training school at nearby Thun. There, he threw himself wholeheartedly into every aspect of his training, and, as one of his contemporaries wrote:

> "He applied himself with ardour to all parts of a soldier's duty; toiling and faring as the private, working with spade and barrow; climbing, with a knapsack on his back, the steepest glaciers; and the activity of his spirit led him to prefer always the most arduous adventure."[119]

In the summertime, he and his mother holidayed in Rome where he studied Italian history, art and culture, and, to the amusement of those who knew him, made no secret of his dream of returning to France to restore the Bonapartes' fortunes. The future British Foreign Secretary, the Earl of Malmesbury, met him at that time and thought him a 'a wild harum-scarum youth...riding at full gallop down the streets to the annoyance of the public, fencing, and pistol-shooting, and apparently without serious thoughts of any kind, although even then he was possessed with the conviction that he would one day rule over France.'[120]

Other witnesses were equally scornful of his lofty ambitions, as, dressed in shabby, worn-out clothes, he looked insignificant and bore no resemblance to a potential Emperor.

> "Louis-Napoleon's legs," sneered one observer, "seemed to have been an afterthought of his Creator – they were too short for his body, and his head appeared constantly bent down, to supervise their motion; consequently, their owner was always at a disadvantage when compelled to make use of them."[121]

If Louis were aware of such derogatory descriptions, he might well have found comfort in the knowledge that the mighty Emperor Napoleon, had once been similarly mocked by his fellow officers, and known by the affectionate nickname, 'the Little Corporal.'

In 1830, Hortense and Louis were delighted to hear of the July Revolution and Louis Philippe's accession to the throne. Surely, they thought, since the Citizen King himself had known the pain of exile, he would take pity on them and lift the order of banishment. Unfortunately, although Louis Philippe was sympathetic to their situation, under pressure from his extended family, he felt obliged to refuse their request. Dejectedly, Louis returned to Italy but his spirits were soon lifted by a reunion with his recently married brother, Napoleon, who confided in him that he was about to participate in an uprising of the Papal States in the hope of helping to bring about Italian unification.

Eager for adventure, Louis agreed to accompany him, but, knowing that his mother would try to dissuade him from such a dangerous mission, he made his preparations in secret, and left her a note on the day of his departure.

> "Your love will know how to appreciate our motives. We have taken great duties upon us, and

much responsibility, and have gone too far to return. The name we bear binds us to assist all those who are oppressed and call upon us for help. Please tell my sister-in-law that it was I who persuaded her husband to accompany me, for Napoleon dislikes the idea of having hidden from her the slightest action of his life."[122]

As Louis had expected, Hortense was horrified to discover what had happened, and she frantically contacted Louis' father and numerous other relations, begging them to find any means of rescuing her sons from danger. Impatient for news, she became so desperate that she decided to follow the army, determined to find her boys and bring them home. When, at last, she caught up with them, she found that they were both confined to bed with measles, and shortly after her arrival, her elder son succumbed to complications of the disease and died on 17th March 1831.

Under Hortense's tender ministrations, Louis gradually recovered but the death of his brother affected him deeply and left him with an even greater desire to fulfil his own destiny by returning to France. So obsessed had he become by this dream that Hortense realised she could no longer restrain him and agreed to go with him to Paris incognito in the hope that she might obtain a personal interview with Louis Philippe and persuade him to lift the ban. The King welcomed her warmly and assured her that, if it were solely his decision, he would gladly allow her and her son to live in France. Greatly encouraged by his kindness, Hortense handed him a plaintive letter from Louis, in which he offered to enlist as an ordinary foot soldier in the French army.

Louis Philippe asked her to return to her lodgings to give him time to consider the situation, and, the following morning, he sent the President of the Council of Ministers to deliver his response. Hortense, he said, would be permitted to stay, but as Louis was now the Emperor Napoleon's heir, he would only be allowed to enlist in the army if he were willing to change his name. Affronted by the suggestion, Louis left at once for Arenberg, more determined than ever to return one day in glory.

For the next few years, his plan seemed nothing more than a pipe-dream as he quietly studied politics and philosophy, and published several books and pamphlets of his political and military musings. All the time, though, he kept abreast of events in France, and, by 1836, was convinced that Louis Philippe had become so unpopular that, if he returned, he would be welcomed as saviour by the French people.

One morning in October, after telling his mother that he was going hunting, he embarked on a hare-brained scheme to stage a coup. On 29th of the month he arrived at the garrison in Strasbourg and exhorted the officers to follow him to Paris. While some appeared interested, the majority ridiculed his suggestion before reporting him to their superior officers. From then on, the plot descended into more of a farce than a coup as Louis Philippe's agents followed his every move. When he entered the city, proclaiming 'Long live the Emperor!' no one believed that he was Napoleon's nephew, and a lowly lieutenant arrested him for assuming a false name. Once he had proved his identity, the authorities were so convinced of his lack of support that his punishment consisted of being sent on a journey throughout the country to see how little attention he attracted. Due to his mother's intercession, he avoided a trial, but when the humiliating excursion was over, he was quietly put on a ship bound for America.

He arrived in Norfolk, Virginia, on 30th March 1837 and, after spending some time in New York, planned to follow in Louis Philippe's footsteps by undertaking a tour of several states. A month later, however, he received a letter from his mother, telling him that she had been seriously ill and was about to undergo surgery.

"If it should fail," she told him, "receive in this letter my last blessing. We shall meet, doubt it not, in a better world. In this, I leave little to regret but thy love, which has been to me the chief charm of life…I press thee to my heart, my beloved! I am quite calm, quite resigned: I trust that we may see each other yet once more even in this world. The will of God be done!"[123]

In the event, her doctors advised her that surgery was unnecessary, knowing that her 'internal complaint' was incurable. Louis, meanwhile, set sail at once for Europe, and with great difficulty gained permission to travel overland to Arenberg. When he arrived, he found that his mother was dying, and for several days he barely left her side. On 5th October 1837, she suddenly sat up and threw her arms around him, then leaned back on her pillow and died.

Louis was alone in the world – the only surviving member of his immediate family being his father, whom he was not permitted to visit in Italy. His grief was compounded when it was revealed that Hortense had asked to be buried beside her mother in Paris, but the French authorities refused him permission to enter the country for her funeral. He remained, therefore, in Arenberg throughout the winter, but, in early 1838, the French government again asked the Swiss to expel him. Initially, they refused to do so until Louis Philippe sent troops to the border, which so alarmed them that they apologetically ordered Louis to leave.

This time, he travelled to England where, according to his critics, he idled away his days at the races and his evenings in low taverns. His supporters, though, gave a more accurate account of how he spent his time in conversation with renowned intellectuals, who encouraged him to produce further academic papers. Thanks to his natural charm and scintillating conversation, he was frequently entertained by the aristocracy; and his skill and courage as a horseman gained him a reputation as a champion of pageants and mock-tournaments. Still, though, he nurtured his dream of returning to France as hero, and allegedly told an English acquaintance:

"I like you very well as a people, but I must wipe out Waterloo and St. Helena!"

In view of his undisguised ambition, Louis Philippe viewed him as a serious threat and kept him under constant surveillance; but the British, for the most part, dismissed his plans, seeing him as nothing but a dreamer.

The return of Napoleon's ashes to France in 1840 led to a resurgence of interest in the late Emperor, which Louis believed would result in his gaining greater support than he had done during the Strasbourg fiasco, and so, in August, he hired a small boat, the *Edinburgh Castle*, to take him and a few faithful companions across the Channel. He imagined that he would receive the same rousing welcome as had greeted Napoleon following his escape from Elba, but, once again he was disillusioned when he strutted into the guard house at Boulogne, crying, 'Vive l'Empereur', and the astonished soldiers, having no idea who he was, simply ignored him. He marched on into the town where, raising the imperial standard, he distributed leaflets urging the townsfolk to march to Paris with him. Bemused but unmoved, they stood and watched as the police, alerted to the commotion, arrived with a squadron of soldiers, who, following a scuffle, took him into custody.

"Did you ever know such a fool as that fellow is?" an English statesman commented. "Why, he really believes he will yet be Emperor of France."[124]

This time, following a trial, which 'excites no interest whatever'[125], he was imprisoned in the Chateau de Ham in Picardy, where he was to remain in relative comfort for the next six years, enjoying the company of a little dog named Ham, and his faithful valet, Charles Thenin. He was permitted to receive visitors, and given access to books and papers, so, rather than bewailing his fate, he spent his time producing articles on such diverse subjects as how to eradicate poverty, the best methods of sugar cultivation, and how the French could colonise South America. So fruitful were his studies that he would later joke that he had attended the University of Ham, but, even as he appeared to have resigned himself to a life in captivity, a visit from the prominent statesman and historian, Louis Blanc, revealed that he had not abandoned hope of yet becoming Emperor.

"Remember the Empire was the Emperor," Blanc warned him. "Can the Emperor rise again?... Remember that France let Napoleon fall because his power had grown too heavy to be borne any longer. Had he not been abandoned by France, he would never have met his doom at Waterloo. Remember how he died; remember where he died!...Give up, then, that part of a Pretender for which you lack a stage. Trust your disinterestedness with the care of your destiny. Dare to become and to declare yourself a Republican."[126]

Louis' eyes filled with tears but, despite giving the appearance of having heeded Blanc's words, he remained so confident of future glory that, when he was offered his freedom on condition that he left the country and relinquished his claims to the throne, he replied resolutely,

"I prefer being a captive on the soil of France, to being a free man in a foreign land."[127]

Shortly before Christmas 1845, when word reached him that his father was seriously ill, Louis wrote to the King, asking for permission to visit him in Italy with the assurance that he would then return to his prison. As his request was refused, he decided that he had no option but to escape, and, enlisting the help of Thenin and a companion named Dr Connau, it was not long before an ideal opportunity arose.

As fortune would have it, workmen happened to be carrying out repairs to the chateau, and Thenin was able to obtain a painter's smock and a pair of sabots for his master. Louis shaved off his moustache and donned the disguise before calmly mingling with the workmen as he made his way out of the prison. To distract the guards, Thenin encouraged Louis' dog to charge around barking – a ploy that he repeated as they passed each subsequent sentry. Meanwhile, Dr Connau had placed a mannequin in Louis' bed and let it be known that he was ill and needed complete rest to aid his recovery.

Once free from the chateau, Louis walked to a nearby village, where Thenin had arranged for a carriage take him to the railway station at Valenciennes. From there, armed with a Belgian passport, he took a train across the border into Belgium, and boarded a ship bound for England, in the hope of making his way from there to Florence. By this time, though, his escape had been discovered and the French authorities contacted both the Austrian Ambassador in London and the Grand Duke of Tuscany, asking them to deny Louis a passport that would enable him to visit his father. Although his plan had been foiled, as his father died before he could reach him, he inherited a substantial fortune and was permitted to remain a free man in England.

Dividing his time between London and his house, Brasted Place, in Kent, he produced further writings including a treatise on the necessity of abolishing the African slave trade.

> "Slavery itself once destroyed," he wrote, "the slave-trade must of necessity perish by the same blow; and the claims of humanity would be satisfied. Whereas, up to the present day, while we are busy in sowing hatred between master and slave, the commerce in human flesh continues, and becomes all the more atrocious the more we attempt to repress it."[128]

Once again, Louis' timing was fortuitous, for his sojourn in England coincided with the affair of the Spanish marriages and the consequent antipathy of the

British towards Louis Philippe. Although few Englishmen believed that Louis would ever be in a position to take the throne, he was popular simply because he was a rival to the hated French King.

Undeterred by others' doubts, Louis clung to his dream, and, as soon as the revolution erupted in 1848, he set out for Paris, expecting a warm welcome from the new Provisional Government. Although not displeased to see him, the ministers feared his presence might add to the turmoil that was already prevalent in the country, and so he wisely returned to London to bide his time and watch how events would unfold.

In England, much the amusement of his friends, he continued to speak of achieving his ambition, prompting Queen Victoria's cousin, George of Cambridge, to write cheerfully:

> "Louis Napoleon is a wonderful fellow; he does the most extraordinary things, apparently with impunity, and has gained popularity by them. Still I fancy he cannot go on long in this way, and though I think he certainly has a great deal of tact and talent, still I think he has not enough to carry him through so vast an undertaking, and that he will consequently break down in the attempt of making himself Emperor...which he is evidently driving at."[129]

The revolution in France sparked similar uprisings across much of Europe, and it was feared that Britain, too, might soon be affected. So earnestly did the Prince Consort take the threat that he boarded the windows of Buckingham Palace and prepared escape routes in case the Royal Family should be forced to flee the city. Louis, determined to demonstrate that he stood on the side of the law, enrolled as a special constable but his services were rarely required as, apart from 'a few little riots', Queen Victoria's popularity prevented any serious disturbances.

While still in England, Louis put himself forward as a candidate for the French National Assembly in

September 1848, and, to his immense delight, he was elected. On returning to France, though, he discovered that the Provisional Government was in such disarray that he proposed himself as President of the new French Republic, and, in December, he was elected with a far greater majority than any of his opponents.

From exile and imprisonment, he had attained the highest office in France but had still not lost sight of his ultimate goal, and he knew that the agreed four year term of office would not allow him time to implement all of his plans. For two years he continued as President, becoming increasingly frustrated that squabbles between different parties hindered his schemes, until in the winter of 1851, he decided he must take action. In the middle of the night of 1st-2nd December, he arranged to have all his opponents arrested so that by morning he was in complete command of the government. High Court judges hastily convened to declare him guilty of high treason but, before they were able to pass sentence, troops entered the meeting and dispersed them.

Republicans called the Parisians to action in an attempt to prevent his seizure of power but, as barricades rose in the streets, Louis declared that the city was under siege.

> "…He deluged its streets with blood;" the *Times* reported, "he terrorised France by wholesale transportation. He finally asked for a sanction or condemnation of his deed of violence. Seven millions and a half of Frenchmen against little above half a million gave sentence in his favour."[130]

The coup d'état was complete and those who had mocked his ambition could only gape askance as he was proclaimed 'Napoleon III, Emperor by the Grace of God and the Will of the People.'

Chapter 8 – Of Course, One Cannot Marry Her

Having seized power, Louis immediately set about securing his position by winning the support of the people and the army by donating vast sums to popular causes and pardoning over two hundred imprisoned soldiers and sailors. On a wider scale, though, he knew it would be more difficult to obtain the acceptance of his fellow monarchs, some of whom viewed him as an opportunistic usurper, while others feared that he intended to emulate his late uncle's military conquests.

Tsar Nicholas I of Russia refused to acknowledge him as an Emperor; King Leopold of the Belgians warned that he intended to dominate Europe; and Queen Victoria, who would have preferred one of the Orléans princes to re-establish the monarchy, warned King Friedrich Wilhelm IV of Prussia that his decision to restore the Imperial Eagle to regimental standards suggested that he was preparing for war.

The Queen's ministers and attendants were equally antipathetic towards him. The diplomat, Lord Cowley, suggested that he was growing 'far too big for his boots'; and one of the Duchess of Kent's[p] ladies-in-waiting declared that she was deeply distressed that he dared to call himself His Majesty. The Earl of Clarendon was even more outspoken:

> "I have no sympathy with L. Napoleon," he wrote, "who has committed wholesale high treason and trampled his own obligations and the rights of others under foot with an audacity that has no parallel in history."[131]

The British Ambassador in Paris advised his government that it would be wise to fortify the defences along England's south coast; while the British press

---

[p] The Duchess of Kent was Queen Victoria's mother.

simultaneously feared and mocked him, claiming that he spent his time:

> "…day by day, or, rather, night by night, dressed in white culottes with diamond buckles, dancing with all his might. His whole court dances along with him: eight balls to be given by eight high functionaries in the next ten days are advertised in the papers. Splendour and adulation surround him on every side. He treads on silver, and is served on gold."[132]

This story had little foundation as his close acquaintances were surprised by his simple tastes and dislike of ostentation. The rooms he inhabited were practical rather than luxurious; and he generally wore plain black clothes with a rather old-fashioned hat. His habits, too, were far more abstemious than his critics imagined, for he rose early to work through the business of the day, writing speeches, responding to memos, and studying all manner of subjects which, he hoped, would be of benefit to his people.

Equally false were the scare-mongering stories reported by other journalists, who warned that his ascent to power portended disaster for the whole of Europe.

> "If this man's reign is destined to continue even for a brief duration," read an article in the *Times*, "the world will witness the most heterogeneous jumble of despotism and demagogy, of socialism and corruption that history has ever chronicled."[133]

Distressed by these unflattering reports, Louis asked the British Ambassador why the English and their Queen, were so disdainful of him. The Ambassador could only reply that his method of seizing power was anathema to the people of a country with a constitutional monarchy.

He did, however, have one or two prominent foreign supporters. The American author, Henry de Puy, claimed that:

> "Whatever may be thought of the character of Louis Napoleon, it cannot be denied that he is a

man of remarkable ability. He has shown the utmost self-possession, firmness, courage and prudence during his administration. He began his career amid the scoffs of Europe, and now his movements are watched with an interest which indicates a full recognition of his capacity and his power. He possesses, in an eminent degree, that promptness in decision, that inflexibility of purpose, and that energy in the execution of his designs, that seems to be the indestructible inheritance of his race."[134]

More significantly, Britain's Foreign Secretary, Palmerston, who had struck up a friendship with him during his exile, considered him a stabilising influence on an otherwise turbulent country. Rejoicing in the downfall of his 'inveterate enemy', Louis Philippe, Palmerston stated that 'no other person at present is competent to be at the head of affairs in France; and if Louis Napoleon should end by founding a dynasty, I do not see that we need regret it as far as English interests are concerned.'[135] When, though, he went so far as to tell the French Ambassador, Count Walewski, that he supported the coup d'état, his words were reported by the French press, and appeared to compromise British neutrality. Queen Victoria was incensed by his indiscretion, and the Prime Minister, Russell, wrote him a castigatory letter, all but demanding his resignation. Palmerston calmly replied that he had not made a public declaration in his capacity as Foreign Secretary but had merely expressed a private opinion, which he was entitled to do. His explanation failed to satisfy the Queen, and the Prince Consort immediately wrote to Russell on her behalf:

"The distinction which Lord Palmerston tries to establish between his personal and his official acts is perfectly untenable. However much you may attempt such a distinction in theory, in practice it becomes impossible."[136]

Instead of accepting the reprimand with good grace, Palmerston played on the Queen's fondness for the Orléans family by claiming that he had evidence that they were involved in a conspiracy to bring down the new Emperor. While feigning illness, he said, Joinville had secretly left Claremont for Lille, where, supported by his brother, Aumale, he had attempted to raise an army to stage a coup d'état. Deeply disturbed by this revelation, the Queen ordered a thorough investigation into the claims, and she could hardly conceal her sense of triumph when she discovered that Aumale had been in Naples at the time of the alleged plot, and, as she informed Russell, she 'had been able satisfactorily to ascertain that the report about the French Princes rested upon no foundation whatever.'[137]

A few days later, Palmerston resigned, much to the delight of the Queen, who wrote to the King of the Belgians that the news would surely 'give you as much satisfaction and relief as it does to us, and will do to the whole of the world!'[138]

Nonetheless, the incident highlighted the delicacy of her position regarding Louis' accession. As Queen, she had a duty to respect a fellow sovereign, but, at the same time, she refused to break off 'our very near and numerous relationships with the Orléans family.' Wisely, she contacted the respected statesman and future Prime Minister, Lord Aberdeen, to seek his advice on how best to balance her personal and public roles. Could she, for example, pay an unofficial visit to the Duchess of Aumale; and could she continue to invite other members of the family to Osborne or Balmoral?

"…We have," she wrote to Aberdeen, "invariably received the poor Orléans family…from time to time here and in London, and…the Queen has always from the first year done this openly but unostentatiously. It is by no means her intention to change her conduct in this respect…but we think that perhaps it would be wiser not to see them

100

here, at any rate till after the meeting of Parliament, though it is very painful to the Queen to hurt their feelings by apparent neglect."[139]

There was also, she noted, a danger of appearing to be pandering to the 'will and pleasure of Louis Napoleon' if she failed to maintain the long standing friendships with the former Royal Family. Moreover,

> "It goes much against the Queen's feelings of generosity and kindness to neglect the poor exiles...but the present moment is one of unparalleled excitement and of great political importance, which requires great prudence and circumspection."[140]

Lord Aberdeen replied that he could see no reason why she should alter her former arrangements, providing that she continued to meet the Orléans family openly to avoid any suggestion of secret intrigues against Louis Napoleon.

While the Queen was busily balancing her public role with her private friendships, Louis was preoccupied with an equally delicate issue of his own. Although he had enjoyed numerous affairs, at the age forty-four he was still unmarried but needed a wife to establish his dynasty. So far, though, his attempts to marry had been unsuccessful as he had suffered the humiliation of two broken engagements – the first to a young English lady who severed all connection with him when she discovered he was simultaneously conducting a liaison with a certain Miss Howard; and the second to his cousin, Princess Mathilde Bonaparte. Mathilde's father, Jerome – Napoleon I's youngest brother – had been eager to bring the couple together. They were clearly attracted to one another, and Jerome felt it would enhance his own position if his daughter were to marry the great Napoleon's heir. When, though, he heard of Louis' reckless Strasbourg escapade he wrote disappointedly to his brother:

101

"All that you say about Louis' extravagant ideas is quite true. We only know here what is in the papers, and that is sufficient to make us groan over so ridiculous an enterprise."[141]

In spite of Mathilde's desperate pleading and her assurance that Louis' courage and spirit of adventure had made her love him even more, Jerome broke off the engagement and forbade the couple from meeting or even writing to one another. Consequently, several years passed before they met again, and, while imprisoned in Ham, Louis learned that Mathilde had married a Russian nobleman. Nonetheless, following his return to France in 1848, he sought her out and she loaned him a substantial sum of money to assist him in his struggle for power. As their friendship was restored, Louis frequently turned to Mathilde for advice, particularly in the matter of finding a suitable wife to secure the succession.

Mathilde agreed with Louis' ministers that it would strengthen his standing and benefit the country if he were to marry a foreign princess, such as the beautiful nineteen-year-old, Princess Carola of Sweden. He duly sent a message to that effect to Stockholm, but Carola's father, predicting that Louis' reign would be brief, politely declined the proposal on her behalf. Wasting no time, Louis turned his attention to Queen Victoria's niece, Princess Adelaide of Hohenlohe-Langenburg. Although he had never met Adelaide, he believed the marriage would help secure good relations with Germany and England, and he was happy to learn that her mother – Queen Victoria's half-sister, Feodore – was not entirely opposed to the idea. Unfortunately for him, Queen Victoria considered the idea preposterous, and persuaded Feodore to reject the proposal.

Unwilling to face further humiliation, Louis abandoned his plan of marrying a foreign princess – a decision made all the easier by the fact that he had already set his heart on Eugénie de Montijo, the fiery and beautiful twenty-six-year-old daughter of a Spanish grandee, whom he first met while visiting Mathilde. Intelligent and well-travelled, Eugénie had spent her youth in Spain, England and France, and had followed Louis' career with a childlike fascination. At the time of the coup d'état, she had written to him, effusively expressing her admiration – a compliment which he remembered at their first meeting.

Although he was instantly attracted to Eugénie, he initially considered her too low-born to marry, and intended instead to take her as his mistress. She, though, under the guidance of her mother and her mentor, had the foresight to spurn his undeniable charms, insisting that she could not sleep with him unless they were married. This did not prevent her, though, from tempting him with passionate letters until he decided to abandon convention and make her his wife. Not until several years later did it transpire that her billets-doux had been dictated by her mother and her mentor, both of whom were inspired more by ambition than by affection.

Louis was so delighted when Eugénie accepted his proposal that it came as a blow to realise that his extended family failed to share his exultation.

"It is quite natural and proper to love Mademoiselle de Montijo," wrote one of his cousins, before adding laconically, "but of course one cannot marry her."[142]

Mathilde was even more shocked by his 'violent passion' and reputedly fell to her knees to implore him to withdraw his proposal. The majority of journalists and ministers likewise thought the idea ridiculous, one reporter commenting:

"It is not the kind of alliance which those who support the Emperor, his servants, and personal friends have wished. A diplomatic union might have been of some utility to the State; a union with a French lady would have been agreeable to the people…On the other hand a union with a Spanish lady meets with no sympathy from the nation, and

103

can only be the result of personal gratification. The head of a great State like France, anxious to found a new dynasty, should entertain more serious thoughts and higher aims than to satisfy a whim and succumb to a young woman's beauty."[143]

Undeterred by the criticism, Louis calmly explained that history showed how many foreign princesses had been unhappy in France, and how many alliances forged by marriage created difficulties for the country. What was more, he said, 'I have preferred a woman whom I love and respect to a woman unknown to me, with whom an alliance would have had advantages mixed with sacrifices.'[144]

In January 1853, only a week after the announcement of their betrothal, Louis and Eugénie were married in a lavish ceremony in the Salle des Marechaux at the Tuileries, but although Eugénie was now officially the Empress, several wedding guests refused to treat her with due deference. Louis' uncle, bowing to the groom but completely ignored the bride; and even Mathilde, who had once been her friend, refused to travel in a carriage beside her. These slights continued throughout the days of celebration that followed, as one cousin, whom Eugénie attempted to put at ease, retorted sharply, 'Madame, you are very good, but you seem to forget that I was born and brought up at Court';[145] while another openly described her as stubborn, frivolous and extravagant.

Even in England, ministers considered the marriage a mésalliance, one British diplomat reporting that it was, 'a fatal measure; he would have done far better if he could have married the Hohenlohe girl, who was dying to be Empress.'[146]

Amid all the criticism, only the aging procureur-general, André Dupin, spoke in defence of the Emperor, stating that he:

"...acts more sensibly by marrying the woman he likes than by eating humble-pie and bargaining for some strait-laced, stuck-up German princess, with feet as large as mine. At any rate, when he kisses his wife, it will be because he feels inclined, and not because he feels compelled."[147]

If Eugénie failed to obtain the support of Louis' family, she was more successful in winning the hearts of his people. Her countless acts of generosity did not pass unnoticed, nor did the fact that, when offered a choice of wedding gifts, she requested that all political prisoners in exile should be allowed to return to France. Still more impressive was her response when, on hearing that the Municipal Council of Paris had voted to purchase her diamonds worth six-hundred-thousand francs, she graciously asked that the money be given instead to the poor. She was equally generous with her own private funds, donating vast sums to build hospitals and convalescent homes, as well as sending varying amounts to individual petitioners. Often, in the winter, she visited the sick incognito; and, when a cholera epidemic broke out in Amiens, she wandered among the sufferers, disregarding the warnings of the nurses who feared that she might contract the disease. On meeting two children who had been orphaned by the epidemic, she arranged payments to support them for the rest of their lives.

In the early years of her marriage, her kindness and sparkling appearance so enchanted the public that spontaneous applause erupted whenever they saw her. Within the court, too, ministers who had originally viewed her with disdain were struck by the charm and intelligence of her scintillating conversation. The Minister of Foreign Affairs had been so opposed to the marriage that he had threatened to resign, but, after spending some time with Eugénie, he tore up his letter of resignation.

"She did not at first appeal either to the senses or the imagination of men," wrote Princess Radziwill. "...Later on, however, when one had opportunity to see her more frequently, and especially to talk with her, her personality grew upon one with an especial charm that has never been equalled by any other woman."[148]

Even her warmest admirers, though, were bemused by her unpredictability, considering her a 'baffling conundrum'[149] whose character was marked by countless contradictions. She was known, for example, for her piety and devotion to the Roman Catholic faith, which she practised almost to the point of superstition, having amassed a fine collection of relics for use in any emergency. When a courtier lay dying, she insisted that he could be cured by hanging a thread from John the Baptist's swaddling band on his bedpost. 'Her simple childlike faith,' wrote a visitor, 'wrung the last grim smile from the tortured lips of the dying courtier.'[150] Her piety was tempered though by a love of frivolity, fine clothes and courtly entertainments, including, contrary to the Church's teachings, séances and meetings with mediums, who invoked spirits which, in her opinion 'were probably embryonic, undeveloped spirits, since they did such childish things rapping tables, making chairs walk about, and so forth.'[151] Nor did her adherence to her faith prevent her from defying the Pope if his rulings ran contrary to her own convictions. When the Bishop of Orléans, with papal authority, opposed a plan to open university places to girls, claiming it favoured 'the designs of impiety by new and unheard-of attempts, and imprudently putting the last hand to the ruin of social order,'[152] Eugénie openly criticised him and, in a show of defiance, arranged for her nieces to attend lectures at the Sorbonne.

She and Louis were equally quick to stand up against the Church and civil authorities when, while staying at Biarritz in 1858, they received a deputation of the citizens of the Pyrenean town of Lourdes. A local shepherdess named Bernadette Soubirous claimed to have witnessed a series of visions of the Virgin Mary in a grotto known as Massabielle, and several healing miracles were said to have occurred at the site. As crowds began to gather, the authorities, with the backing of the bishop, ordered the construction of barricades around the grotto to prevent the building of an unauthorised shrine, but when Eugénie and Louis, who had visited a similar site at nearby Betharram, were told what was happening, they sent an order for the immediate removal of the fences to allow the people to continue their devotions.

Eugénie, who was, in Louis' opinion, devout but not bigoted, refused to accept that Catholicism was the only true religion. 'There is,' she said, 'but one justice before God; and it belongs to all men alike, rich or poor, black or white, Catholic or Protestant, Jew or Gentile.'

Her dismissal of the Bishop of Orléans' objections to girls' education was indicative of her belief in the need to improve the lot of women in society. Withstanding a great deal of criticism, she successfully fought to allow women to work in the Post Office; and, irked that they were barred from the Legion d'Honneur, she made a point of patronising female artists and musicians. This crusade sprang from her own frustration at being denied any significant role in affairs of state, particularly since she had always been fascinated by politics.

"Nothing...used to irritate me more," she wrote, "than to hear myself denied a political sense because I was a woman. I longed to reply: 'Indeed! Women have no political sense? What about Elizabeth? Maria Theresa? Catherine II?' And after all, was there not before my eyes...at Windsor, Queen Victoria? For more than twenty years she had been the personification, as noble as she was vigorous, of all the principles, all the traditions, all the tendencies of the British people."[153]

Famous women fascinated her, and when, within days of her wedding, Louis showed her many souvenirs of Marie Antoinette, she developed an interest in the tragic Queen, which would continue to the end of her life.

Her lack of bigotry was matched by her loyalty to her friends, several of whom were known to have been sympathetic to Louis Philippe. When a courtier questioned the wisdom of surrounding herself with such women, she replied that they had been friends before her marriage and she had no intention of abandoning them simply because her position had changed. At the same time, though, a close acquaintance noted that she was 'capable, even in the case of old friends and old servants, of a curious hardness that would amaze and puzzle. What had touched that chord you could not imagine.'[154] She found it impossible to forgive even the smallest slight, and, once she mistrusted someone, nothing could be done to convince her of their sincerity.

Her profoundly romantic nature allowed for no sentimentality; and, although she was generally regarded as brave, the slightest crisis could throw her into a panic. She often appeared cold and uncaring and yet could empathise with suffering creatures and would not even allow an insect to be killed without a good reason. On one occasion she stopped to stroke a lamb being carried by a shepherd and, on hearing that he was taking it to be slaughtered, she was so appalled that she insisted on buying it to enable it to live out its days in the freedom of a pasture. Bafflingly, though, she had grown up enjoying the dubious pleasures of bull-fights, and even attempted to introduce them into France. At her insistence, Louis accompanied her to one such spectacle, which turned out to be a particularly bloody affair.

> "…From the moment that the first horse was killed," a witnesses noted, "the Emperor never raised his eyes for a moment from the bill of the performance, which was lying in front of him: indeed the man who had finally to despatch the bulls was obliged to come quite underneath the Imperial box to ask permission; and even then the Emperor appeared at first not to see him."[155]

Happily for the bulls, Louis' dislike of the spectacle was shared by the majority of his subjects and, as a result, the popularity of bullfights was confined to the south of the country.

Chapter 9 – A Remarkable, An Unusual Man

Descriptions of the charming Emperor, his glamorous court and his sparkling Empress, intrigued the naturally inquisitive Queen Victoria; and, although her attachment to the Orléans family, left her reluctant to admit it, she eagerly awaited an opportunity to meet the fascinating couple. She did not have long to wait, for, within twelve months of Louis' marriage, a crisis in the East drew him into an alliance with Britain.

Louis could not forgive Tsar Nicholas' refusal to acknowledge him as the rightful Emperor, and, soon after his accession, he ordered his ambassador in Constantinople to undertake the repair of the roof of the Church of the Holy Sepulchre in Jerusalem, which was under the joint control of the Orthodox and Roman Catholic Churches. As the work was carried out at French expense, Louis then declared that henceforth the church would remain solely under his jurisdiction. This assertion not only angered the Tsar but also shocked other European sovereigns, some of whom accused Louis of petulance, claiming that he was sulking because Nicholas refused to address 'Mon Frère' – the customary form of communication between monarchs. In view of the outcry, Louis was forced to withdraw his declaration but not before the Tsar had reluctantly agreed to accept him as France's legitimate sovereign.

In spite of the compromise, relations between France and Russia remained tense, and the rising hostility accelerated when, in 1853, the Tsar embarked on a campaign to take control of the Dardanelles and Constantinople, ostensibly to protect the Orthodox Christians in the rapidly crumbling Ottoman Empire. The Turks attempted to repel the invaders and, in November 1853, the Russians destroyed the entire Turkish fleet in the harbour at Sinope. The French balked at such aggression; and the British, fearing for their trading links with Turkey and India, and called it an act of unqualified treachery and barbarism by the Tsar, who was 'a brigand of the first water.'

The event brought about an unlikely alliance between the old rivals, Britain and the France, but, as both Louis and Queen Victoria were eager to avoid war, they urged the Tsar to accept a compromise.

> "Let your Majesty adopt that plan, on which the Queen of England and myself are perfectly in accord," Louis wrote to Nicholas, "and tranquillity will be restored, and the world satisfied. There is, in fact, nothing in this plan that is not worthy of your Majesty, nothing that can wound your honour. But if, from a motive difficult to be comprehended, your Majesty should refuse, in that case, France, as well as England, would be obliged to leave to the fate of arms, and to the hazards of war, what might be decided at present by reason and justice."[156]

The Tsar refused to back down, and, in March 1854, France and Britain declared war on Russia. Queen Victoria immediately sent her cousin, George, Duke of Cambridge, to Paris to discuss with Louis the details of the unfamiliar alliance. He was received with great warmth and driven through streets beside the Emperor in a display of unity, before being taken to watch a review of the troops who were about to depart for the Crimea. So impressed was the Duke that he was able to report that he had formed 'a very favourable opinion of the French Army' and a conviction of 'the cordiality of feelings which now so happily exists between the two nations.'[157]

His assessment of the preparedness of the French troops was evidenced during the first winter of the war when, unlike their British counterparts, more of whom were dying of disease than of injuries, Louis' soldiers were amply supplied with warm coats and tents, and were accompanied by mobile bakeries to ensure that they adequately fed. Their provision for the wounded was also superior to that of their British allies, as one English officer recorded:

> "After the Battle of the Alma they were able to assist us by the loan of ambulance waggons for the carriage of our wounded to the shore for removal to Scutari, when we were without a single ambulance waggon for the purpose...Their transport animals were looked after by men who had been trained to take proper care of them. From time to time they took down our sick to Balaclava – sometimes in very large numbers together – on well-trained and well-cared for mules, conducted by men of the corps d'infirmiers."[158]

George, though, had been mistaken about the 'cordiality of feeling' between the allies, who so mistrusted one another that the British Commander-in-Chief, Lord Raglan, who had lost an arm at the Battle of Waterloo, went so far as to refer to the French as the enemy[q]. Louis exacerbated the rivalry when he wrote an article for a prominent newspaper, claiming that the victory at Alma was entirely due to the French, who had resisted the 'more timid counsels' of other commanders. The British were so insulted that the diplomat, Lord Cowley, was sent to remonstrate with the Emperor, who assured him that he had meant no offence but wished 'merely to acknowledge the energy displayed by [his Commander-in-Chief] when differences of opinion arose between him and officers of the French army and fleet.'[159]

In reality, Louis had written the article in the hope of gaining greater support for the war, for, in spite of the allies' early successes, many of his countrymen believed he had entered into the conflict primarily to increase his

---

[q] Xenophobic slanders were not aimed solely at the French. When war broke out, rumours were rife that the German Prince Albert had been arrested as a traitor and imprisoned in the Tower of London! Several British ministers believed that Napoleon III was behind the rumours, having paid British journalists to denigrate the Prince.

own popularity at a time when there was a growing conviction that his reign would be of short duration.

In an effort to boost enthusiasm among his own people, he invited Prince Albert to witness a review of the troops at St Omer in the hope that his presence would demonstrate Britain's commitment to the campaign. With the Queen's full support, the Prince accepted the invitation, despite his private concerns about Louis' method of seizing power and his semi-autocratic regime. Arriving in France in the autumn of 1854, the Prince was happily surprised to find that his host was 'benevolent and anxious for the good of the people,' and, after only a few brief conversations, he concluded that Louis was possibly the only man who could hold his country together.

The Emperor was even more impressed by Prince Albert, whom he described as 'one of the highest intelligences of our time,' although he had to admit that he was disappointed that his guest refused a cigar after dinner, and later, in the gardens, declined the offer of a cigarette. Before the visit was over, Louis casually mentioned that he had not been able to entertain the Prince as well as he would have wished, since he was not at home in Paris, but he would be honoured if he would return to France with Queen Victoria at their earliest convenience. Prince Albert graciously accepted the invitation and returned the compliment by saying that he and the Queen would be delighted to entertain the Emperor and Empress in England.

While Louis was revelling in his new friendship, his Generals were becoming increasingly frustrated by his constant interference in their plans. From the safety of St Cloud, he bombarded them with instructions, despite having no first-hand experience of the conditions under which they were fighting. His letters to the ordinary soldiers displayed such a complete lack of understanding that they were more likely to inspire derision than allegiance. When, for example, he was told that entire platoons were being wiped out by disease, he wrote to remind them that plague had struck the armies of Napoleon I, whereas they had '*only* the cholera.'

> "Try to keep your feet dry and warm," he advised. "Take care of your health. Mine is very good. Biarritz is a nice place of residence. But I shall soon join my army, and share its labours."[160]

The mention of his plan to go to the Crimea to take command of the army sent a ripple of alarm through the French High Command; and when he told his allies that his presence was 'the only way to bring to a rapid conclusion an expedition which otherwise must result in disaster to England as well as to France,'[161] the British were thrown into a complete panic. During the Emperor's absence, there was a strong possibility that France might descend into yet another revolution and, if he were toppled or killed in battle, Britain would be left facing the Russians alone.

> "Napoleon," said the British Ambassador to Constantinople, "thinks that he is endowed with the political genius of Richelieu and the virtues of St. Louis. But he will be found out at last. His real measure will be taken. His subjects talk of nothing but the war at present. But his time will come. Only one of the last five sovereigns of France preserved his crown to the end of his life. A storm may any day arise in Paris, and not many more French troops can be expected for the [Crimean campaign]. They will be kept back for home requirements. That is the question of the greatest urgency for England at this moment."[162]

The Foreign Secretary, Lord Clarendon, was duly dispatched to Boulogne to dissuade him from carrying out his plan, by explaining that British troops would find it difficult to serve under a French monarch. Louis dismissed the argument by assuring Clarendon that he would discuss his strategies with Lord Raglan, and that 'the honour of the British flag would be his first consideration, even beyond that of his own.'[163]

Shortly after this meeting, Louis wrote to Queen Victoria, asking whether his proposed visit to England could take place in April that year. The Queen, realising that this would give her an opportunity to dissuade him from going to the Crimea, responded cordially and, a few weeks later, a fleet of warships was sent to escort him and Eugénie to Dover.

Crowds turned out in their thousands to welcome the Emperor and Empress to England, where journalists who had once written so derogatorily of him, now hailed Louis as a brother-in-arms.

At Windsor, Queen Victoria waited eagerly to set eyes on the charming French Emperor and his beautiful wife, but her excitement was tempered by the recollection of recent meeting with Queen Amélie, of whom she had written:

> "It made us both so sad to see her drive away in a plain coach with miserable post-horses, and to think that this was the Queen of the French, and that six years ago her husband was surrounded by the same pomp and grandeur which…surround his successor."[164]

Her spirits were quickly lifted, the moment that she set eyes on her guests. Louis was not classically handsome, for his head appeared too big for his body and his eyelids drooped as though he were permanently tired, but he was charming and dapper, speaking English with barely a trace of an accent, and, as the Queen observed, he was 'civil, tactful and amiable.' Eugénie, too, impressed her, being 'full of courage and spirit, and yet so gentle, with such innocence…she has the prettiest and most modest manner.'[165]

The naturally passionate Queen Victoria could not fail to be charmed by so romantic a figure, whose manner among ladies had, according to Princess Radziwill, 'a tinge of chivalry that savoured of olden times, and generally succeeded in winning for him all that he wanted.'[166]

Over the next few days, the Queen's admiration increased, as she wrote in effusive detail to her cousin:

"[The Emperor is] a remarkable, an unusual man; on all occasions both publicly and in private, when he was quite alone with us, his manner was dignified, decorous, tactful and unbelievably calm...His manners have something which in English we call 'fascinating'; he is natural, very frank, melancholy and sometimes even enthusiastic."[167]

The Empress, too, she said, had 'a charming profile and figure with a sweetness and friendliness that win all hearts.'[168] More surprisingly and much to Queen Victoria's amusement, Eugénie succeeded in winning the admiration and affection of Prince Albert, who rarely enjoyed such friendly relations with women. So obvious was his enchantment that he felt obliged to inform his former mentor, Baron Stockmar, that, fond as he was of the Empress, their relationship was entirely moral and honourable.

Not everyone at Windsor was quite so impressed by the visitors. One lady-in-waiting reported that the servants found their presence irksome, and complained that 'the noise and route and confusion of the French people...is not to be told – all the doors open and screaming and talking – the ladies dressing with open doors.'[169] Lord Greville was equally disappointed by the Emperor, for, while acknowledging that he was extremely well-mannered, he added that 'everybody is struck with his mean and diminutive figure and vulgar appearance.'[170]

Unaware of the jibes and criticism, Louis revelled in the Queen's attention, and was delighted when, at the conclusion of an opera performance, she rose in full view of the audience and curtsied to him.

"Nothing could be better done, nor have produced a greater effect," one witness recorded. "The cheers that followed this simple act were deafening; and even the Emperor's sombre countenance visibly brightened in accepting this great compliment."[171]

To the relief of his hosts, Louis agreed to abandon his plans to go to the Crimea, as the recent death of Tsar Nicholas[r] raised the possibility of a swift conclusion to the war. Instead, he reissued an invitation to the Queen and Prince Albert to visit France a few months later; and before he left England he was honoured to be invested with the Order of the Garter.

'I am a gentleman at last!' he declared in triumph.

On returning home, determined to maintain his friendship with the Queen and her people, he immediately wrote to thank her for her hospitality and sent gifts for all the British officers who had served in his escort.

"It is so sweet," he concluded, "to think that aside from political interests Your Majesty and your family feel some affection for us, that in the first rank of my preoccupations I place the desire always to be worthy of this august friendship."[172]

A month later, the allies sent a force of seventy-thousand men to the strategic city of Sebastopol where the greater part of the Russian army was stationed. Although the joint British and French troops could easily have taken the city, orders were given to halt the advance and to put the place under siege. As a result, the Russians had time to regroup, and, as thousands more lives were lost at the battles of Balaclava and Inkerman, the French became so disillusioned that, in Lord Greville's words, 'the unpopularity of Louis Napoleon increases and his discredit likewise, and as soon as the unpopularity shall extend to the army, it will be all over with him.'[173]

Louis, however, was more concerned with preparing for Queen Victoria's visit than with events in the Crimea, and he was glad to hear that she and Prince Albert would be accompanied by their two eldest

---

[r] Tsar Nicholas I caught a chill which developed into pneumonia, and he died in St Petersburg on 2nd March 1855.

children, Vicky and Bertie[s]. In August 1855, the royal party arrived on the French coast and, following a brief delay due to a thick fog, were escorted amid cheering crowds to Paris.

> "I am delighted, enchanted, amused, and interested," the Queen gushed to the King of the Belgians, "and think I never saw anything more beautiful and gay than Paris, or more splendid than all the Palaces."[174]

Still more gratifying was the warmth of the French people, who, despite the Queen's dowdiness with her dull straw bonnet and ill-matching parasol and handbag, cheered so loudly that Maréchal Magnan claimed the reception was 'much greater and much more enthusiastic even than that for Napoleon on his return from his victories.'[175]

While the Queen was admiring the Emperor, and Prince Albert and Vicky were struck by the beauty of Paris, fourteen-year-old Bertie was more enchanted by the attention he received from the beautiful Empress and her ladies-in-waiting, whose low-cut gowns and glamorous appearance contrasted sharply with that of his frumpily-dressed mother. So enamoured was he that he asked if he might stay and live with the Empress, and, when she replied that his parents would miss him, he answered that this was not the case, since they had many other children at home.

To add to the joy of the visit, reports arrived of the allies' progress in the Crimea, a sure sign in Louis' opinion, of the success of the alliance of Britain and France. For her part, Queen Victoria felt so comfortable with the Emperor and Empress that she was able to speak freely to them of her affection for the Orléans family. Although Louis had refused to restore their French estates, he assured her that he felt no personal antipathy

---

[s] Victoria, later the German Empress Frederick; and Albert Edward, later King Edward VII.

towards them and had destroyed nothing which Louis Philippe had created. To emphasise his point, he took her to various sites associated with the former King, including a trip to the shrine that had been built on the site of the Duke of Orléans' fatal carriage accident.

Once again, though, members of the Queen's suite were far less impressed by their French adventure. One lady-in-waiting complained that a footman's attentions were so intrusive that she could not even bathe without him rattling the door handle in an attempt to enter the room; while another claimed that the servants in general were disorganised, rude and 'most disobliging and uncivil.'[176]

By the time she returned to England, Queen Victoria was convinced that the visit had achieved the 'complete Union of the two countries...in the most satisfactory and solid manner, for it is not only a Union of the two Governments – the two Sovereigns – it is that of the two Nations!'[177] At the same time, she was careful not to offend the Orléans family, but immediately invited the Duke and Duchess of Montpensier to Osborne, and sent Queen Amélie a full report of her visit to the Duke of Orléans' shrine.

Within a month, Sebastopol fell to the allies, leading Louis to suggest that this would be an opportune moment to arrange an honourable peace, which would enable him to do restore more congenial relations with Russia. He organised a congress, attended by the Duke of Cambridge and an array of military and naval commanders; and, four months later, in March 1856, the Treaty of Paris was signed, by which the Russians ceded the land that they had occupied, and, in return, the Sultan agreed to protect the rights of all his Christian subjects.

If Louis anticipated praise for his efforts, his hopes were quickly dispelled. Several British officers accused him of acting too hastily in bringing about an armistice before Russia was totally defeated; and at home many of his people believed that French blood had been shed in vain.

Even Louis began to question his own motives:

"Was this worth the terrible waste of life and treasure," he asked, "...to say nothing of the equally great losses to Russia, in blood and money! I fear not."[178]

Ultimately, the conflict, which he had hoped would increase his popularity at home and cement good relations abroad, had failed on both counts; and the death of nine-hundred-thousand soldiers lay heavily on Louis' conscience.

Chapter 10 – A Worthy Man and Prince

Notwithstanding his disenchantment with the war, Louis had every reason to rejoice in the spring of 1856, for, two weeks before the signing of the Treaty of Paris, Eugénie gave birth to a son, 'Loulou', the Prince Imperial.

After three years of marriage, the forty-eight-year-old Emperor had almost given hope of producing an heir, and his disappointment was all the more acute because he genuinely loved children, and had told Queen Victoria that he envied her and Prince Albert for possessing such a remarkable family. When he discovered that Eugénie was pregnant, he could hardly control his elation; and, as her labour began on 15th March, he flew to her room, determined to be present at the birth. For fifteen hours he remained at her side, working himself into such a nervous frenzy that he could not stand still but paced around incessantly, sobbing into his hands. When, at last the baby was born 'he was so overpowered with joy that he rushed into the next room and embraced the five first persons he met. Then recollecting that his behaviour was not dignified, he said, 'Je ne peux pas vous embrasser tous.'"[179]

The whole of France shared his joy, as spontaneous celebrations erupted across the country; and, two months later, over three-hundred-thousand people participated in a procession to Notre Dame for the baby's Christening.

> "There were people at every window along the quays," wrote a lady-in-waiting, "people on the roofs, on the chimneys even, people standing on trestles along the road, on the parapets by the Seine, on the arches of the bridges, in every possible corner, cramped and crushed, but heedless of discomfort; an inquisitive, sympathetic, innumerable crowd, buzzing, swaying, like bees in a swarm, thirsting for a sight which it knew would be magnificent, unique, in

fact, on account of the splendour of the procession and the great pomp which was to be observed."[180]

At the conclusion of the ceremony, the Emperor and Empress stood on a balcony of the Tuileries, receiving a rapturous and extended ovation, but, amid the cheers, few people realised the effect that the painful and potentially fatal confinement had had upon the Empress. One visitor, who saw her at the christening told a friend that she had aged dramatically and the trauma of childbirth had 'faded, coarsened, and yellowed the skin of her face, which I had thought so fine, transparent, and youthful.'[181]

While honouring a promise she had made to build a chapel dedicated to her patron saint in thanksgiving for the safe delivery of her son, she stated that the birth had been so traumatic that she would have no more children, and allegedly refused to sleep with her husband ever again. Her detractors, and even some of her admirers, claimed that this was merely an excuse to avoid him as she had never truly loved him and was entirely devoid of passion.

> "People have said that her skill, as Caesar's wife, in avoiding the breath of scandal, is a great proof of her 'cleverness,'" wrote the composer, Ethel Smythe, "but I suspect it was still more a case of absence of temptation from within. She was not tender, for one thing, nor imaginative; and imagination plays a great part, I think, in women's love affairs. Above all, not to beat about the bush, there was no sensuality in her composition."[182]

Deprived of his wife's embraces, Louis returned to the arms of his many mistresses, on whom he lavished gifts of jewels and beautiful houses. Several followed him on his tours around the country, scandalising his ministers who were doing their utmost to keep his promiscuity from the public, and deeply distressing Eugénie who refused to suffer in silence. Louis seemed incapable of understanding why she was offended when he blatantly

121

took her best friends and ladies-in-waiting as lovers; nor could he comprehend why she flew into a rage when they openly flaunted their liaisons before her. On one occasion, while she was attending an art exhibition, a member of the court suggested that she and the Emperor might like to purchase a series of statuettes of a woman, representing the four seasons. As soon as she saw the exhibit, she recognised that it was modelled on her husband's most recent mistress in various positions, which threw her into such a tantrum that she stormed from the room.

With each passing month, her jealousy intensified to the point where Louis could not even speak with a guest without her appearing and scowling at the door to ensure that he was not entertaining a woman. Her rages became the talk of Europe, and the constant bickering embarrassed their visitors, as one British Prime Minister observed, while joining them for dinner. Eugénie made a superficial comment to which Louis rather unkindly joked,

"What is the difference between you and a mirror?" – the answer being that a mirror is reflective and his wife was not. Eugénie responded equally sharply,

"And what is the difference between *you* and a mirror? A mirror is polished and you certainly are not."

Often, even when they restrained their tongues, visitors were aware of their underlying domestic disharmony.

"I myself," wrote an attendant after first meeting the couple, "was sensible of a somewhat painful impression when I entered this vast salon, in the middle of which their Majesties showed as two melancholy and isolated specks. It seemed to me there was a lack of life; great rooms too big for two persons alone…no equality, no familiarity – it is enough to kill one with boredom."[183]

In the early years of their marriage, the differences in their characters had been barely discernible, but now they became ever more apparent. Louis was calm, quiet,

122

contemplative and, according to his critics, so scheming that it was impossible to read his intentions in his face. Eugénie, on the other hand, was dogmatic and impulsive, dominating every conversation, and making no secret of her prejudices as well as her genuine kindness. It disturbed Louis and his ministers that she spoke freely on all manner of sensitive subjects, regardless of whether or not her hearers were to be trusted.

"Her many intimacies with ladies who bore her no real sympathy," wrote Princess Radziwill, "...did her much harm and caused her many annoyances which she could well have avoided had she shown herself more careful in what she did or said."[184]

Several close acquaintances concluded that the couple would be happier were they to separate or even divorce, but, as neither would consider such an option, their marriage became a matter of 'daily warfare', in which Louis was subjected to so many angry outbursts that his home filled him with terror and disgust.

"The Empress," wrote one of her detractors, "showed herself essentially tactless in the relations of married life. Of a cold, unimpassioned temperament, she had nothing to offer but false protestations of love; she thus became powerless to keep the affections of her husband, who could no longer doubt that in the first exaltation of his feeling, in the blindness of his hope, he had given far more than he had received...With a little conjugal tact, the Empress might certainly have lessened for herself, as well as for the Emperor, the loneliness of their domestic life. She might have aroused in her simple-hearted husband, if not a new love, a feeling of remorse which would certainly have checked the increasing coldness between them."[185]

What many observers failed to notice, however, was the fact that, beneath the tensions and discord, Louis' deepest feelings for Eugénie remained unchanged. Often, he was caught gazing at her affectionately; and fifteen years after their wedding, he wrote a long description of her talents and beauty. One close acquaintance stated that, notwithstanding their many differences, Louis was 'forever charmed by the brilliancy of her conversation, and still more so by the sincerity of her character and the purity of her ideals in all matters of conduct.'[186] Moreover, he so appreciated her political acumen that he came to rely on her advice before making any important decisions. Although his ministers were irked by what they saw as her interference, Louis knew that Eugénie had taken great pains to study all aspects of government. From the time they were married she had insisted on being present at all of his meetings with diplomats and ambassadors so that she could take notes of the proceedings to which she could later refer. She had set herself, too, a rigid reading schedule to learn about all the major issues that affected the French people, and had such a quick grasp of the most complex subjects that Louis often trusted her judgement more than his own. When, for example, he considered negotiating a formal alliance with Tsar Alexander II after the Crimean War, she warned him that, since the British, and more particularly Queen Victoria and Prince Albert, mistrusted the Russians, it could seriously damage Anglo-French relations, and so, acting on her advice, he cultivated instead an unofficial friendship with the Tsar.

The more he came to rely on her, the more Louis' ministers disliked her. One went so far as to claim that she had a 'fatal' influence upon him, having emasculated him by 'bringing about a certain lack of force and a weakness of will-power', which led to 'the omnipotence of the Empress, and which also helped to lay at home and abroad the foundations of a despicable policy, the formal expression of an authority which emphasised the weakness of Napoleon III."[187]

Their determination to curb her influence was never more in evidence than in 1857 when, following a visit to the Isle of Wight, Louis travelled to Stuttgart to meet the Tsar. Eugénie planned to go with him but, shortly before she was due to leave, she was told that, as the Tsarina would not be present, and so it would be inappropriate for her to attend. Not until it was too late did she hear that the Tsarina had changed her mind and gone to Stuttgart, but no one had thought to inform the French Empress of the change of plan.

Ironically, while the birth of their son brought Louis and Eugénie closer together, his upbringing became a source of constant bickering between them. Soon after the Prince Imperial was born, Louis told a friend that they both were 'resolved to make him a worthy man and prince' before adding that, 'the Empress is especially interested in this good work. When she puts her heart and mind in anything, she always succeeds.'[188]

The baby was only four months old, however, when his parents had their first major disagreement about him. Louis, appreciating the benefits of fresh air, asked Loulou's nurse to take him to a terrace by the river where Louis Philippe's children had often played. Eugénie, with the support of her doctors, claimed that the river air was unhealthy, and wanted him to be taken instead to the Tuileries gardens. Louis, fearing that he would be too much in the public gaze, refused to allow this to happen, and, consequently, the little Prince was kept permanently indoors in ill-ventilated rooms in stifling heat.

Soon afterwards, Louis was obliged to leave Paris on official business, while Eugénie, who was still recovering from the effects of childbirth, was advised to travel to Biarritz for the good of her health. Initially, it was agreed that Loulou would remain in Paris in the charge of his English nurse, Miss Shaw, but, at the last moment, Eugénie decided to take him with her. Louis argued that the baby was far too young to travel such a distance, but, Eugénie insisted on having her way, compromising only so far as to take a specifically-appointed physician with her.

Loulou's parents at least agreed on the appointment of nursery attendants, including a wet-nurse, whose diet consisted of a selection of meat and vegetables as well as a bottle of wine a day; and the English Miss Shaw, who came on the highest recommendation of Queen Victoria. Loulou quickly became attached to Miss Shaw, whom he fondly called 'Nana' but other members of the household thought her to be an unsettling influence. When a tutor, Augustin Filon, was appointed to replace her, she remained with the family, leading Filon to conclude that, 'her only fault was to imagine herself necessary after she had ceased to be useful. I saw her sometime after my arrival display certain signs of belated coquetry, and show a great desire to become young again.'[189] Loulou's doctor was equally concerned about her behaviour, for, although he conceded that she 'understands her business admirably,' he was disconcerted to see her medicate the prince for even the most minor ailment.

> "I do not like to accustom children to drugs," he wrote to his wife. "By habit the body loses its sensibility to remedies, and when it becomes necessary to make it obedient, one has to strike heavy blows, which are not always without unpleasant consequences…This was precisely contrary to the wishes of Miss Shaw, who, imbued with the prejudices of English nurses, drugged the Prince continually and said nothing about it."[190]

In her defence, Miss Shaw might have argued that she was merely fulfilling the Empress' instructions, as Eugénie was so fretful about the baby's health that every time he vomited she was convinced that he had been poisoned. She regularly summoned the physicians, claiming he was too hot, too cold, too pale, too flushed, too slow in learning to crawl, or too awkward in his movements; and, as he grew older, she became irrationally anxious if he were hot or excited, and frequently interrupted his games because she feared that he was becoming over-heated.

More damaging to the child was her conception of a 'worthy man and prince' as one who is in every way superior to his fellow human beings. On her orders, there was to be no familiarity from his attendants, and he was denied the company of other children except during their annual holiday in Biarritz, where he was permitted to select his own playmates.

> "He knows nothing," reported his doctor, "of the laughter, the jumping, the change of expression, the tears, the angers, and the delights, which vary life when a number of children are together."[191]

Although Eugénie insisted on keeping Loulou sheltered from his peers, she wanted him to be aware of his privileged position by introducing him to the poor, whose squalid dwellings she visited on a weekly basis. When, however, she tentatively suggested that he might accompany her, ministers and officers strongly advised her against it, warning that his safety could not be guaranteed. Consequently, in the words of his tutor, he 'did not visit the poor, and continued to study modern life in the pages of De Viris and Cornelius Nepos. He knew none of the valuable lessons of charity, which would have been so good for his intelligence and for his heart.'[192]

Louis, on the other hand, wanted his son to enjoy as normal a childhood as possible, and was keen to encourage him to join in the rough and tumble games of other boys. On one occasion, as he and Loulou were walking hand-in-hand through the Tuileries, he spotted a small band of urchins playing noisily nearby and told his son to join in their game. Loulou had so much fun that, on returning home, he eagerly told his mother all that had happened, at which she scolded his father for allowing him to mix so freely with such 'ill-bred' companions.

Nor was Loulou exempt from Eugénie's legendary temper, and at times she flew at him in such a rage that one contemporary reported that she treated him with a severity bordering on tyranny. This attitude led to many 'violent discussions' between her and Louis, whom she regularly berated for failing to support her strict regime. On one occasion, for example, when she had told the barber to dress Loulou's hair in a particular style, she was angry to observe that, no matter how carefully the barber followed her orders, the Prince would deliberately ruffle it up with his fingers. Exasperatedly, she took him to the Emperor, expecting that he would deliver a severe reprimand, but when Loulou burst into tears and said that he refused to be made to look like a girl, his father was so impressed that he stated that henceforth he must be allowed to give his own instruction to the barber. It was a rare occasion, though, when Loulou dared to stand up to his mother, for, as he told his father, he thought that she said many foolish things but he was rather frightened of her.

Fortunately, Loulou retained a strong and loving relationship with Louis, who, in spite of Eugénie's restrictions, introduced him to activities which he knew would interest him. He encouraged his love of drawing and acting – skills for which he showed a remarkable talent – and granted him a military commission when he was only nine years old. The following year, he took him hunting, and began to give him prominent positions on ceremonial occasions with the intention of preparing him for his future role as Emperor.

Indulgent as he was, however, Louis was quick to reprimand him for any sign of arrogance. He upbraided him for speaking rudely to his tutor, and insisted that he must refer to his equerry as *Monsieur* rather than calling him by his surname. He was equally adamant that he must not misuse his position or title, telling him that he must be 'humble and wise' and reminding him that, 'as yet you have everything to learn, my child.'[193]

With his father's charm and his mother's looks, Loulou was such an attractive child that the Crown

Princess of Prussia, who seldom praised her own seven children, gushed to Queen Victoria:

> "What a darling he is! I think he is the prettiest most interesting child I ever saw. With very regular features, a beautiful complexion, most sweet expression and fine large blue eyes with a fringe of black eyelashes and black hair...he seems very forward and intelligent."[194]

Queen Victoria agreed that he was 'very nice' but rather churlishly added, 'but excessively short for his age'.

Chapter 11 – From the Alps to the Adriatic

Shortly after eight o'clock, on the evening of 14th January 1858, Louis and Eugénie set out to the Paris Opera for a performance of *William Tell,* and *Mary Stuart,* featuring the renowned Italian tragedienne, Adelaide Ristori. As they neared the entrance to the theatre, four men ran forwards and hurled grenades beneath their carriage, instantly killing several bystanders and members of the mounted guard together with twenty horses. Remarkably, apart from a scratch on Louis' head and a cut on Eugénie's cheek, they sustained no serious injuries, and, as the attendants rushed to their aid, the blood-spattered Empress, brushed them aside, saying:

"Do not bother yourselves about us; it is our trade; take care of the wounded."[195]

To rapturous applause the couple walked calmly on into the theatre where one member of the audience observed that, although the Emperor looked pale and rather nervous, he and the Empress sat through the entire performance as though nothing untoward had happened. The following day, to demonstrate their refusal to be cowed by the incident, they rode the full length of several Parisian boulevards with only one officer in attendance.

The police, meanwhile, were been busily gathering information about the conspirators, one of whom, Giuseppe Pierri, had been arrested prior to the attack when he was recognised as a known insurgent by an alert policeman. A second man, Charles de Rudio, was apprehended shortly afterwards; and, when a hapless servant named Gomez was discovered to be searching for his missing master, the police ordered him to take them to his house, where the leader of the group, an Italian nationalist named Felipe Orsini, was lying wounded, having been injured by his own grenade.

This was not the first time that an Italian insurgent had made an attempt on Louis' life. Three years earlier, while he was riding on the Champ Elysees, a man stepped out in front of him and discharged two bullets from a pistol. Fortunately for Louis, the would-be assassin missed his target, and a detective, brandishing a dagger, quickly disarmed him. A few months later, another Italian nationalist pointed a gun towards the imperial carriage as it arrived at a theatre, but a diligent officer, seeing what was about to happen, seized the assailant's arm forcing him to misfire. Unbeknown to the gunman, however, Louis was not in the carriage, which was occupied only by three ladies-in-waiting.

Orsini's attack was more damaging and gained greater notoriety on both sides of the English Channel. Queen Victoria followed the 'dreadful' details of the subsequent investigation, and was shocked to read that the French police had discovered that the plot had been hatched in England, where the grenades had been manufactured with the help of an exiled anarchist – the French surgeon, Simon Bernard. Irked that the British authorities were slow to arrest Bernard, the French Ambassador, Count Walewski, was even more disconcerted to discover that, under British law, there was no serious charge to bring against him. He approached the Prime Minister, Palmerston, and asked him to make Conspiracy to Murder a capital crime, and, within a short time, Palmerston introduced a bill to that effect to the House of Commons. To his surprise, the majority of Members of Parliament vehemently opposed his suggestion, arguing that it would be wrong to change British law to satisfy French demands, and that it would threaten the country's reputation as a haven for political refugees. The debate became so heated that Palmerston was jeered in the streets, and, at length, to Queen Victoria's delight, he felt obliged to tender his resignation.

In the meantime, Bernard was brought to trial and, following a six-day hearing, his defence lawyer summed up his case in a speech which cleverly captured public opinion.

"Tell the French Emperor," he urged the court, "that he cannot intimidate an English jury: tell him that the jurybox is the sanctuary of English Liberty...tell him that though six hundred thousand French bayonets glittered before you; though the roar of French cannon thundered in your ears; you will return a verdict which your own hearts and consciences will sanction, and approve: careless whether that verdict please, or displease, a foreign despot; or scares, or shocks, and destroys for ever the Throne, which a Tyrant has built upon the ruins of the Liberties of a once free and mighty people."[196]

Predictably, Bernard was acquitted and a large crowd gathered outside the court to cheer him as though he were a hero. Appalled by the scene, French journalists produced a barrage of Anglophobic articles, which led to such a wide-spread hatred of all things English, that there were calls for Louis to launch an immediate invasion. Even Louis' half-brother, the Duke of Morny[t], contributed to the feeling of outrage when, in a widely-publicised letter, he referred to London as 'a lair of assassins' in which nothing was done to prevent murderers from preparing their heinous crimes.

This wave of anti-British feeling could not have come at a more inopportune time for Louis, who feared that the recent marriage of Queen Victoria's eldest daughter, Vicky, to the heir to the throne of Prussia, signified a strengthening of relations between the two countries, which could be detrimental to French interests.

Orsini, meanwhile, appeared in court, where, with impressive eloquence, he accepted full responsibility for the crime. He had been motivated, he said, by a desire to rid Italy of Austrian and Papal control – a plan which had been thwarted by Louis' support for the Pope in 1849[u].

---

[t] Charles, Duke of Morny was the illegitimate son of Louis' mother, Hortense, and her lover, the Comte de Flahaut. .

His arguments were so persuasive that even Eugénie was 'deeply moved by the nobility of his language, the heroism of his attitude, the supreme dignity of his bearing before the assize courts.'[197] She wept openly on hearing that he had been sentenced to death, and was so concerned about him that she talked of nothing else for days, leading some members of her household to believe that she had quite lost her senses. As the day of his execution approached, she fell on her knees before her husband, pleading for his life, and insisting that he had only carried out the attack because Louis was a friend of the Austrian Emperor, who was viewed as the greatest hindrance to Italian unification. Her behaviour so shocked Louis' advisers, than the Minister of the Interior told her bluntly that she should mind her own business so that he could get on with his; and warned her that, if Orsini were freed, she would not be able to appear in public without inciting the anger of the crowds. Already, he told her, this unseemly defence of a would-be assassin had led to all kinds of outlandish rumours, including the suggestion that she wished 'to get rid of the Emperor in the same way that Marie de Medici tried to get rid of Henry IV. After obtaining the crown she throws other women into his arms, and asks for the pardon of assassins.'[198]

Louis, however, also wished to grant a pardon to the conspirators, and Eugénie's pleading only increased his desire to release them. Nonetheless, under immense pressure from the senate and the legislative bodies, he was forced to sign the death warrants, and Orsini and Pierri were duly executed; while de Rudio and Gomez were sentenced to hard labour for life.

Soon after the executions had been carried out, Louis received a letter which Orsini had written during the final days of his imprisonment. Although he repented of having carried out so violent a crime, he was convinced that his cause was just, and he urged the Emperor to

---

[u] See below

support Italian unification, without which, he claimed, Europe would never know peace.

> "Let your Majesty remember that the Italians…joyfully laid down their lives for the great Napoleon; that they were faithful to his cause to the hour of his fall. Let your Majesty reflect that peace cannot exist, either for your Majesty or for Europe, while Italy is enslaved. Let your Majesty accept the last prayer of a patriot on the foot of the scaffold, and win the blessings of twenty-five millions of citizens by the deliverance of their country."[199]

His words made such an impression on Louis that, according to Eugénie, on that day 'he resolved, in his innermost conscience, on the Italian war.'[200]

Italy had long been a conglomeration of states and kingdoms which, since the Congress of Vienna in 1815, were dominated by the Austrian Habsburgs. At the time of his accession in 1830, Louis Philippe had promised to support the nationalists in their struggle for complete independence, but affairs at home prevented him from honouring his promise. The revolution which resulted in his downfall, also gave greater impetus to the nationalists' cause, as the Milanese drove the occupying garrison out of their city, and the King of Sardinia declared war on Austria. He had, though, underestimated the strength of his enemy, and, following a resounding defeat, he abdicated in favour of his son, Victor Emmanuel II.

Meanwhile, an ardent patriot and general, Giuseppe Garibaldi, led an army into Rome, declaring the city a republic and forcing Pope Pius IX to flee the Vatican. Louis – then President of France – hurried to the Pope's support, placing Rome under siege until papal authority was restored.

As support for the uprisings dwindled, the nationalists withdrew, but calls for Italian unification continued and, over the next five years, Louis began to recognise the benefits of a united Italy. In 1856, the Piedmont-Sardinian Prime Minister, Count Cavour, sent his beautiful cousin, Virginie, Countess of Castiglione, to Paris in the hope that she would seduce the Emperor and persuade him to support a new Austro-Sardinian War. Notwithstanding Louis' penchant for seductive women, the Countess made little impression on him when they first met at a ball. She was beautiful, he commented, but, as her appearance was far superior to her intelligence or spirituality, he dismissed her as 'insipid and insignificant.' She made an equally poor impression on several other observers, one of whom remarked that she was:

> "...very beautiful indeed, but to my mind her beauty was of the body and not of the soul. This kind of woman seems to me to be rather an object of art, a very fine ornament to the drawing room, but scarcely capable of touching the heart."[201]

Others thought her pretentious, lacking in style and substance, and little more than a high class harlot. In spite of his initial reaction, however, Louis soon succumbed to her charms and, within a few months, they were rumoured to be lovers. The affair not only caused a scandal but also attracted the attention of the French police, who feared that she had been sent from Italy to assassinate him.

By then, Louis had become so enamoured of his mistress that neither criticism nor warnings could distract him from her charms. He lavished so many gifts upon her that her complaisant husband boasted that he was growing rich at the Emperor's expense until the scandal became too humiliating for him and he demanded a separation, to which Virginie responded by sending him a photograph of herself fiercely wielding a dagger!

As the affair coincided with Louis increasing support for Italian unification, it was widely believed that the Countess was responsible for his espousal of the cause, but, in fact, he was such a fickle philanderer that, within a few months, he was tired of her company, and sent her back to Piedmont, laden with expensive jewels. When she eventually reappeared in Paris, it was clear that, although she and the Emperor were on friendly terms, they were no longer lovers.

Irked by the failure of his plan, Cavour decided to take a more direct approach, and arranged a meeting with Louis at Polombières-les-Bains in the summer of 1858. Although the full details of their conversation were never disclosed, it was widely believed that Louis urged the Sardinians to do everything possible to provoke the Austrians into declaring war, which would be seen as an act of aggression, and would provide the French a valid reason to come to their aid. In return for military assistance, Louis would be given the regions of Nice and Savoy, and, as a means of cementing the alliance, he wished to arrange a marriage between his cousin, Prince Napoleon, and King Victor Emmanuel's daughter, Clotilde of Savoy.

Thirty-seven-year-old Prince Napoleon – brother of the Emperor's erstwhile fiancée, Mathilde – was far from the ideal choice of a husband for the retiring fifteen-year-old Clotilde. Known to his family as 'Plonplon', his promiscuous lifestyle had made him so unpopular in France that few believed that he would remain faithful to his shy young bride. Moreover, as he had been Louis' heir until the birth of the Prince Imperial, he was widely suspected of being responsible for instigating a series of rumours that the Emperor was not, in fact, Loulou's father, and the child was a crippled imbecile.

Unsurprisingly, when King Victor Emmanuel received the proposal he refused to sanction the wedding, but Louis cheerfully reminded him that, in spite of his reputation, his cousin had always treated his mistresses well and had even left a jolly carnival in Paris to pay his respects to one whom he had not seen for several years when he heard that she was dying. This failed to impress the King but his ministers, eager to please the French Emperor, urged him to reconsider for the sake of his country. Eventually, he agreed to explain the situation to Clotilde and allow her to make the final decision. When his daughter was told of the plan, she reduced her father and Cavour to tears, as she nobly responded:

> "The marriage is desired by my father; I know therefore in his opinion this union must be useful to my family and to my country, and therefore I have no hesitation in giving my consent."

Plonplon duly signed an alliance on behalf of the Emperor, promising French support in the event of an Austrian attack, and when, a few days later, the wedding took place in Turin, most of Europe viewed it as a declaration of war.

"Things look bad all over Europe," Lord Greville reported, "and it will be very difficult to avert a general war if Louis Napoleon wants one."[202]

The marriage was widely condemned in France and Sardinia, where many believed that the unfortunate Clotilde was being used as a pawn in a political game. To make matters worse, the French people had no desire to enter into another expensive war, particularly one from which they felt they had very little to gain. Queen Victoria, too, wrote to Louis, urging him to abandon any belligerent plans, and suggesting that the Italian situation could be better resolved through peaceful negotiations or an international conference. The Pope agreed with Queen, as did many of Louis' own Generals, one leading officer begging him 'to consider how detrimental [war] would be to France and to your dynasty.' Even Eugénie warned him against acting too hastily, as:

> "...The Italians will not thank you for the blood you will shed for them. And if you think to secure friends by serving their ambition and their vanity, you are in error. If danger threatened you, they would turn their backs on you."[203]

Why Louis insisted on adhering to his 'secret' alliance with Cavour remains a matter of conjecture. At the time, many commentators, including the British diplomat, Lord Cowley, believed it was due to his fear of assassination by Italian nationalists, 'which haunts him perpetually, and has robbed him of all his former courage and coolness.' Cavour, according to Cowley, constantly preyed on this fear by warning him that he could only protect himself from the Italians' murderous intentions by allying himself to their cause.

Others, however, disputed this, suggesting that Orsini had inspired in him the recollection of the part that he and his late brother had played in the struggle for Italian independence. Moreover, according to the historian, Trevelyan, his own personality drove him to involve himself in the campaign because he was 'at once a selfish and scheming adventurer who murdered liberty in his own country and protested against its natural manifestations in neighbouring lands, and a romantic idealist who wished to extend the principles of the French Revolution over Europe.'[204]

Whatever Louis' reasons, the Sardinians adhered to the plan and, in the spring of 1859, began a series of provocative manoeuvres along the Austrian border. As predicted, the Austrians issued several warnings, all of which were ignored, and 19th April they sent King Victor Emmanuel an ultimatum: unless he disarmed within three days, their countries would be at war.

The King rose to the occasion, rousing his troops with stirring speeches, and assuring them of French support which would result in ultimate victory in this 'just and sacred enterprise.' When his ministers heard that he intended to lead his army in person, they pleaded with him not to place himself in such danger, but he responded calmly that he could not send men to die in battle 'if I were not prepared to show them by my own example that the cause was one worth dying for?'[205]

Louis' advisers were equally alarmed to hear that he, too, intended to take personal command of his army, and they were even more distressed when they heard that, during his absence, Eugénie would act as his regent, with absolute power over the Privy Council, the Council of Ministers and the Senate. Like Victor Emmanuel, Louis' address to his troops was designed to arouse strong patriotic feeling, and he assured his allies that, when the campaign was completed, Italy would be free 'from the Alps to the Adriatic'.

The anxious Crown Princess of Prussia, wrote desperately to Queen Victoria, pleading with her to maintain Britain's neutrality. In Berlin, she explained, there were rumours that, if Austria were defeated, the unpredictable French Emperor might turn his belligerent attentions on the German states. Her fears that Britain might support him were, however, unfounded for Louis had become so unpopular in England that even his erstwhile champion, Palmerston, commented that 'his mind is as full of schemes as a warren is full of rabbits.'[206]

The campaign began well for the French and Sardinians, who achieved a resounding victory at Magenta on 4th June 1859. Although they were vastly outnumbered, the speed of their attack took the Austrians by surprise, and the success was all the more significant since it gave the allies direct access to the strategic city of Milan, into which Louis and Victor Emmanuel rode triumphantly four days later.

As had happened in the Crimea, though, rivalry soon developed between the allied armies. The Sardinians felt that the French treated them as inferiors; and their Generals resented having to yield to French commanders. It was demeaning for Victor Emmanuel, they claimed, the have his own battle-plans disrupted or altered by his allies; and, when the stories of discord reached Britain, the press was only too quick to put the blame on the French Emperor.

> "The newspapers," wrote Lord Greville, "are beginning to make remarks on the difference between Victor Emmanuel and Louis Napoleon – the former fighting for three consecutive days at the head of his soldiers, and bivouacking with

them on the field of battle, whilst the latter picnics with Madame C[astiglione]. However untrue this may be, there is no doubt that the French are giving the

Sardinians the roughest portion of the business to perform."[207]

Nonetheless, the allies pressed on and, on 24th June, they launched a second major assault in the sweltering heat of Solferino. Again, the Austrians were taken by surprise, and during a nine-hour battle they lost fifty-thousand men before laying down their arms in surrender. Once more, as had happened in the Crimea, Louis soon lost interest in the project, and, sickened by the sight of so much blood, he was relieved when the Austrian Emperor petitioned for a truce.

Without consulting his allies, he agreed to Franz Josef's request, but knowing that this would mean that he had failed to achieve his stated aim of driving the Austrians out of Italy, he attempted to pass responsibility for his actions onto the British. He wrote privately to Palmerston to ask for arbitration but Palmerston saw through the ruse and wrote to the Foreign Secretary, 'why should we incur the opprobrium of leaving Italy laden with Austrian chains and of having betrayed the Italians at the moment of their brightest hopes?'[208]

Louis had no option but to meet Franz Josef at Villafranca, where they agreed a treaty whereby Austria would retain Venetia but surrender control of Lombardy. Parma would be handed over to Louis; and the Dukes of Modena and Tuscany, who had been overthrown when their peoples rose up to support the Sardinians, would return to their duchies and resume the positions they had held before the war.

The willingness with which Louis accepted these terms shocked his allies, and left his Generals bemused as to why he had not taken greater advantage of their victories.

"If after the Battle of Solferino was over," one senior officer explained, "the Emperor had cared to follow up his success, he could have done so easily enough, for in my own division there were seventeen battalions perfectly intact, and which had never been used, but such was the state of confusion at the headquarters' staff that the enemy, although flying in every direction, were not pursued."[209]

Louis responded by explaining that, on the morning of the battle, Eugénie had sent him a warning that Prussian forces were moving along the Rhine. Had he continued to lead his army towards Vienna, there was a strong possibility that the Prussians would take advantage of his absence to launch an invasion of France. If that had happened, he claimed, it could have led to a general European war, which he, as a man of peace, was desperate to avoid.

The Sardinians dismissed his excuses and were so angry that he had reneged on his promise to guarantee Italy's freedom from the Alps to the Adriatic that they nicknamed him 'the Great Betrayer'. Their furious Prime Minister openly confronted him, and was 'so violent and insolent in his language, that the Emperor threatened to have him arrested.'[210] King Victor Emmanuel, sighed, 'Poor Italy!' but, although he privately complained that Louis had treated him like a dog, he wrote him a gracious letter, telling him that, 'I shall always feel grateful for what you have done for Italian independence, and you may count on me as a friend.'[211] His people were far less forgiving, and when he and Louis rode into Turin together, the King was greeted with flowers and cheers while the Emperor was met with only a stony silence.

Although the rest of Europe viewed the Italian campaign as a failure, the French hailed it as a victory, and welcomed the Emperor back to Paris as a conquering hero. As he handed out medals to all those who had seen active service, he reminded the crowds that Eugénie deserved praise for the competent way she had run the country during his absence. Henceforth, she would be given an even greater role in political affairs, and would resume the responsibilities of regent when Louis embarked on foreign tours, most notably when he toured Algeria, which he had annexed to France in 1857.

Chapter 12 – An Empire Carved Out Of A Block Of Silver

Contrary to his critics' fears, Louis had little hope of expanding his empire throughout Europe, but, since his imprisonment in Ham, he had been convinced of the benefits of gaining a foothold in the Americas. In 1857, he told the future British Prime Minister, Benjamin Disraeli, that it would be advantageous to establish a European monarchy in Mexico, which had for several years been torn apart by civil war. Disraeli dismissed the idea on the grounds that the Americans had adopted the Monroe Doctrine – a policy by which they would vigorously oppose all European attempts to colonise any part of the continent – but, never a man to allow a seemingly insurmountable obstacle to stand in the way of his dreams, Louis continued to nurture his plan and waited for an appropriate time to bring it to fruition.

His opportunity arose when a Liberal President, Benito Juarez, seized power in the country, and immediately cancelled the repayment of all European loans, which amounted to approximately one-hundred-million dollars. Louis called on the British and Spanish to support his demands for the return of their money and, in 1861, a convention of the three powers was held in London. The outcome was an agreement to dispatch a joint fleet to South America on the understanding that, once the repayment had been secured, they would withdraw without seeking financial or territorial gains, or interfering in the internal politics of the country.

Although Louis outwardly accepted the terms, he had every intention of going far beyond the recuperation of the debt, as, with Eugénie's support, he intended to establish a monarchy in the country. Eugénie's interest in the project had begun the previous year when, while holidaying in Biarritz, she met several Mexican emigres who convinced her that a monarchy was the surest means of bringing stability and strengthening the Church's authority in their country. They explained to her that, although the majority of Mexicans were Roman Catholic, Juarez had seized all Church lands and banned the wearing of clerical garb in public. He had also requisitioned much of the land of the native Indians, causing poverty and despair among the indigenous population. Eugénie became so fascinated by the subject that filled the Tuileries with pictures and books about all aspects of Mexican life, and constantly encouraged Louis to select an appropriate King to place on the throne.

The outbreak of the American Civil War added impetus to her vision, for, while the Americans were preoccupied by the conflict, they would be unlikely to enforce the Monroe Doctrine. Moreover, Louis was convinced that the Southern (Confederate) States would eventually be victorious, and, in return for his help during their campaign, they would be willing to accept his plan for Mexico's future.

Neither the British nor the Spanish shared Louis' ambitions, nor were they deceived by the philanthropic gloss that he placed over his scheme. He intended, said one of his apologists, 'to deliver the Mexican people from that condition of anarchy and helplessness under which they had groaned for forty years'[212] by establishing a stable government; but his detractors believed that he simply wanted access to the 'inexhaustible mineral and agricultural wealth' of the country, in order to replenish his coffers following the expense of the Italian campaign.

Aware of what was being said, Louis sent Queen Victoria a long letter explaining his intentions, and succeeded in convincing her that 'his plans are not for any advantage France is to derive from it.'[213] She realised, though, that few of her ministers would share that opinion, particularly when they heard that Louis had informed a Confederate officer that, with British help, he intended to effect an armistice in the American Civil War. The British government was so angry that Lord Russell wrote a firm letter to the Emperor, informing him that Britain had no intention of interfering in the American conflict. Louis accepted the reprimand with good grace, but did not allow it to distract him from his plans, and, six months later, when the British and Spanish withdrew from the venture, he boldly declared that France would continue alone.

Trusting to the word of the monarchists whom they had met in Biarritz, Louis and Eugénie naively believed that, when the French troops launched an invasion, the Mexicans would welcome them as liberators. What they had failed to realise was that, although many of the indigenous people wanted a change of government, many others were fiercely loyal to Juarez. Consequently, the campaign was more prolonged and hazardous than anyone had anticipated, and the vagueness of its objectives led to a good deal of confusion. Many officers still believed that their sole purpose was to recover the repayment of the loans, and, to that end, in March 1862, they marched towards Juarez' base in Mexico City. The President, aware of the plan, sent his army to intercept them, and when they paused at Puebla, the Mexicans launched a successful attack, leaving the French humiliated and defeated.

When news of the defeat reached Paris, the majority of ministers called for an end to the campaign, which they viewed as a vainglorious waste of resources. Louis, though, horrified by what had happened, insisted that they must restore French pride by marching on until they had conquered the entire country. In the months that followed, the army was blighted by disease and exhaustion, but, despite frequent calls to end the mission, Louis adamantly refused to bring the army home. In March 1863, his soldiers returned to the scene of their defeat and placed the city of Puebla under siege. For over six weeks, as the Mexican launched ferocious attempts to break through their lines, a French courtier reported that 'our army at Puebla is almost without ammunition. Only

145

93 rounds are left for each gun; there are no mortars, and the bullets are nearly exhausted.'[214]

Even so, Louis refused to accept that he was beaten; and Eugénie remained so committed to the venture that she told an American diplomat:

"…if Mexico were not so far, and if my son were not still a child, I should wish to see him lead the French Army, whose sword is at present engaged in writing one of the finest pages of the history of the century."[215]

A fortnight later, to Louis' delight, the eighteen thousand inhabitants of Puebla finally surrendered, giving the French direct access to the capital. As soon as Juarez heard of the approaching army, he and the majority of his supporters fled towards the Texan border. Those who remained in the city were largely opponents of the President and so, when the French troops arrived on 10th June, they received a rapturous welcome from the citizens, who spread flowers on the road before them and rang the church bells in thanksgiving for their liberation.

Rejoicing in the success, Louis was determined to implement the next stage of his plan as quickly as possible. He approached several European princes, offering them the crown of the new Mexican Empire but few were prepared to accept such a precarious throne. Louis Philippe's son, the Duke of Aumale; and Queen Victoria's cousin, Ferdinand of Saxe-Coburg-Kohary had already declined the offer, when Louis decided upon the Roman Catholic Archduke Maximilian, a younger brother of Emperor Franz Josef of Austria.

"I have carved you an Empire out of a block of silver," Louis told him in the autumn of 1863, but, like Aumale and Ferdinand, Maximilian had many reservations. The country had known so much turmoil that he might well be placing himself in great danger; or worse, Louis might be intending to use him as a French puppet. On the other hand, as he had fallen out of favour with Emperor Franz Josef, he was idling his time away at his castle, Miramar, near Trieste, with no prospect of a more profitable position; and his wife, Charlotte[v], overjoyed at the prospect of becoming an Empress, assured him and anyone else who would listen that he was being called to fulfil a sacred mission.

Over several months, Maximilian met with bankers, priests and ministers to discuss the pros and the cons of accepting the crown, but it was not until a group of Mexican monarchists arrived at Miramar to assure him that the people were eager to receive him, that he finally agreed to become their Emperor. Before proceeding, he prepared a list of stipulations which were to be included in a formal treaty. Among other guarantees, he required an assurance that the French would make no claim on silver-rich region of Sonora; the gradual withdrawal of Louis' troops from the country; and the support of the French Foreign Legion for the next six years to enable him to establish control and train an effective native army. Louis travelled to Trieste to sign the Treaty of Miramar, and, in April 1864, Maximilian and Charlotte – now calling herself Carlotta – set sail with an idealistic vision of all that they would achieve in their new Empire.

King Leopold of the Belgians had complete faith in Charlotte's abilities and told Queen Victoria that, although the mission was fraught with danger, he was confident that she and Maximilian were equal to the task, and 'if it succeeds it will be one of the greatest and most useful of our time.'[216]

The Queen was far from convinced, as she considered the venture reckless; while Charlotte's grandmother wailed hysterically, 'They will be killed! They will be killed!'

A more rational American diplomat commented:
"The Archduke Maximilian...firmly believes that he is going forth to Mexico to establish an

[v] Queen Victoria's cousin, Charlotte, was the only daughter of King Leopold I of the Belgians.

American empire, and that it is his divine mission to destroy the dragon of democracy and re-establish the true Church...Poor young man!"[217]

Even one of Maximilian's most devoted officers feared the worst. The new Emperor was, he observed:

"...frank, candid, and open, a man of the nicest honour, and a gentleman in the noblest sense of that evilly-entreated word – thoroughly honest and sincere in his wish to regenerate his adopted country...[but his] one great defect was inability to believe in the hideous depths of corruption and baseness to which some specimens of human nature can descend."[218]

The couple's arrival in Mexico quickly dispelled any illusions, for, contrary to their expectations, they met with a cool – and in some places openly hostile – reception. Far from the Austrian palaces, their accommodation was a rat-infested ruin, and, the country was so poor that they would be obliged to use their own private funds to pay for their daily living expenses. Undeterred, they were ready to make a success of the venture, and, as Maximilian set about establishing order, creating trading links, abolishing child labour and corporal punishment, and introducing reforms to benefit the poor; Charlotte gave her time and money to numerous charitable causes, often trudging over muddy tracks to visit some of the lowliest hovels, prisons and hospitals.

Their efforts brought them few rewards. The aristocracy opposed Maximilian's liberal reforms; and the supporters of the exiled Juarez made frequent attempts to re-establish a republic. For the first year of his reign, at least, Maximilian could rely on Louis' promise of military support, and, by April 1865, French troops had driven Juarez' supporters back to the Texan border.

Unfortunately, a month later, the American Civil War ended and President Andrew Johnson announced that he would revert to the Monroe Doctrine. Refusing to acknowledge Maximilian's empire, he sent several regiments to the border to frighten the French into leaving the country. Initially, Louis tried to reach a compromise by offering to withdraw his troops in return for official recognition of Maximilian as Emperor, but a formal note from Washington put paid to his designs.

"The United States have not seen any satisfactory evidence that the people of Mexico have spoken, and have called into being, or accepted, the so-called empire, which it is insisted has been set up in their capital."[219]

By then, as so often happened, Louis was already losing interest in the project, as affairs in Italy and the impending Austro-Prussian War[w] were absorbing all his attention. At the same time, his ministers continued to complain about the expense of a mission the initial purpose of which was to recover a debt but now had turned into a costly misadventure. In a half-hearted effort to abide by the Treaty of Miramar, Louis sought to delay the withdrawal of his troops but simultaneously wrote to Maximilian to tell him that the adventure was over and it was time for him to come home.

This news fell like a thunderbolt on Maximilian and Charlotte, and the prospect of returning to Austria was all the more humiliating since Emperor Franz Josef had deprived his brother of all his Austrian titles and his position in the line of succession when he accepted the Mexican throne. What was more, 'his character was too noble and too pure to suspect the honesty of others'[220] and, consequently, he could not believe that Louis would go back on his word. Certain that if he understood the precarious of his position, Louis would relent, Maximilian asked Charlotte to go to France to explain the situation more fully.

Unfortunately, her arrival in Paris coincided with the conclusion of the Austro-Prussian War, which had so shocked Louis that he had fallen ill and taken to his bed in

---

[w] See Chapter 14

Saint Cloud[x]. For three days, he was not well enough to receive her, and, when he eventually granted her an audience, he blamed Maximilian for the disaster, claiming that he had failed to endear himself to the Mexican people. In such circumstances, he concluded, all he could do was guarantee him safe passage back to Europe.

Agitated and distressed, Charlotte returned to her hotel but, throughout the next week, she continuously petitioned Louis for a further meeting. He finally gave way and visited her at her hotel, where she threw herself weeping at his feet, pleading with him for mercy, before suddenly sitting upright and staring into space as though unaware of his presence. When he repeated all he had said at their previous meeting, she flew into a frenzy, hurling so many curses and accusations upon him, that, not knowing how to react, he left abruptly.

Dejectedly, Charlotte decided to return to Miramar but her eccentricities became so excessive that her companions persuaded her to rest near Lake Como, where doctors prescribed her sedatives to settle her nerves before continuing her journey. By the time that she reached the castle, she appeared to have recovered her senses until she received a letter from Maximilian, urging her to go to Rome to seek the support of the Pope. On arriving at the Vatican, she behaved with complete composure, discoursing in several languages with cardinals and various dignitaries, but four days later, she suffered a relapse and threw herself at the Pope's feet, telling him that Louis had sent his agents to poison her. Over the next few days, her paranoia was so extreme that she covered her face with a black mantilla for fear of being recognised; and refused to eat anything except meals prepared for her by one trusted maid, which she took at a table to which a number of hens were tethered to protect her from assassins and spies.

---

[x] See Chapter 14

When word of her insanity reached Belgium, her brother, King Leopold II[y], set out for Italy to take her back to his palace at Laeken. There, for her own safety, she was confined in a suite of rooms and would never see Mexico or her husband again[z].

"She who was so quiet and self-possessed," wrote the Crown Princess of Prussia, "so calm and serious and yet of cheerful disposition I cannot understand how such a thing could happen. I love her so much...What she must have suffered, what she must have gone through to come to that."[221]

Several weeks passed before news of her condition reached Maximilian, who was so distressed that for ten days he barely left his room. When he did emerge, he discovered that the country was in a state of chaos, as opposing republican and monarchist factions were on the brink of civil war. In view of his personal and political situation, he briefly considered abdicating, until a group of powerful monarchists assured him that the greater part of the country remained loyal and desperately needed him to stay. In February 1867, therefore, he set out with an army of eight-thousand men and, following a few skirmishes, marched into the city of Queretaro to a rousing reception. His triumph was short lived. In mid-March republican forces besieged the city and, after two months, food supplies were dwindling and dysentery was rife. Maximilian's only option was to escape unseen through the enemy lines to rally his troops in other parts of the country, but the night before he was due to leave, a treacherous colonel secretly approached the republican commander, General Escobedo, offering to lead a column of his troops into the city in return for a substantial financial reward. By the time that Maximilian discovered

---

[y] Charlotte's father, King Leopold I, had died in December 1865. Her grief at his death might have added to her mental instability.

[z] Charlotte never fully regained her sanity and remained virtually incarcerated for the rest of her life.

what was happening, Queretaro was filled with enemy soldiers, who arrested him and two of his companions. Following a show trial all three were sentenced to death by firing squad.

When news of the sentence reached Europe, Queen Victoria and several of her fellow monarchs sent representations to Juarez, pleading for a reprieve. With genuine regret, the President replied that he could not interfere in the court's decision and a date had already been set for the executions.

Maximilian endured his captivity and impending doom with such courage and resignation that even his gaolers were deeply impressed.

> "...After having been so long about him," one of them later recorded, "and having witnessed how good and nobly he behaved in his misfortune, and looked in his true, melancholy blue eyes, he felt the greatest sympathy, if not love and admiration, for him."[222]

The execution, on 19th June 1867, was a particularly gruesome affair. Maximilian's two companions died instantly but four out of the five soldiers making up the firing squad, missed the Emperor's heart, rupturing his windpipe and causing blood to gush into his lungs. As he fell, choking and drowning, to his knees, he pointed to his chest, pleading with the fifth soldier to kill him outright, but the man panicked and, dropping his gun, ran away. Five agonising minutes passed before an officer, witnessing the scene, succeeded in firing the fatal shot.

> "Oh that horrible murder of Max," Queen Victoria. "...Awful, too awful! Everything was done, messages and representations sent but all in vain!"[223]

Louis, meanwhile, was busily entertaining foreign dignitaries at the International Exposition in Paris[aa], and

---

aa See Chapter 15

was handing out prizes to the exhibitors when, on a sweltering afternoon, 30th June, a telegram arrived telling him of the shocking events in Queretaro. The Austrian delegates immediately withdrew from the exposition, but Louis continued the prize-giving as though nothing had happened.

On returning home, he cancelled all subsequent celebrations and summoned his Chief of the Secret Police, Hyrvoix, to ask him how the people were reacting to news. With great reluctance, Hyrvoix answered that there was a general feeling of discontent and many blamed 'the Spanish woman' – Eugénie – for the fiasco which had cost the lives of six thousand French soldiers and enormous sums of money.

Immediately on the defensive, the enraged Eugénie cried out, 'The Spanish woman! the Spanish woman! I have become French, but I will show my enemies that I can he Spanish when occasion demands it!' and, storming from the room privately arranged for Hyrvoix to be exiled to the provinces. When, though, some days later, she met the widow of one of the men who had been executed with Maximilian, she burst into tears and sobbed to a minister who had opposed the Mexican venture,

> "Why was your advice not heeded? Had your counsels prevailed Maximilian would to-day be leading a happy life under the shades of Miramar, with Charlotte by his side. Instead of which he is but a corpse, and his poor Consort a raving lunatic. What a ghastly ending to it all."[224]

So intense was her distress that she claimed that, were the Prince Imperial not still a child, she would encourage her husband to abdicate in his favour. Later, though, when her anguish had subsided, she insisted that she and Louis had acted in good faith and could not be held responsible for the tragic events in Mexico. Many years later, when a diplomat broached the subject, she responded angrily:

153

"I am not ashamed of Mexico. I deplore it; but I do not blush for it. I am even always ready to discuss it, for it is one of the themes which injustice and calumny have most wrongly exploited against us."[225]

In spite of her protestations, Mexico would lie heavily on her heart to the end of her life.

Chapter 13 – For His Own Aggrandisement

Louis' disastrous Mexican venture confirmed his detractors' opinion of him as an untrustworthy schemer. 'The prince, who was shot in America, was the victim;' wrote one British politician, 'the Emperor, who survived at Paris, was the instigator of the crime.'[226] Even those who viewed him less harshly felt that 'the French expedition to Mexico and its tragical end are a sad blot on Louis Napoleon's career;'[227] while many others believed it was evidence of his 'overreaching ambition'.

The prospect of where his ambition might lead continued to trouble British politicians, many of whom believed he still cherished the dream of avenging his uncle's defeat at Waterloo. From Paris, senior diplomats repeatedly sent warning to London that he was not to be trusted and they must not 'relax' but should continue strengthening the defences along the Channel coast. The Earl of Lytton considered him sincere but unscrupulous, and thought him 'doubtless ambitious for France; but the ambition of France is a menace for Europe; because from geographical and physical causes it must be a territorial ambition.'[228] The appropriation of Algeria in 1857, increased this suspicion; and his determination to annex Nice and Savoy was seen as further evidence of his plans to extend his empire.

Although Britain had remained neutral throughout the Italian campaign, the majority of ministers hoped for an Austrian defeat and were shocked when Louis ended the war before driving the Austrians out of Italy. The Treaty of Villafranca prompted such vitriolic language in the House of Commons that Queen Victoria intervened by reminding her ministers that:

"We did not protest against the war; we can hardly now protest against the peace."

When, however, she discovered that Louis was demanding Nice and Savoy as a payment for his part in the campaign, she empathised with those politicians who reacted with suspicion and anger. Most of the Savoyards, Louis argued, viewed themselves as French, and, more importantly, he needed the territories to create a mountainous buffer between France and the increasingly militaristic Prussia[bb]. The British dismissed his argument as a convenient disguise for his true ambitions, and noted that, since the Crimean War, he had increased his standing army to five-hundred-and-fifty-thousand men. Feelings ran so high that one Member of Parliament warned that the annexation of Nice and Savoy would, 'spread distrust and suspicion throughout Europe, and has reminded the French Government that it probably, or possibly, implies on the part of the Emperor of France the adoption of a policy which has already been most fatal to the fortunes of his family.'[229]

The Foreign Minister, Lord John Russell, advised against jumping to erroneous conclusions as there was no evidence that proposed annexation was anything more than a rumour. To discover the facts, he asked the British Ambassador in Sardinia, James Hudson, to discuss the matter with Count Cavour, who told him that no official agreement had been reached, but added that the Savoyards could be given a referendum on the matter. This unsatisfactory response led to such tensions between Britain and France that Queen Victoria used her customary New Year greeting to stress to Louis the importance of maintaining peace and acting only in the best interests of the Italians.

> "There will be," she wrote, "many divergent opinions and apparent hostile interests to be reconciled, but with the help of heaven, and a firm determination to seek only the welfare of those whose destiny we have to direct and shape, one must not despair of a satisfactory result."[230]

[bb] See Chapter 14

Just a few months later, in March 1860, the annexation was effected by the Treaty of Turin, after which the people of Nice and Savoy were given a free vote, resulting in an overwhelming show of support for the decision.

The Savoyards might have been content with the outcome, but the treaty provoked much condemnation in Sardinia and across the rest of Europe. One of Victor Emmanuel's leading Generals, Giuseppe Garibaldi, was so incensed that he declared that the referendum had been illegal and accused the French police of pressurising the voters into acquiescing to Louis' wishes. The British were equally outraged, fearing that the move would compromise Swiss independence, and that the resolution had been brought about by threats and intrigue.

A widely-circulated rumour claimed that French Ambassador, Count Benedetti, had met Cavour in secret and told him that, unless the Sardinians agreed to the annexation, Louis would withdraw his troops from Lombardy, enabling the Austrians to return. When Cavour replied that he would be happy to see the French depart, Benedetti allegedly pulled from his pocket a private letter from the Emperor, and told him bluntly, 'I have orders to withdraw the troops, but not to France; they will occupy Bologna and Florence.'[231]

Queen Victoria was deeply shocked by Louis' double-dealing, complaining to the Foreign Secretary that, 'we have been made regular dupes;' while Lord Russell warned that the treaty would produce 'great distrust all over Europe' and, more disturbingly,

> "...such an act as the annexation of Savoy will lead a nation so warlike as the French to call upon its Government from time to time to commit other acts of aggression."[232]

Although he stopped short of threatening war, the tone of his speech was so belligerent that the French Ambassador approached Palmerston, asking him to distance himself from the comments. Palmerston replied that Russell had his full support and recommended that the Ambassador should read the entire speech to his Emperor. When the shocked Ambassador suggested that this was tantamount to a declaration of war, Palmerston shrugged and replied that, if that were the case, Britain was fully prepared.

Cavour, meanwhile, desperately tried to extricate himself from the affair by claiming that:

> "When I assured Sir James Hudson that the cession of those two provinces would not take place, I spoke in good faith; but matters have since changed."[233]

For all their bellicose speeches, the British ministers were powerless to reverse the annexation, but they hoped that the severe tone adopted by Parliament would deter Louis from attempting to make further territorial acquisitions. Nonetheless, the fear of a French invasion intensified with further calls for the strengthening of Britain's coastal fortifications, despite Disraeli's repeated assurance that Louis' power was waning.

Although Queen Victoria had supported Italian unification, she reached the conclusion that Louis was not to be trusted; and Pope Pius IX was equally quick to condemn him when he reneged on the terms of the Treaty of Villafranca. He remained silent when several duchies annexed themselves to Sardinia; and when Victor Emmanuel asked his permission to march his troops through the Papal States[cc], he acquiesced on condition that Rome be left intact.

The Papal States had long been seen as a major hindrance to Italian unification, and many attempts had been made to free them from the Pope's rule. Since the uprisings of 1849, a French garrison had been stationed in Rome to protect the Holy See from further insurrection, but, despite this apparent support for the Pope, Louis

---

[cc] States under the direct sovereignty of the Pope.

believed that his temporal authority should be confined to Rome. In a widely-read article he patronised, 'the less territory he has, the greater will be his sovereignty; what he loses in material power he will gain in spiritual prestige.'[234]

This assertion paved the way for many more articles to appear in the French press, objecting to the fact that the Pope's authority was maintained by, and reliant upon foreign armies. Consequently, Pius IX could only watch anxiously as, unchecked by the French, Sardinian troops occupied his states of Bologna and Romagna, both of which declared that Victor Emmanuel was now their King. When Louis failed to come to his aid, the Pope and his supporters accused him of being a dishonest traitor.

Knowing of the low opinion in which he was held across the continent, Louis sought to restore his reputation in Britain by creating some form of alliance, but when he hinted to the British Ambassador that it would be wise to join forces to protect Italy following the anticipated unification, the British Government dismissed his proposal on the grounds that he was an unreliable partner who would abandon his allies at his own convenience as he had done to the Sardinians after Solferino.

> "If we know anything of the sentiments of our countrymen," *The Times* scathingly reported, "nothing is more certain than that this nation would not endure any Ministry which should propose to pledge England to an offensive alliance with France against the rest of Europe. We wish well to Italy, but we do not go to war for an idea...If we did so, we should prefer to have...some confidence that our allies would fight out the whole fight with us, and not make peace at inconvenient seasons...We will honour, glorify, sympathise, admire, but in this quarrel, and under these conditions, we will not fight."[235]

Queen Victoria agreed and warned Lord Russell that it would be,

"...most dangerous for us to offer to bind ourselves to a common action with the Emperor...whilst he has entered into a variety of agreements with different parties...of which we know nothing, and has objects in view, which we can only guess at, and which have not the good of Italy in view, but his own aggrandisement, to the serious detriment of Europe."[236]

With the failure of his attempts to create a military alliance, Louis, turned his attention to the formation of a free trade deal. Initially he had opposed the idea for fear of angering the French protectionists and damaging trade with other European powers, but now, under pressure from his ministers, he agreed to a treaty to reduce tariffs on imports of British coal and iron, in return for a reduction of duties on exports of French wine and brandy. The Prince Consort, who was not wholly in favour of the plan, commented to a friend that, 'the treaty will give the Emperor our coals and iron, which he will want if he should come into collision with us' – an observation which would gain greater significance almost a decade later.[dd]

Nonetheless, the deal went some way to ameliorating relations between Britain and France, and Louis took the opportunity to assure the Queen that he would continue to do everything in his power to cement closer ties between their countries. It was not, though, until March 1861, when Victor Emmanuel was declared King of the newly-unified Italy, that the British ministers began to view him more favourably. To their surprise, he staunchly stood up to the Papists in his government, and, in spite of his Roman Catholicism, he placed the good of the Italian people above that of the Pope. Queen Victoria's Protestant ministers were filled with admiration.

[dd] See Chapter 14

"He has," wrote Lord Greville, "well-nigh recovered in this country the confidence and the popularity which had become exchanged for distrust, suspicion, and alarm ... He certainly has exhibited great courage and above all boundless confidence in his own power and authority in his own country."[237]

Not everyone was quite so convinced that he was now a true friend of Britain, as many believed he still harboured a secret plan to launch an invasion. Shortly after the unification of Italy, his former champion, Palmerston commented:

"Till lately I had strong confidence in the fair intentions of Napoleon toward England, but of late I have begun to feel great distrust and to suspect that his formerly declared intention of avenging Waterloo has only lain dormant and has not died away. He seems to have thought that he ought to lay his foundation by beating with our aid or with our concurrence, or our neutrality first Russia and then Austria: and by dealing with them generously to make them his friends and in any subsequent quarrel with us."[238]

In reality, Palmerston's suspicions were probably groundless, as there is no evidence to suggest that Louis ever had designs on Britain, particularly when he was well aware that it would be far easier and more advantageous to him, to expand his territory into the Prussian Rhineland.

Chapter 14 – Begging For A Tip

In the summer of 1865, the Machiavellian Prussian statesman, Otto von Bismarck, travelled to Biarritz, where Louis was taking his annual holiday, to gain as assurance that, in the event of a war between Prussia and Austria, France would remain neutral. Viewing Louis a 'good-natured' man 'of limited intelligence', he had little doubt that he would obtain the desired guarantee, and would then be able to create the Austrian conflict, which would take him closer to fulfilling his dream of a unified Germany dominated by Prussia. His argument was ingenious and convincing, as he flattered Louis into believing that Prussia needed French support to become a strong power in Europe. A strong Prussia, he explained, would happily enter into a peaceful alliance with France, but a weak Prussia, constantly fearing a French invasion, 'would be always looking for allies against its powerful Western neighbour.'[239]

'Limited' as Louis' intelligence might have been, he immediately saw through Bismarck's machinations, and he knew, too, that not all of the German states shared the statesman's vision for a unified Germany. While the majority of the northern states were in accord with Bismarck's ideas, most of the southern states feared Prussian domination, and favoured instead a union of all German-speaking peoples, under the leadership of Austria. Consequently, should war break out, the southern states would rise up in defence of Austria, which, according to Louis' calculations, would result in an Austrian victory. That prospect, Louis decided, could prove very beneficial to France, for, while the Prussians were reeling in defeat, he could send in his troops to seize part of the Prussian Rhineland.

Alternatively, Louis decided, a Prussian victory could prove equally advantageous to France, as he could expect some recompense for his country's neutrality, and so he hinted to Bismarck that he would not interfere in the conflict, in return for which he expected to be given 'certain territories'. Neither party gave the other a firm commitment but, by the time that Bismarck left Biarritz, he was convinced that he had achieved his objective.

In the days that followed, Louis continued to muse on the situation, and came to the conclusion that a Prussian victory would be most advantageous, since, as a reward for his neutrality, he would obtain the Rhine provinces without having to go to the trouble of seizing them by force. In order to ensure this outcome, he secretly persuaded King Victor Emmanuel to form an alliance with Prussia, so that the Austrians would find themselves confronted by two separate armies. When the Austrians discovered the alliance, they were so alarmed that, unaware of Louis' involvement, they pleaded with him to persuade Victor Emmanuel to withdraw from the agreement in return for Austrian-occupied Venetia. When, however, the proposition was put to the Italian King, he nobly replied that he was not a man to break his word or renege on a promise.

In June 1866, the conflict began, and, following a few early losses, the Prussians gained success after success, suggesting that they would ultimately be triumphant. Although this was the outcome for which Louis had been hoping, he was deeply disconcerted by Prussians' progress, for, as the Crown Prince led his troops towards such an easy victory, it occurred to Louis that he could march with equal ease into France.

"The future King a good General, too!" he gasped. "That is the last straw!"[240]

Only seven weeks after the outbreak of war, the Austrians suffered a resounding defeat at Königgrätz and Emperor Franz Josef pleaded with Louis to mediate in peace negotiations. Louis duly approach Victor Emmanuel and Wilhelm I of Prussia, whose initial response was to disregard the request and march on to Vienna. Bismarck, though, heard a rumour that Louis was preparing to seize the Rhineland, and, on further investigation, discovered that the story was not without substance. Prince Chlodwig of Hohenlohe-Schillingsfürst, the Prime Minister of Austria's ally, Bavaria, received a deputation from the Rhine Palatinate, complaining that Louis' agents were actively inquiring of the local population whether their people would be happier if they were French.

> "The characterless people there," wrote Prince Chlodwig, "who have never clung to any sovereign, any more than to Germany, will readily allow themselves to be made French. This makes the patriots furious, and they are sending deputations to implore protection. But where are we to get an army from to keep the French troops off? Our troops have enough to do to keep off the Prussians; there are none left for the Palatinate."[241]

There could not have been a more propitious time for Louis to prevent Prussia from becoming the most dominant force in Europe, particularly when several of his ministers were warning that the Prussians were so fixated with power that, once they had defeated Austria, they would turn their guns on France. During a cabinet meeting two days after Königgrätz, the Foreign Minister, Drouyn de Lhuys, urged Louis to send eighty-thousand men into the Rhineland to launch a pre-emptive strike; and the Minister of War confidently stated that two-hundred-and-fifty-thousand French troops could be in the region within twenty days.

The Minister of the Interior, La Valette, disagreed, warning that any attack on Prussia would give the impression of support for Austria which would undoubtedly lead to a breach in relations with Italy. It would be far better, he said, to remain on friendly terms with the Prussians, who would surely reward French neutrality with a gift of various provinces.

Louis remained silent throughout much of the meeting, but Eugénie, incensed by La Valette's naiveté, cried out,

> "When the Prussian armies are no longer tied up in Bohemia and can turn back against ourselves, Bismarck will simply laugh at our claims!"[242]

Her outburst roused the ministers to such a pitch that, by the time the meeting was over, Louis had ordered a full mobilisation and had agreed to send a warning note to Berlin the following day.

The ministers gradually drifted away, but La Valette and few like-minded advisors remained behind, and once they were alone with Louis, they persuaded him to abandon the plan, and to trust King Wilhelm, who would, they said, honour the unwritten agreement he had made with Bismarck in Biarritz.

In fact, Bismarck fully expected Louis to take advantage of the situation, and had, therefore, convinced his King to accept Franz Josef's request for an armistice. He was so surprised that Louis did not march his armies in to the Rhineland that, even years later, he told a French diplomat:

> "I don't understand yet why the French army did not cross the Rhine in July, 1866, while we were entangled in the passes of Bohemia. And when I say 'the French army,' I'm wrong: one single division, fifteen thousand men, would have sufficed! The mere sight of your red trousers in the Duchy of Baden and the Palatinate would have raised the whole of Southern Germany against Prussia...And that would have been the end of us. I do not know if we could even have covered Berlin."[243]

During the ensuing peace negotiations, Franz Josef accepted all the Prussian terms, including ceding Venetia to the French Emperor on the understanding that he would hand the province over to Italy. The Austrians were also forced to accept the Prussian seizure of the disputed

Danish territories of Schleswig-Holstein; and, as the jubilant Prussians revelled in their spoils, Bismarck was hailed as the hero of the hour.

"I rejoice as a Prussian at the heroic conduct of our troops," wrote Queen Victoria's daughter, the Crown Princess of Prussia, "but my joy is damped with the fear that they have shed their blood in vain. With such a man and such principles at the head of our Government how can I look forward to satisfactory results for Germany?"[244]

Louis was far more optimistic, and cheerfully sent his envoys to Berlin to discover which provinces he would be given as payment for his neutrality. Bismarck, however, had no intention of adhering to their agreement, and pompously insulted the emissaries, whom he accused of 'begging for a tip.'

Louis, thoroughly disheartened, not only had to endure his ministers' criticism for failing to seize the Rhineland provinces, but also was faced with the realisation that he had helped to empower Prussia and Italy, while gaining nothing for France. Depressed and sickened, he retired to the spa town of Vichy, where, for several days he was so lethargic that his doctors believed he was dying[ee].

Eugénie, refusing to accept the humiliation, insisted that he must salvage some semblance of success from the situation and urged him to instruct his Ambassador, Vincent Benedetti, to ask again for recompense for France's recent neutrality. This time, Benedetti was to ask for the Grand Duchy of Luxembourg, and an assurance of Prussian neutrality if France should attempt to annex Belgium.

"But all this," Louis wrote to be Benedetti, "should only be insinuated amicably. The treaty must remain secret. The question of Luxembourg

---

[ee] It was at this time that Charlotte arrived, seeking help for Maximilian in Mexico.

will come out of itself as soon as the negotiations begin. That is the most pressing."[245]

Convinced that the proposal would help to restore the balance of power in Europe, Benedetti presented the idea to Bismarck as though it would be easily accomplished, for, although Luxembourg, in which a Prussian garrison was stationed, was officially ruled by the Netherlands, the impecunious Dutch King would be willing to sell it at a reasonable price. The annexation of Belgium, Benedetti continued, would be effected at an opportune moment, and, at Louis' suggestion, he also recommended that Prussia should annex Protestant Saxony, and give the Roman Catholic Saxon King a separate Kingdom on the opposite bank of the Rhine.

This time, Bismarck responded more favourably, and, after a brief discussion, asked Benedetti to put his terms in writing. When Benedetti had done so and signed the document, Bismarck gave his word that, in return for Louis' recognition of Prussia's recent territorial gains, he would withdraw the Prussian garrison from Luxembourg, and provide whatever assistance might be needed in the annexation of Belgium. When Benedetti had left, Bismarck filed away the handwritten agreement, which he himself had deliberately omitted to sign.

Weeks passed, and when no further word arrived from Berlin, Louis decided to take matters into his own hands by offering the King of the Netherlands five million guilders for the Grand Duchy of Luxembourg. This was exactly what Bismarck had expected to happen, and, as soon as the Dutch King had accepted Louis' offer, he leaked the story to the press and included a copy of Benedetti's note regarding the proposed annexation of Belgium.

'This publication,' said Eugénie, 'kindled the anger of the whole of Europe against us, as if we had been planning an act of brigandage.'[246]

When King Leopold II of Belgium wrote to his cousin, Queen Victoria, expressing his fears that his

167

country would be invaded, she assured him that Britain would come to his assistance if any attempt were made to compromise Belgian neutrality. So intense was the outcry that, for a while, it appeared that war would be inevitable, but, thanks partly to Bismarck's gloating intervention, an international conference was arranged to settle the matter peacefully.

> "I have no serious reason to love Napoleon III," he told a French diplomat later, "...but I would not fight him...All those about the King were for war; I was the only one to reject it."[247]

The delegates met in London in May 1867, and agreed that the Prussian garrison would withdraw from Luxembourg, the neutrality of which was guaranteed although it would remain united to the Netherlands. The neutrality of Belgium was also re-affirmed and guaranteed by all the participating powers.

The immediate threat of war had passed but the incident had inspired in Louis and Eugénie a deep mistrust of Bismarck, and provoked in the French an intense hatred of all things Prussian.

> "Nobody really knows what the Emperor intends to do," one French minister recorded. "The middle class look upon war with horror, but the masses, especially in the eastern departments, are ready to eat the Prussians."[248]

Louis himself believed that at some point a war with Prussia would become inevitable, and he privately ordered his Generals to make all the necessary preparations.

> "From this moment," he said, "we ought to think of the future, and in peace to be always ready for war; so that, should an event occur similar to the one we have just had to deal with, we may not be found living in a fool's paradise, and absolutely unprepared to defend ourselves."[249]

Convinced that his army was far superior to that of the King Wilhelm, he believed that he could achieve an easy victory as long as Prussia had no support from its allies. To that end, he set about trying to create discord between Austria and Russia, in the hope of distracting them from a Franco-Prussian conflict.

Four years earlier, the French had enthusiastically supported an anti-Russian uprising in Poland, which so captured Eugénie's imagination that she had urged Louis to adopt the cause of Polish independence. 'I even wanted the restoration of the ancient Kingdom of Poland under the sceptre of an Austrian Archduke,'[250] she later confessed, but her hopes were dashed when the rebellion was crushed and, declining Louis' suggestion of an international conference, Tsar Alexander II declared that he was God's appointed ruler of the region.

Now, though, it occurred to Louis that, if Austria were to lay claim to Warsaw, the Russians would be so incensed that it could lead to a convenient Russo-Austrian War. He, therefore, advised Emperor Franz Josef to embark on a tour through his Galician territories in the hope that he would receive such a warm welcome from his Polish subjects that the Russian Poles would rise up again and claim him as their King. Preparations for the tour were virtually completed when Louis' plan was thwarted as Franz Josef discovered that the Tsar was also on his way to Warsaw. Not only did the Austrian Emperor cancel his visit, but went further by sending his brother-in-law to congratulate Alexander on his arrival in the capital.

"I am glad," the Tsar replied, "that his Austrian Majesty has relinquished his contemplated journey to Galicia. Of course I have no right to express an opinion on the internal politics of Austria; but if that journey had been undertaken, not for domestic interests, but as a political demonstration against myself, it would scarcely have left me indifferent."[251]

His intentions frustrated, Louis decided instead to court the Tsar in order to obtain his support during any subsequent conflict, and there would be no greater opportunity of cultivating his friendship than during the Great Exposition of Paris in 1867.

Chapter 15 – Tranquillity & Contentment Pervade All Classes of Society

Proud as he was of his uncle, and much as he desired to emulate his successes, Louis understood that he risked being compared unfavourably to the great Napoleon, and that unrealistic expectations might be placed upon his shoulders. Soon after the coup d'état, he warned, 'I cannot do for you all the Emperor did; I have neither his genius nor his power'[252]; and, as the years went by, he became increasingly concerned about how his people viewed him, and it worried him that he failed to live up to the example of his renowned predecessor.

Often, he attended festivals simply to discover how well he was received; and it was typical of him that his first response to Maximilian's execution was to summon the Chief of Police to find out how the public had reacted to the news. Although his own tastes were relatively simply, he had made his court as glamorous as possible because this was what he believed the people expected; and whenever the tide of opinion turned against him, he became depressed and lethargic, not least because he believed that he had always acted for the good of his people.

"The Emperor's was essentially a kind nature," wrote Princess Catherine Radziwill. "During the eighteen years of his reign he did an enormous amount of good, and certainly France owes to him a good deal of her present prosperity. He thought about his people's welfare more than had any previous Sovereign…He wanted his country to be strong, rich, an example to others in its energetic progress along the path of material and intellectual development."[253]

As soon as he came to power, he set about implementing the plans which he had formulated during his imprisonment in Ham, many of which were based on his observations in other countries. In England, he had observed that the growing economy owed much to the advent of the railways, and one of his first acts as President of the National Assembly was to issue a series of concessions to several French companies to enable them to build reliable networks around Paris, and across the country from Calais to Marseilles. For almost two decades, he continued to support the construction of further lines so that, by the mid-1860s, a highly-efficient system operated throughout most of France. He arranged, too, for the improvement of the docks, and replaced many of the merchant fleet's wooden vessels with steamships.

Like Prince Albert in England, Louis took a keen interest in the housing conditions of the working classes, and, at his own expense, he built numerous new dwellings and introduced better sanitation to the poorest parts of the country. On a larger scale, he had many discussions with architects and planners regarding the best means of creating healthier and more attractive towns, and his plans paid off, as one British journalist observed when returning to Marseilles in 1865.

> "The town, as I knew it first, was about the dirtiest and most evil-smelling mass of houses, inhabited by a population as unwashed and as malodorous as could well be conceived. At least [Napoleon III] had cleansed Marseilles. At least he had sanitated it. At least, under his sway, magnificent new streets had been built, and the historic Cannebifere endowed with palatial hotels in lieu of the filthy and comfortless inns of yore, reeking with the fumes of garlic and bad tobacco."[254]

The people of Marseilles were so delighted by his improvements that they presented Louis with a handsome residence in the town so that he might 'always have one foot in the sea.'

171

At the start of his reign, the silk-manufacturing city of Lyons, had been a rundown insanitary place, but, thanks to his improvements it became 'adorned with streets as stately as the Avenue de l'Opéra, and possessing hotels as sumptuous as the Grand, or the Louvre, in Paris.'[255]

"Under his sway," wrote one English author, "France enjoys an unusual degree of prosperity, and unwonted tranquillity and contentment pervade all classes of society."[256]

It was a view shared by countless foreign visitors who returned home with stories of the number of new buildings that had been erected, and the obvious affluence of Napoleon III's subjects. In Paris, rents were surprisingly low; goods were inexpensive; and even working people were able to purchase all kinds of luxuries that were beyond the dreams of their English counterparts. Moreover, the city attracted many artists, musicians and intellectuals, making it one of the most cultured places in Europe.

Nonetheless, in the fifty years prior to Louis' accession, industrialisation and overcrowding had turned large parts of Paris into a shabby collection of alleyways, factories and slums. During his imprisonment in Ham, he had dreamed of a capital that signified a nation in the ascendancy, with wide thoroughfares, attractive buildings, and public parks, like those through which had ridden in London.

As soon as he became President, he set about bringing his dream to fruition by appointing George-Eugène Haussmann as Prefect of the Seine with a mandate to renovate the city, beginning by clearing the slums, which had become a breeding ground of anarchy and revolution. Haussmann eagerly undertook the commission and drew up plans to move the factories to the outskirts, where new dwellings would be built to house the workers whose slums had been demolished. Alleyways and courtyards would be replaced with wide boulevards lined with uniform buildings; and beneath the streets, the sewage system would be renovated, and pipes laid to carry gas and fresh water through the various arrondissements. Through regular meetings with Haussmann, Louis involved himself in every stage of the preparations, and was convinced that the enormous expense of the project would be offset by the fact that it would create employment over several decades for thousands of workers.

Unfortunately, in Paris the Emperor had never achieved the popularity that he had gained throughout the rest of the country, and, while it was agreed that the appearance of the city was greatly improved, the constant noise and disruption as well as the expense led to numerous complaints and a general air of dissatisfaction. One leading political figure, Jules Ferry, accused Haussmann of having deliberately underestimated the cost of his schemes, and called for his dismissal, but Louis, determinedly loyal to the Prefect, responded quickly:

> "That is nominally true, but in reality Haussmann has not underrated the cost of the improvements, he has only underrated the greed of the Paris bourgeois, just as he would have underrated M. Ferry's impudence if he had attempted to transform him into a fair critic and a gentleman."[257]

Haussmann repaid his loyalty by bringing about a complete transformation of the city, and when, in 1864, he was praised for his endeavours, he humbly replied that the Emperor had designed and planned everything, whereas he – Haussmann – was merely a collaborator.

Immensely proud of the achievement, Louis longed to show the city to the rest of Europe, and it occurred to him that a world fair, similar to the Great Exhibition which Prince Albert had organised in London in 1851, was the ideal way of drawing in crowds, including the princes and kings of neighbouring powers. He appointed his cousin, Prince Napoleon, to preside over a commission to organise the event, and, within two years, over fifty thousand artists, designers and inventors had agreed to exhibit their wares in the great 'Exposition' in the Champs de Mars.

The event was to run from April to November 1867, and, as preparations were underway, Louis made regular visits to the site to ensure that everything lived up to his highest expectations. Inevitably there were setbacks, not the least of which was the building that was to house the exhibition, which Louis considered so dull and ugly that he referred to it as the 'grandiose gasometer.' Prince Napoleon's sudden resignation came as another blow; and, as foreign exhibitors arrived, they found the commissioners were 'very rapacious, grasping and greedy...constantly quarrelling with the Foreign Commissioners, and doing their best to extort more and more cash from the concessionaries of the different shows and places of refreshment in the annexes.'[258]

A further disappointment was the absence of the Prince Imperial from the opening ceremony, particularly since the boy had been created the nominal president of the exhibition. Shortly before the event, he had developed a painful abscess on his hip, and, following surgery, he was obliged to remain immobile. Rumours, believed to have been started by Prince Napoleon, soon spread that he was seriously ill or that he had died, but within a few weeks he was sufficiently recovered to stem the gossip by reappearing in public.

In spite of the hitches, Louis and Eugénie were determined to use the exhibition not only to show off Paris' beauty but also to cement useful ties with other countries. Louis made a point of expressing his thanks to all the foreign exhibitors, and was particularly keen to praise the English displays. To his embarrassment, he himself won the prize for the most innovative display of hygienic housing, and, much to the delight of the crowds, his award was accepted on his behalf by the Prince Imperial.

No fewer than two emperors, eight kings, a sultan, a viceroy and six reigning princes attended the exhibition, and all were treated to lavish hospitality. Notwithstanding their recent dispute, Bismarck and King Wilhelm were among the guests, as was Queen Victoria's daughter, the Crown Princess of Prussia, who was deeply impressed by the warmth of her reception.

> "The real kindness of the Emperor and Empress, the charming way in which they do the honours, and the trouble they give themselves to see all their guests, left a most pleasing impression on me. They spoke so often and with such real attachment of you and dear Papa – and asked so much after you."[259]

The Princes of Wales, Prussia, Orange, Saxony and Italy were driven to the site in the state coaches of Louis XVI, which had been preserved at Versailles and recommissioned for the occasion; and all past wars and disputes were forgotten as the crowds cheered loudly as each royal personage passed by. When it became known that Louis had sent an invitation to Tsar Alexander II, a delegation of Poles petitioned him to rescind the offer, but Louis not only ignored their request, but also, to the annoyance and amusement of his other guests, went out of his way to treat the Tsar as his most important visitor.

Sadly, his efforts backfired when, in preparation for an opera performance, he arranged for two thrones – one for himself and one for the Tsar – to be placed at the front while the rest of the princes, princesses and kings were to sit on ordinary chairs behind them. When Alexander realised what he had done, he walked passed the throne and sat down beside the Queen of the Belgians. At the races, the following afternoon, observers noticed that the Tsar was particularly taciturn, and the King of Prussia was equally out of sorts, but worse was to come the next day when, during a carriage ride through the Bois de Boulogne, a Pole stepped out from the crowd and discharged a pistol. The bullet struck one of the horses before passing directly between Louis and the Tsar, but when the attacker raised his arm to fire again, the gun exploded in his hand.

> "The horse's blood spurted all over the Russian princes," the *Daily Telegraph* reported, "and at that instant the Czar looked alarmed. Napoleon got up, waved his hat, and then said to the Czar, 'Sire, we have been under fire together.'"[260]

His apparent composure concealed how deeply he had been shaken; and, when Eugénie heard what had happened, she sobbed all evening that she wished her husband had been slightly injured for then it would appear that he, and not the Tsar, was the target of the would-be assassin. 'To receive an imperial guest is one thing;' Louis sighed after Alexander's departure, 'to have him die on your hands is quite another affair.'[261]

The episode did little to further Louis' plans for a strong Franco-Russian alliance, for when the gunman came to trial, his defence argued that he had been driven to such violence by the cruelty of 'the butcher of Poland,' and consequently he was spared the death sentence.

'It certainly looked as if some evil spell had been cast over our relations with Russia,'[262] Eugénie complained, convinced that all hope of an alliance was at an end.

The execution of Maximilian in Mexico also cast a shadow over the celebrations, and, in spite of Louis' hospitality, the exposition did little to ease the rivalry between France and Prussia. Sensing an impending conflict, Louis used the final day of the exhibition to urge his people:

> "Let us be great by the arts of Peace, as of War: let us place our confidence in God; to enable us to triumph over the difficulties of the Present, and the Chances of the Future."[263]

'The difficulties of the present' were becoming increasingly apparent to Louis, who had not only failed to secure the alliances for which he had been hoping, but was also aware of the growing discontent within his government. His ministers were openly working to deprive him of many of his autocratic powers, and he had no doubt that they intended to reduce his authority further, until he became little more than a cypher.

By the early 1860s, in spite of his efforts to improve conditions for workers, Marxist ideas were flooding into the cities, where illegal meetings were frequently held amid calls for a return to a republic. An increasing number of liberal reformers were elected to the Chamber, and, in May 1869, when strikes erupted across the country, Louis was forced to yield to demands to grant freedom of the press and give greater powers to parliament. These seemingly minor concessions failed to satisfy the protestors, and, four months later, he was compelled to hand over control of the treasury and legislature to his ministers.

On 2nd January 1870, a new government was formed under the premiership of a former republican, Emile Ollivier, one of whose first acts was to reduce the number of men in the army by ten thousand a year. Anticipating an imminent war, Louis, who had studied the training techniques of the Prussian forces, agreed with the Minister of War that there was a need for compulsory conscription into the regular army or the National Guard. Formerly, the Emperor would have had the strength and ambition to reverse Ollivier's decision, but by 1870, he was becoming increasingly depressed and weighed down by a painful illness.

Louis had always been prone to an allegedly inherited stomach complaint, which had also affected Emperor Napoleon I, but his more debilitating problems began in 1864, triggered by a carriage accident. He, Eugénie and Princess Anna Murat were on their way to visit his mother's grave, when the horses suddenly bolted throwing the passengers on to the road. Princess Anna fractured her jaw and damaged a facial nerve, while Eugénie escaped with relatively minor cuts and bruises. Louis, however, had sustained more serious injuries,

177

including an internal haemorrhage, which his doctors struggled to stem. So as not to alarm the people, it was reported that Eugénie had been badly hurt, and Louis' attention to her explained his prolonged absence from public events.

From that time onwards, he was plagued by severe internal pains, which flared up at regular intervals. On the advice of his doctors, he replaced his Havana cigars with cigarettes and adopted a marginally more abstemious lifestyle, but none of this relieved his excruciating abdominal cramps, which some of his physicians suspected were caused by a kidney stone. Eugénie, though, later stressed that neither she nor Louis had any idea of the cause of his illness, as the doctors were unable to agree on a diagnosis.

> "I had been familiar with, vesical spasms, intense pain in the loins, frequent haematuria, etc....and their origin is attributed to a stone in the bladder. But the other consultant physicians...did not completely bear out his opinion."[264]

His sufferings were all the more intense, due to a condition which his doctors referred to as 'hypeaethesia' – an unusual sensitivity to pain, which made the slightest inflammation unbearable. Moreover, since childhood, he had been prone to haemorrhages, and, according to his dentist, had once nearly bled to death after having a tooth extracted.

Determined to conceal his illness for fear that any sign of weakness would give greater impetus to the republicans' cause, he insisted on carrying out his duties as though nothing were wrong. When, though, in early 1870, the Crown Princess of Prussia spent a week in Paris she was shocked by his depressed and sickly demeanour; and, two months later, Lord Malmesbury, who had not seen him for three years, met him at a dinner and observed that he was 'much altered in appearance, and looking very ill' and 'had had grown prematurely aged and broken.' It occurred to him that the Emperor's willingness to accept a more constitutional government:

> "...was more the result of bodily suffering and exhaustion from a deadly disease than from any moral conviction; and that he felt, as he must have done, that the life left him was short, and that his son would have a better chance of quietly inheriting his throne under a parliamentary and irresponsible regime."[265]

At the time when Ollivier announced his intention of reducing the size of the army, Louis was suffering a particularly agonising bout of his illness, and, in conversation with Malmesbury, he said he felt so ill that it was a blessing that Europe appeared to be at peace. Ironically, just three months later, as his sufferings became even more intense, he would find himself in the midst of the most devastating war of his life.

Chapter 16 – The Unfortunate Affair May Set Europe in a Blaze

In 1868, following a revolution, the deposed Spanish Queen, Isabella II, asked Louis' permission to settle in France. He graciously placed the Chateau of Pau at her disposal and sent three officers of his household to escort her from the border to his residence at Biarritz where he and Eugénie were staying. In Isabella's absence, Spain briefly became a republic, with a Provisional Government presided over by Marshal Prim – an officer who had recently returned from Mexico, where he had opposed Louis' plans to place Maximilian on the throne.

Although the Spaniards no longer trusted Isabella's dynasty, they wished to retain a monarchy and invited suggestions of potential candidates for the vacant throne. Louis Philippe's son, Montpensier, was among the most prominent contenders, alongside Isabella's recalcitrant brother-in-law, Don Enrique, Duke of Madrid; and Queen Victoria's second son, Prince Alfred, Duke of Edinburgh. The Prussians proposed Prince Leopold of Hohenzollern-Sigmaringen, a thirty-five-year-old member of King Wilhelm's extended family; or his younger brother, Fritz; or his father-in-law, Queen Victoria's cousin, Ferdinand of Saxe-Coburg-Kohary.

Bismarck guilefully watched the proceedings, convinced that he twist the situation to goad the French into a declaration of war. Suspecting that Louis despised the entire Orléans family, he initially attempted to provoke him by expressing support for Montpensier but his plan was thwarted when Louis sent his Foreign Minister to Madrid to state that he had accepted this suggestion, and had no desire to meddle in Spanish politics.

The Spaniards' preferred candidate was Ferdinand of Saxe-Coburg-Kohary, the widower of the late Portuguese Queen, but when he expressed reluctance to accept the offer, Don Enrique blamed Montpensier, claiming the he was 'making himself very popular at the Portuguese capital by trying to disparage Prince Ferdinand.'[266]

The allegation was well-founded, as Montpensier had tried to discredit his rival by telling the Papal Nuncio in Madrid that Ferdinand was unsuited to the role of a Catholic sovereign since he was openly living with an opera singer and actress named Elise Hensler. When the Nuncio questioned Ferdinand on the matter, he replied that he intended to marry Elise and, since the Spaniards refused to accept her as his consort, he had no intention of accepting the crown.

With Ferdinand removed from the contest, Bismarck forcefully pressed for the selection of Leopold of Hohenzollen-Sigmaringen, leading to an outcry in the French press, and outright condemnation from the celebrated author, Victor Hugo.

"The Hohenzollerns have reached such audacity that they aspire to dominate Europe. It will be for our time an eternal humiliation that this project has been, we will not say undertaken, but only conceived."[267]

Louis, too, saw Leopold's candidacy as a deliberate provocation, since his appointment would leave France surrounded by Hohenzollerns. He, therefore, summoned the Prussian Ambassador to Paris and told him bluntly:

"The Montpensier candidature is merely anti-dynastic; it only strikes at me and I can permit it. But that of the Hohenzollern prince is essentially anti-national. It is aimed at France and the country will surely resent it; so it must be prevented at all hazards. Return to Berlin, talk the matter over with Bismarck, but be careful to use no expressions which might lead him to think that we are seeking a quarrel."[268]

181

For a while it seemed that the matter would be resolved peacefully with Montpensier's accession, but Don Enrique, who despised 'the bloated French pasty cook,' continued to defame him and, in early 1870, he published a letter claiming that Montpensier was a 'charlatan in politics' and had used all his wife's money to dethrone Queen Isabella so that he could seize power. The letter created such a furore that Montpensier wrote to Don Enrique, asking him to confirm that he was the author, and when Don Enrique replied by sending him a signed copy of the original letter, he was so incensed that he challenged him to a duel.

To the alarm of the friends of the portly short-sighted Montpensier, Don Enrique enthusiastically accepted the challenge, and, although duelling was officially illegal, the authorities failed to intervene when a date – 12th March 1870 – was set for the meeting. Lots were drawn as to who should fire the first shot, and Montpensier's chances of survival decreased dramatically when Don Enrique drew the longer straw. To the surprise of their seconds, both men missed the target with their first two bullets; and it seemed inevitable that, at the third attempt, Don Enrique would find his aim. Once again, though, he failed to hit the target, and, to the relief of the seconds, it seemed that the duel would end without bloodshed. No one was more shocked than Montpensier when his last bullet killed his opponent outright, filling him with such horror that for several days he was confined to bed with a fever. Racked with remorse, Montpensier offered to adopt, or pay for the upbringing of, Don Enrique's children but the offer was politely declined.

Queen Victoria could hardly believe what had happened, and telegraphed Montpensier's brother, Aumale, to discover if the story were true. On being told all the details, she wrote to her daughter in Prussia:

"The poor Duke of Montpensier is quite blameless in this dreadful affair. Don Enrique was a horrid,

182

low, republican scamp and forced poor Montpensier who is as myope [sic] as a mole and totally unaccustomed to pistols into the duel. But it is most painful for him."[269]

When Montpensier had sufficiently recovered to stand trial for duelling, he was sentenced to a month's banishment from Madrid, and a fine of several hundred-thousand pesetas to be paid to Don Enrique's family. More significantly, the escapade put an end to any possibility of his ascending the throne, which enabled Bismarck to redouble his efforts to promote Prince Leopold of Hohenzollern-Sigmaringen.

In fact, Leopold had no desire to accept the throne; and King of Prussia opposed the idea, knowing that his candidacy would infuriate the French. Bismarck, though, refused to give way, and, using all his legendary guile, he eventually convinced them both that the Hohenzollern prince was the first choice of the Spanish people.

Once King Wilhelm had given his consent, Bismarck began secret negotiations with Prim, and a confidential message to that effect was sent to the Cortes[ff] in Madrid, stating that Leopold had accepted the crown. By chance or design, when the news arrived, the Cortes was in recession, and as Bismarck waited for the ministers to return, the story was leaked to the press.

On July 2nd, a Parisian newspaper printed the story, which, said Eugénie, 'exploded like a bomb', and left Louis so dumbfounded that he urgently sent an envoy to King Wilhelm at the spa town of Ems, urging him to prohibit his nephew from accepting the throne. Other monarchs were equally stunned. The Tsar, foreseeing an imminent war, offered to mediate; the King of the Belgians described the move as a deliberate provocation to France; and Queen Victoria, who 'thought all that had been given up,' was even more surprised when she received a telegram from Louis, seeking Britain's support

---

ff The Spanish Parliament

in resisting Leopold's candidacy. At the same time, articles appeared in French newspapers, claiming that the British Government was secretly in league with Prussia, and when the editor of the *Times* refuted the allegation, he also condemned the French Emperor for interfering in Spanish affairs.

Uncertain how to proceed, the Queen sought the Foreign Secretary's advice and was relieved when he said that Britain must remain neutral to avoid becoming embroiled in any subsequent war. Privately, though, she suspect that Bismarck was involved in some form of subterfuge, and wrote to her daughter, the Crown Princess, asking what role, if any, Prussia had played in the affair. Affronted by the implied criticism of her adopted homeland, the Crown Princess replied indignantly that, while all of Berlin objected to French interference in Spain, the Prussians had played no part in the negotiations, and no one was more surprised than King Wilhelm when the news of Leopold's appointment appeared in the press.

Unconvinced, Queen Victoria replied the next day: "The unfortunate affair of Leopold H. may set Europe in a blaze. If only he would retire of himself it would be a blessing, though the conduct of the French is most preposterous and shameful. If the King [of Prussia] too would say he had nothing to do with it."[270]

The French Foreign Minister, Benedetti, meanwhile, had arrived in Ems, where he found King Wilhelm in a most conciliatory mood. Significantly, he had ordered Bismarck to stay away from the meeting, and agreed with Benedetti that the best solution would be for Leopold himself to renounce any claim to the throne, and promised to arrange for Leopold's father to send a letter to Madrid via Paris to that effect. When Benedetti went further, demanding an assurance that no other Hohenzollern candidate would come forward, the King refused to commit himself but amicably concluded the meeting.

There, the matter might have ended but Bismarck, desperate to create a war that would ultimately lead to German unification, was not prepared to let the opportunity slip from his hands. Having obtained King Wilhelm's permission to present a transcript of the meeting to the press and to foreign governments, he set to work doctoring the document.

> "The French Ambassador," he wrote, "having insisted on guarantees for the future, after Prince Leopold's desistance, His Majesty refused to receive him anymore, and sent word to him, by the aide-de-camp on duty, that he had nothing further to communicate to him."[271]

The message, which distorted the friendly tone of the meeting, implied that the King had insulted the French Foreign Minister; and, at the same time, Bismarck had several anonymous and inflammatory articles published in prominent Prussian newspapers, accusing Eugénie of having been involved in the revolution that overthrew Isabella, so that she and Louis could create a war of succession. Other articles were equally provocative:

> "Is Spain," asked one, "to inquire submissively at the Tuileries whether the King whom she desires to take is considered satisfactory? Is the Spanish throne a French dependency?"[272]

As Bismarck had intended, the articles aroused French anger, and several ministers declared that, in the face of such insults, there was no alternative but to issue a declaration of war. Ill and weary, Louis had no desire to commit to a conflict but, on July 14th, during a meeting of the Ministerial Council at Saint Cloud, the Minister of War threatened to resign unless the Prussians were punished for their effrontery. Eugénie, fearing for her husband's position if he failed to respond to the mood of the country, agreed that something must be done to satisfy French honour.

185

"We had felt the blow of an insult, direct, brutal, and mortifying," she later explained. "We had to pick up the gauntlet! We no longer had any choice save between war and dishonour!"[273]

Her detractors would later claim that she had driven Louis into war, and had placed the interests of her native Spain above those of France. She, however, always denied the allegation, and as late at 1904, she was still protesting that this was far from the truth.

"I am quite ready to assume the responsibility of all my acts," she stated. "I admit that I exerted my influence in favour of the unfortunate Mexican expedition, but I stoutly deny that I ever approved of the struggle between Germany and France. Quite the contrary, I did what I could to prevent it."[274]

Lord Malmesbury disagreed, stating that he had been told by Duke of Gramont, who was present at the meeting, that the Empress had been most vociferous in insisting that France's honour was at stake; but Gramont's claim is dubious since he also stood accused of being the most belligerent attendee at the meeting.

A declaration of war was prepared and, when it had been read aloud in the council, Louis applauded, seeking only the assurance that France had a good chance of victory. The Minister of War confirmed that this was the case, reminding him that the infantry was equipped with the most modern firearm – the breech-loading Chassepot rifle, which was far superior to the Prussians' Dreyse needle guns.

The following day, the declaration was presented to the Legislative Chamber, where a rowdy debate ensued. Adolphe Theirs, Louis Philippe's one-time Prime Minister, who had repeatedly spoken of the inevitability of a war with Prussia, argued that, since Prince Leopold's name had been withdrawn from the candidacy, there was no legitimate reason to issue the declaration.

"Well, gentlemen," he concluded, "do you want people to say, do you want all Europe to say that, the main point being granted, you have resolved, for a mere question of form, to shed torrents of blood? As for me, let me tell you in two words, to explain both my actions and my language, let me tell you that I look upon this war as supremely imprudent."[275]

When his remonstrations were jeered by the majority of the council, Louis asked why he had waited until the last minute to raise these objections. As no reply was forthcoming, a vote was taken as to whether or not the declaration should be sent to Berlin, and as it gained virtually unanimous support, Louis signed the document and sealed his own fate.

Chapter 17 – Without Weakness But Without Enthusiasm

Unaware of the extent of Bismarck's machinations, the whole of Germany viewed the French declaration as an unprovoked act of aggression. The southern states rose up in support of Prussia, and so powerful a wave of patriotism swept through the country that even the Crown Princess of Prussia, who had known Louis and Eugénie since childhood, was caught up in the fervour.

> "We have been shamefully forced into this war," she wrote to Queen Victoria, "and the feeling of indignation against an act of such crying injustice has risen in two days here to such a pitch that you would hardly believe it; there is a universal cry 'To arms to resist an enemy who so wantonly insults us.'"[276]

Her younger sister, Alice, wife of the heir to the German Grand Duchy of Hesse, was equally quick to lay the blame at the feet of the French:

> "...The provocation of a war such as this is a crime that will have to be answered for, and for which there is no justification...There is a feeling of unity and standing by each other, forgetting all party quarrels, which makes one proud of the name of German."[277]

Aghast at Louis' 'act of mad folly', Queen Victoria agreed with her daughters, but as her government immediately declared neutrality, she was unable to voice her fears that her beloved Germany could be facing defeat. 'Can there be a more cruel position than the unhappy Queen's?' she asked her Foreign Minister, and she privately empathised with the Crown Princess' plaintive sigh,

> "Oh that England could help us! I wish no ill to France, nor to anyone, but I wish Europe could

unite, once for all to stop her ever again having it in her power to force a war upon another nation."[278]

The French, meanwhile, delighted at the prospect of crushing Prussia, gathered to cheer to the departing soldiers; and wild celebrations erupted across Paris. This provided an ideal excuse for Louis to avoid the city as he set out to join the army at Metz, for, while he claimed that he did not wish to give rise to even greater excitement, the truth was that he was barely fit to be seen, let alone to participate in any military action.

His closest acquaintances, seeing how ill he looked, pleaded with him to remain at Saint Cloud; and, shortly before his departure, Princess Mathilde was so alarmed by his ashen complexion and stooped shoulders that she warned him that he was incapable of commanding an army. He could not, she said, ride a horse or even endure the jolting of a carriage, how then would he be able to acquit himself well in battle? Louis dismissed her concerns as exaggerations, but raised no objections when Eugénie insisted on packing numerous medicines with his luggage.

Louis and Eugénie agreed that the fourteen-year-old Prince Imperial should accompany his father, but for entirely different reasons. While Louis believed that presence of his beloved son on the battlefield would assure his men of his belief in an imminent victory, Eugénie, fearing that defeat could lead to a revolution, wanted the boy to be as far away as possible from Paris. Moreover, she decided that, if, at such a young age, he were able to endear himself to the ordinary soldiers, he would gain an army of supporters should he attempt to regain the throne.

'Do you duty' she called tearfully as, dressed in a lieutenant's uniform, Loulou marched proudly to the carriage, clutching the hilt of his sword.

The Emperor and Prince received a hearty welcome at Metz but the journey had been excruciating for Louis, who was so plagued by shooting pains in his legs and abdomen that for several days he was hardly capable of standing upright. His incapacity prevented him from launching an immediate surge into the Rhineland; and, as his soldiers remained inactive, the speed of the Prussian advance put paid to the rest of his plans. His troubles were compounded by the news that, since the southern German states had come out in favour of Prussia, the Austrians refused to participate in the war; and his former ally, King Victor Emmanuel, also insisted on remaining neutral.

Still more disconcerting was the realisation that he had been misled about the capability of the army, for, even in the midst of the cheers as they set out for battle, several observers had noticed that, for all their enthusiasm and bravado, the soldiers appeared ill-disciplined and incapable of understanding the seriousness of their task. Many were puny and looked unfit for service, while others were so intoxicated that they marched out of step, with women on their arms. Now, as Louis wandered among them, he could not help but think of the perfectly disciplined Prussian troops, who had carried out skilful manoeuvres with consummate ease.

Nonetheless, it was not long before he and Loulou had a first taste of victory when they rode into Saarbrucken and drove the Prussian vanguard from the town. In spite of the ferocity of the fighting and the danger in which he found himself, the Prince Imperial impressed the troops by his remarkable composure, and that evening Louis wrote to Eugénie:

> "[He] has just received his *baptême du feu.* He was admirably cool, and in no way affected. We were in the front line, and the cannon-balls and bullets fell at our feet…Some of the soldiers shed tears to see him so calm."[279]

The joy of victory was fleeting. From then onwards, defeat followed defeat and the anxious French ministers concluded that this was due to the Emperor's incompetence and his lack of an efficient war plan.

Without consulting him, they dispatched Marshal Bazaine to take over the command, and, despite his shock at this insult, he felt powerless to raise any objections.

Bazaine certainly appeared to have the credentials to lead the French to victory, for he had served with great distinction in the Crimea; and, for his successes in Mexico he had been created a Knight Grand Cross of the Légion d'Honneur. His strategies against the Prussians, though, greatly alarmed the Emperor, and, as he failed to achieve the desired victories, the troops became increasingly demoralised.

Following major defeats at Worth and Gravelotte, Louis and the Prince Imperial withdrew to Metz, but had hardly had time to settle in the town when they were told that the Prussians were approaching, forcing them to retreat to Châlons[gg].

Rather than revelling in her husband's victories, the Crown Princess of Prussia could not help but reflect on her former relationship with Louis and his family, while justifying the war by stating that it was the only means of keeping the violent French in check.

> "This present Emperor is not the scourge of Europe as his uncle was," she wrote to her mother, "he has done much that is good and wise and useful. I am sure in his heart he would like better to be at peace, but if the French are to be allowed to fly at their neighbours' throats whenever they think fit...the kindest of Emperors is not only no use but a dangerous individual, as he wields so great an instrument as the French army and into the bargain makes use of it to [distract from discord at home]."[280]

[gg] After Louis' departure, the town, and Bazaine's army, were placed under siege until 27th October, when Bazaine capitulated and surrendered his entire army of almost one-hundred-and-ninety-thousand men.

Queen Victoria watched the German advances with restrained relief but, when her German-born son-in-law, Prince Christian of Schleswig-Holstein, asked her permission to return home to re-join his former regiment, she refused on the grounds that it would appear to compromise British neutrality. Nonetheless, the French, with some justification, bitterly condemned Britain's duplicity, as the press hailed every German victory. The *Times* and the *Telegraph* advised Louis to abdicate; and the *Morning Advertiser* reported that he only remained with the army because he was too ill and too cowardly to face the crowds in Paris. Even those Englishmen who took a more balanced view of the conflict saw benefits for Britain in a French defeat. 'If France ceases to be the first military power in Europe,' wrote Lord Lytton, '...I think it will be an excellent thing for Europe, and especially for England.'[281]

In view of this transparent lack of neutrality, the French Ambassador asked the new Foreign Secretary, Lord Granville, to obtain from the Queen a word of sympathy for his Emperor. When the request was ignored, anti-British feeling ran so high that one expatriate who lived in Boulogne, begged:

> "Tell those travelling Englishmen who so loudly express their pleasure at German victories that they make the position of their countrymen in France most difficult."[282]

Ironically, the Prussians were equally convinced that the British were siding with the French, thanks largely to the commercial treaty that Louis had signed a decade earlier. As British horses supplied the French cavalry; British shells were fired from French guns; and British coal fuelled the French steamers, the Crown Princess told her mother that the English were even more hated than the French, and she and her sister, Alice, were being falsely accused of passing secrets to the Queen, who in turn was passing them on to the French Emperor. Consequently, while her husband was being hailed as hero for the part that he played in some of the bloodiest battles, the Crown Prince was prevented even from helping the wounded in the hospitals.

"It will be long," she told Queen Victoria, "before people believe England means kindly and well by Germany."[283]

Meanwhile, in Châlons, Louis' tribulations continued. He looked so ill and broken that his doctors warned that he would be dead within a month; and, when word reached him that riots were breaking out throughout Paris, his Generals urged him to go home and deal with the situation. Instead, wearing make-up to conceal his sickly appearance, he insisted on re-forming his army, while sending a trusted and popular officer, Louis Jules Trochu, back to France to serve as Governor of Paris, to assist the Empress in restoring order.

It was an unfortunate choice on Louis' part, for Trochu and Eugénie deeply mistrusted each other, and when she suggested recalling the Orléans princes to assist in the struggle, he suspected that the question was a trap, designed to prove him a traitor. He believed, he told her, that it would be better for the Emperor to return to Paris, but, fearing that this would give the impression that he had deserted, she sent an urgent telegram to Châlons:

"Do not think of coming back unless you wish to let loose a terrible revolution…People would say you were running away from danger."[284]

Although her detractors claimed that she wished to him to stay away so that she could retain power, the truth was that she was exhausted and would have been happy to relinquish her responsibilities. Between meeting with ministers three times a day, and following events from the front, every spare hour was taken up with caring for the wounded soldiers whom she had brought into the Tuileries.

With the support of Marshal MacMahon, Louis prepared a plan to relieve the besieged city of Metz, but knowing how dangerous the mission would be, he first sent the Prince Imperial away to the safety of Mézières. In late August, the army set out in the pouring rain over muddy tracks and uneven roads, but before they reached Metz, Louis received a message that the Prussians were aware of their advance and had sent an army to intercept them. Realising that his drenched troops were in no fit state for a battle, he ordered them to withdraw to the historic city of Sedan so that he could reassess the situation.

Unbeknown to the French, the Prussian commander, Helmuth von Molke, had been carefully watching their movements, and on hearing that they had encamped in Sedan, he cried in excitement, 'Now we have them in the mousetrap!'

Oblivious to the danger, Louis believed that the city was so secure that he sent orders to have his son brought back to him, but before Loulou and his escort had reached the outskirts, Prussians were spotted in the vicinity, and the Emperor sent a second order for the Prince to be taken away.

At six o'clock the following morning – 1st September 1870 – the Prussians opened fire, pitting almost a quarter of a million men against a French army of one-hundred-and-forty-thousand. In spite of his physical agony, Louis forced himself onto his horse, much to the distress of his closest companions who were shocked by 'the expression of horrible suffering which passed over his face as he arranged himself in the saddle.'[285]

For five hours, he remained on horseback, placing himself in the thick of the fighting as his men were decimated by the Prussian guns. MacMahon, in a failed attempt to break through the enemy lines, was wounded and carried away in an ambulance; and a shell exploded so close to Louis that it killed two of his officers' horses and seriously injured their riders.

"It is easy to understand the state of his moral being," Louis wrote later, describing himself in the third person. "No longer acting as commander-in-chief, he was not sustained by the feeling of responsibility which animates the mind of him who commands; nor had that exalting excitement of those who are acting under orders, and who know that their devotion may secure victory. The powerless witness of a hopeless struggle…he advanced to the battle-field with that cool resignation which meets danger without weakness but also without enthusiasm."[286]

By evening, the French had sustained seventeen-thousand casualties and a further twenty-one-thousand men had been captured, but all their attempts to breach the Prussian lines had failed.

King Wilhelm, desperate to put an end to the slaughter, sent a message, demanding an immediate surrender, but, when no reply was forthcoming, he ordered his cannon to continue the bombardment. French morale was already reaching its nadir, when a rumour spread that Paris was on the verge of revolution. Hearing the news, many of the soldiers mutinied, or ran away, while others handed themselves over to the Prussians.

This disloyalty was deeply wounding to Louis, for he had always been popular with the army and had devoted himself to the welfare of his regiments and individual soldiers. His men were always well-equipped and well-fed, and he never failed to praise them in defeat as well as in victory. When he heard of an officer who intended who intended to kill himself having lost a fortune at cards, he settled the debts without a second thought; and, on another occasion, when a General slipped and fell at a ball, Louis saved him from humiliation by telling his partner,

"Madame, this is the second time General has fallen in my presence; the first time was at Solferino."[287]

Now, knowing he had lost the support of the troops, he realised that the situation was hopeless and ordered a white flag to be raised over Sedan, before summoning two of his Generals to discuss how best to proceed. The Generals immediately turned on one another, each blaming the other for the fiasco, until Louis calmly silenced them:

> "We have all done our best," he said, "as best we understood it, and as we best could. Don't let us forget the duties we still owe to ourselves, to the army, to France, and to humanity."[288]

On being told of the French capitulation, King Wilhelm sent an officer named Colonel von Bronsart into the city to receive the official surrender. On being taken to Louis' quarters, the Prussian stared at him in astonishment as no one had realised that the French Emperor had been present throughout the battle; but, when he had recovered from the shock, Bronsart assured him that he would be treated with due respect. Louis asked if the Prussian King were in the vicinity, and on receiving an affirmative reply, he wrote him a letter stating that, since he had not died on the battlefield, it was his duty to surrender his sword to the victors.

Bronsart had the letter delivered and also complied with Louis' request for a meeting with Bismarck, who was staying three miles away at Donchery. Horses were readied and Louis set out with Bronsart towards Donchery, but, as one of his Generals observed:

> "The journey from Sedan was a fearful ordeal for the Emperor. He could scarcely keep on his horse, he was suffering such pain. He succeeded in doing so, however, by leaning with both hands on the pommel of the saddle, never allowing a single complaint to escape from him."[289]

As he approached the destination, Louis asked that a message be sent on ahead to Bismarck, explaining that he did not wish to enter the town for fear of being seen by the French mutineers who were being held there as prisoners. Bismarck duly set out to meet him on the road, and, spotting a local farmhouse, suggested it would be a suitable location for their discussion. Once settled inside, Louis explained that, while he was willing to surrender himself and his army, he could not discuss peace terms as he was now a prisoner and all authority lay with the Empress and the Government in Paris.

Bismarck, seeing his obvious discomfort, courteously arranged for him to be taken to the Chateau of Bellevue and, after some hesitation, agreed to ask King Wilhelm to visit him there. The King set out at once and, far from gloating his victory, he greeted Louis with great kindness and respect. He expressed sympathy that he should find himself in such a position, 'more especially as he was aware that it had not been easy to the Emperor to decide for war.'[290] The preliminaries over, Louis repeated that he had surrendered himself and his army, but that, as he was a prisoner, he could not surrender the whole of France. As he left the room after the meeting, he came face to face with the victorious Crown Prince, whom he had not met since the Paris Exposition three years earlier.

> "The King's lofty and august figure," wrote the Crown Prince, "contrasted admirably with the diminutive and depressed form of the Emperor. When Napoleon caught sight of me he gave me his hand, while with the other he dried up the big tears trickling down his cheeks. He referred with much gratitude to the language and generous manner generally with which the King had received him. I spoke, of course, in the same spirit, and asked whether he had obtained any night's rest, to which he replied that anxiety about his family had left him no sleep. On my regretting that the war had assumed so frightfully bloody a character, he replied that that was unhappily only too true, and it was all the more frightful *quand on n'a pas voulu la guerre.*"[291]

From Bellevue, Louis was taken to Schloss Wilhelmshöhe in Kassel, which, ironically, had once been renamed Napoleonshöhe, during the reign of his uncle, Jerome Bonaparte, as King of Westphalia. To his surprise, as he entered the castle, the guards presented arms, and he was told that he could establish his own household and would be given every convenience to make his stay comfortable. In spite of this kindness, Louis was ill, depressed, exhausted and fretting over the fate of his family. He had heard nothing of the Prince Imperial since he was turned back from Sedan; and had received no letters from his wife in over a week.

In England, meanwhile, Queen Victoria was astounded by the French surrender, and torn between relief at the German success, and sympathy for the vanquished, she sent a carefully-worded letter to Eugénie expressing her condolences for all that had happened. Privately, though, she concluded that defeat was a just reward for the 'frivolous' and 'corrupt' French people; and that Louis should take full responsibility, since, if he really had wished to avoid war, he could have abdicated instead of leading his army into such an horrific conflict. To a friend, she wrote bluntly, stating that while she pitied Eugénie:

> "It would have been better for the unfortunate Emperor to have died on the field of battle, but he was too ill for that."[292]

The British press was still more scathing, reporting that none of the deposed royals scattered around Europe deserved less sympathy than this latter-day Napoleon. One journalist described him as the epitome of an over-ambitious despot; while a writer for the *Spectator* laughed that he had spent two-thirds of his life dreaming of power, and the final third not knowing how to wield it. The more sympathetic Lord Lytton foresaw the inevitable outcome of defeat, warning that, 'every fibre of the French nation has been rotted away by lies...[and] when nothing is left but its native ferocity...I suspect that the tiger side will spring forward.'[293]

In Paris, Eugénie was about to experience the full ferocity of that metaphorical tiger.

Chapter 18 – Vive L'Empereur

Vague reports of events at Sedan reached Eugénie on the afternoon of 2nd September. Her husband, she was told, had been captured; her son was missing; and the greater part of the French army had been defeated. Unwilling and unable to believe it, she dismissed the account as a rumour, but the following day a telegram arrived from Louis himself, confirming that all she had been told was true. Not knowing how to respond, she sent for Trochu, the Governor of Paris, but he callously replied that he was busy and tired and needed to eat and sleep. The following morning, he deigned to appear and accompanied her to a meeting of ministers, who warned that the mob was demanding an end to the monarchy, and urged her to hand over all her authority to the Legislative Council.

Eugénie replied that she had a duty to fulfil the responsibility which the Emperor had entrusted to her, and, since the war was not yet over, she was best placed to obtain an honourable peace. The previous day, she explained, she had received a Russian offer to mediate, and, as the Prussians were marching on Paris, there was no time to waste in arranging a transfer of power. When her words met with a stony silent, she asked the opinion of a trusted advisor, Comte de Palikao, who had been with the Emperor at Metz. Reluctantly, Palikao agreed with the ministers, and so, out of 'necessity,' she agreed to relinquish her authority.

> "Her attitude," wrote Princess Radziwill, "was characteristic, and it was in accordance with her nature that she tried to explain the abandonment of her position as Regent by the word 'necessity,' when, in reality, it was the shrinking of a lonely woman, with no one near her to tell her what she ought to do, or to show her how to resist the demands of the mob."[294]

By mid-afternoon, the mob was approaching the Tuileries, and, although the Imperial Guard remained loyal, Eugénie insisted that no French blood must be shed on her behalf. The Prefect of the Police pleaded with her to escape while there was still time, and, mindful of the fate of Marie Antoinette, she agreed to try to make her way to England. The Austrian and Italian Ambassadors offered to help, and arranged for a cab to take her and a lady-in-waiting to the home of a prominent and loyal councillor, but, on discovering the he was not at home, Eugénie gave the cab driver the address of her husband's American dentist, Thomas Evans. When the maid answered the door, she instantly recognised the Empress, and explained that, although her master was out, he was due to return within the hour, and the ladies were welcome to wait for him in the library.

When Evans arrived home, he was astonished to find the exhausted Empress sitting in an armchair. She had not slept or eaten in over twenty-four hours, and, fearing what would happen to her companions if she were arrested, she pleaded with him to find a way to take her to Southampton. After much consideration, he decided that the safest route was via Deauville, where he and his wife happened to own a small villa; and, urging the Empress to try to sleep, he began to make the necessary arrangements.

Early the following morning, Evans, Eugénie and her lady-in-waiting set out in a cab on the long journey towards the coast. After travelling all day, they rested overnight in an inn, arriving at last at Deauville the following afternoon. By good fortune, while the women rested, Evans located an English veteran of the Crimean War, Sir John Burgoyne, who had brought his yacht to Deauville to collect his wife, who had been holidaying in the region. Evans struck up a conversation, and, after being given a tour of the yacht, he explained to Burgoyne the reason for his interest in the vessel. To his surprise, when he asked Sir John to take the Empress to England with him, he refused on the grounds that it was too great a responsibility. Evens responded by playing on his sense of gallantry, reminding him that he could not abandon a lady in such distress. After much cajoling, Burgoyne said that he would let his wife decide, and when the story was related to her, Lady Burgoyne immediately agreed that the Empress would sail to England with them the following morning.

That evening, for the first time in several days, Eugénie sat down to a meal, knowing that her liberation was at hand, but her relief was tempered by the thought that she was abandoning the Prince Imperial. Not knowing where he was or even if he were safe, she clutched a miniature of him, and suddenly burst into tears.

It was decided that it would be safest for Eugénie to board the vessel under cover of darkness, and so, shortly after midnight, she and her companions, trudged through the town in the rain.

> "The condition in which we arrived was deplorable," wrote Evans. "Our shoes were water-soaked, our clothing bedraggled, and we were spattered with mud from head to foot. It had rained heavily during the day, and we had walked quite three-quarters of a mile, a large part of the way over ground covered with sand-drifts, where it was impossible at times, in the shifting and uncertain light, to avoid stumbling against invisible hillocks, or stepping into holes full of water and mud. We had come quickly, considering the roughness of the way, but had proceeded separately and silently, scarcely uttering a word."[295]

Lady Burgoyne did her utmost to make her guests comfortable, providing them with clean, dry clothes and hot punch, and placing cabins at their disposal. As was planned, the yacht set sail soon after dawn, and although a storm raged throughout the entire crossing, they arrived safely in Ryde on the Isle of Wight at four o'clock the following morning. On reaching a hotel, Eugénie's thoughts turned again to her son, as she desperately asked if anyone had any information about him. On meeting only negative replies, she sighed that she could only pray that, if he were being held captive, his gaolers were treating him well.

In fact, the fourteen-year-old prince, had been well served by his attendants, particularly his guardian Comte Clary, who had led him through various towns, gleaning what news he could of the outcome of the Battle of Sedan and the Emperor's subsequent capture. On discovering that Paris was in a state of revolution, he dressed the young prince as a peasant boy and took him over the border into Namur in Belgium, where he learned that the Emperor was being held in Verviers on his way to Wilhelmshőhe. Clary telegraphed at once to assure him that his son was safe, but when Louis replied and asked him to bring the Prince Imperial to Verviers, he felt that fifty-eight mile journey would prove too much for the boy, and instead set out alone to meet the Emperor. Louis, deeply disappointed not to have seen Loulou, urged Clary to take him to England, and so he returned to Namur and collected the Prince to take him to Dover.

The morning after Eugénie's arrival in Ryde, Evans happened to see a newspaper headline stating that the Prince Imperial had arrived safely in Hastings, and although he was not entirely convinced of the truth of the story, he asked Eugénie to accompany him to Brighton in the hope of finding more definite news. To their immense relief, they learned that the Prince had indeed arrived safely in England, and was staying in the rather run-down Marine Hotel in Hastings.

"What a moment in the history of these two persons," gasped Evans, describing their reunion. "This noble woman, who had kept up so bravely during the most trying hours of her flight, could restrain her emotion no longer. The tears of joy flowed abundantly, and her lips murmured words of thanks to Heaven, which had preserved to her that son who had been her pride and delight, and the sight of whom now caused her to forget all she had lost and all she had suffered."[296]

Eugénie and Loulou remained for some weeks in Hastings but their rooms were smelly and uncomfortable, and they were constantly gawped at by the local people. Fortunately, they soon received several offers of better accommodation, including one from a certain Nathaniel Strode of Chislehurst. Strode explained that he had known and respected the Emperor during his exile in England, and he would be delighted if the Empress and Prince Imperial would take up residence in a property, which he owned, named Camden Place. The village, he assured them, was quiet enough to allow for the privacy they craved, and, what was more, there was a Roman Catholic church – St Mary's – in the vicinity.

The house, though spacious and attractive, had a rather chequered history, as, half a century earlier, it had been the site of two grisly murders. The then owner, Mr Bonar and his wife had been sleeping peacefully in their beds when a footman named Nicholson beat them to death with a poker. When arrested, Nicholson claimed that he had no motive for the crime, and was duly hanged at Pennenden Heath in August 1813.

Loulou was fascinated by the story, but Eugénie was more concerned with ensuring that she could pay her own way and immediately sold some of her jewels to ensure she had sufficient funds to meet any obligations. She accepted Stode's offer solely on the understanding that she would be a paying tenant, and, when a nominal sum of £500 a year had been agreed, she and Loulou moved to the village and began to reorder their lives. From Wilhelmshöhe, Louis regularly communicated with her, emphasising the importance of Loulou's education and urging her to do everything possible to raise him with the dignity that befitted his position.

In December, Queen Victoria paid her informal visit and found her looking 'very miserable and intensely sad but still very beautiful and so touching in her simple dignity.'[297] She assured the Queen that, if there had been no revolution, the war with Prussia would have concluded the day after Sedan. As it was, it dragged on for two more months until, following the siege of Paris, the French finally capitulated. In January 1871, King Wilhelm was proclaimed the Emperor of the newly-unified Germany; and by the terms of the subsequent Treaty of Versailles, France was obliged to pay reparation of five million francs, and cede to the Germans the provinces of Alsace and Lorraine.

As soon as the war was over, King Wilhelm ordered Louis' release and, in arranging his departure for England, showed him the same respect which he had shown him throughout his captivity. He sent a carriage drawn by four magnificent white horses to take him from Wilhelmshőhe to the station, where guards presented arms as a military band played rousing music. At Dover, where Eugénie and the Prince Imperial were waiting to greet him, he was given an equally rousing reception. The Mayor of the town stepped forward and, bowing, addressed him as 'Your Majesty', while, all along the route from the harbour, crowds called out, 'Vive l'Empereur!'

The incongruity of the warm welcome he received, and the countless attacks that had been levelled at him since the outbreak of the war, was not lost on a *Times* journalist, who concluded:

> "It must appear, we imagine, to Germans, Frenchmen, and all other people who read the story, that Englishmen lend themselves to the work of the moment with most unthinking minds."[298]

After months in captivity, Louis was finally reconciled with his family in a comfortable home which soon assumed the character of a small French court. Within days, the Prince of Wales arrived to invite him to visit the Queen at Windsor, and less than two weeks after his liberation, he was received at the castle with the same ceremony that had greeted him when he arrived as Emperor sixteen years before. A few weeks later, the Queen and her two youngest children, Prince Leopold and Princess Beatrice, paid a return visit to Chislehurst, prompting rumours of a budding romance between fourteen-year-old Beatrice and the Prince Imperial. Although Queen Victoria was quick to dismiss the story, her friendship with Louis and Eugénie had been fully restored and the ex-Emperor and Empress became regular visitors to Windsor and were often seen by the public at official events and celebrations.

Life at Chislehurst soon settled into a familiar routine. Louis' lifelong friend and doctor, Conneau, arrived with his son, who, similar in age to the Prince Imperial, became his closest companion. Loulou's tutor also moved into the village; and, thanks to Princess Mathilde, who had spotted the animal at a sale of imperial items, the Prince was reunited with his favourite horse, Tambours.

With no Empire to rule and no hope of an immediate restoration, Louis and Eugénie focussed all their attention on their son's upbringing. They agreed that it would beneficial for him to make friends with other boys of his age, and so, alongside his lessons with his tutor, he attended Bertram's Fencing Academy, and was enrolled in a series of classes at King's College in London. The experiment was not as successful as his parents had hoped, as Loulou found it difficult to make friends with his classmates, and, according to his tutor, he 'never entered into conversation with any of them and no one ever approached him. He would always have remained an alien in England if he had spent several years in those surroundings.'[299]

Empathising with his unhappiness, Louis decided to transfer him to the Royal Military College at Woolwich – a prospect which greatly appealed to the sixteen-year-old Prince. He would reside in Woolwich from Monday to Friday in a house furnished by Queen Victoria, and return home to Chislehurst at weekends. At first, in spite of his enthusiasm, he encountered the same problems as had beset him at King's College. His classmates mocked his habit of kneeling to say his prayers each evening; and his poor English hindered his learning, causing him to struggle in academic subjects.

"My poor boy is at Woolwich," his father wrote to a friend, "and finds the apprenticeship somewhat hard."[300]

Nonetheless, with his parents' encouragement, he persisted in his studies, and at the end of the academic year, he came seventh out of a class of thirty-four, and first in fencing and riding. In a short time, too, his warmth and good humour began to win him friends from among his classmates.

"Although on first coming amongst the Woolwich cadets," wrote his tutor, "the Prince was not altogether liked, owing to his ignorance of English ways, yet he was soon beloved by them, and treated as one of themselves. Some were most attached to him, and were ranked amongst the number of his truest friends."[301]

His father, unwilling to interrupt his studies, seldom visited him at the training school but he carefully followed his progress and watched him grow into a charming young man who had all the makings of a fine French Emperor.

Chapter 19 – The Son of Napoleon III

In view of his failing health and all he had been through, Louis might well have settled into a peaceful retirement in Chislehurst, but the spirit of ambition that had once inspired his hare-brained attempt to overthrow Louis Philippe still burned within him, particularly when he contemplated his beloved son's future, and the humiliation of defeat in the Franco-Prussian War.

Much as Louis longed to see his dynasty restored and Loulou crowned Emperor, he felt that it would be unjust to leave him a defeated country, and so came to the conclusion that he himself must retake the throne before abdicating in the Prince Imperial's favour. Picturing himself returning as Napoleon I had done after his banishment to Elba, Louis made arrangements with a member of the Royal Harwich Yacht Club, James Ashbury, to have a vessel at the ready at a moment's notice to take him over the Channel, whence he would proceed to Chalon where an army of forty-thousand men would be waiting to support him. Confiding his plan to a few close acquaintances, he enlisted the help of the Comte de la Chapelle, an ardent monarchist, who had fought alongside him in the Franco-Prussian War, and had written numerous published articles, praising the ex-Emperor. As a consequence of his publications, the Comte was under constant surveillance from republican spies but, by the strength of his fiery personality, he was able to raise a substantial funds to support Louis' mission.

For all their efforts, however, Louis was in no fit state to put his plan into action. Since his return to England, he had suffered from severe rheumatic pains, and his unresolved kidney complaints continued to render him incapable of riding.

"I cannot walk back at the head of an Army," he told an English companion. "It would have a still worse effect to enter Paris in a carriage; it is absolutely necessary that I should ride."[302]

His only hope was to subject himself to a series of surgical operations, which he believed would quickly restore him to health. In November 1872, he assured the Prince Imperial that 'with certain not very drastic remedies I shall be cured in a month's time,'[303] and, shortly before Christmas, he told a friend that within a couple of weeks he would be back in the saddle.

His optimism was premature. By New Year he had shown so little sign of improvement that a disconcerted Queen Victoria sent her own physician, William Gull, to join the renowned surgeon, Sir Henry Thompson, at Chislehurst. On examining the patient, Gull concurred that he was suffering from a kidney stone, and was astounded that, in such a condition, he had managed to endure five hours in the saddle during the Battle of Sedan. When Thompson informed him that he intended to perform a second lithotrity – a surgical procedure to break up the stone – Gull warned that shattering the calculus would release uric acid, which could pass into the blood stream, causing septicaemia. Nonetheless, on the evening of 8th January, Thompson performed the procedure and, convinced it had been successful, prescribed the sedative, chloral hydrate, as an analgesic. Initially, Louis refused the sedative, insisting that he had no pain but Eugénie, on Thompson's advice, persuaded him to take it, and soon afterwards he fell into a deep and peaceful sleep.

The following morning, seeing that he still slept soundly, Eugénie was preparing to visit the Prince Imperial at Woolwich to tell him that the operation had been a success. Suddenly, though, a doctor raced along the corridor, calling for the local priest, Father Goddard, to be summoned. Realising what this meant, Eugénie flew back to the sickroom where Louis opened his eyes and, seeing his friend, Dr Conneau, murmured, 'Were you at Sedan?' before breathing his last.

Investigations into the exact cause of death remain inconclusive. While some of his doctors believed that the chloral hydrate had killed him, Gull insisted he had died of septicaemia, as a result of the lithotrity, but, when Conneau was asked his opinion, he declared that he could neither deny nor support Gull's conclusions.

An urgent message was sent to Woolwich, telling the Prince Imperial that Emperor was very ill and he must return home. Not until he reached Chislehurst did he realise that his father had already died, and, throwing his arms around his mother, he wept before sinking to his knees to recite the prayers for the dead.

Queen Victoria had been receiving daily accounts of the Emperor's progress, and was so shocked by his unexpected demise that, when Gull informed her that the lithotrity had killed him, she declared that surgeons 'are like butchers, nearly all of them without feeling.' She was even more horrified to discover that the 'indelicate details' of his illness were being reported in the popular press, regardless of the effect on Loulou and Eugénie.

> "The poor man suffered terribly," she concluded, "and I believe that a great many things which we thought extraordinary in his behaviour during the last years and during the war, can be explained by his great sufferings!"[304]

Two days after Louis' death, the Prince of Wales travelled to Chislehurst on his mother's behalf, but, as Eugénie was too distressed to see him, he left a simple message conveying his mother's sympathy. The Queen, he said, had ordered the court into three months of mourning, and it was hoped that her fellow sovereigns would do the same.

In view of the political situation and Eugénie's wish for a quiet family funeral, members of Queen Victoria's family arranged to send representatives rather than attending in person, but, on the evening before the requiem, the Prince of Wales returned to the makeshift chapel in Camden Place to pray beside the open coffin, in which the embalmed Emperor lay with rouged cheeks and a stiffly-waxed moustache. He was followed by crowds of

French Imperialists and well-wishers, who flocked into the village to file past the bier.

Regardless of Eugénie's wishes, on the day of the funeral an estimated thirty-thousand people gathered in Chislehurst, including Princess Mathilde, and Louis' cousin Plon-Plon (Prince Napoleon), and his wife Clothilde of Savoy. Had they hoped for a great imperial display they were soon to be disappointed, for, although the packed church of St Mary's was draped in black, there was little evidence that this was the requiem of an Emperor. No uniforms, no insignia and no heraldic crests were visible; and, although Loulou wore his Grand Cross of the Légion d'Honneur, he was dressed in a simple evening suit.

The Prince Imperial bore himself with quiet dignity throughout the Low Mass, conducted by Father Goddard and the Bishop of Southwark, James Dannell. When, however, he left the church, he was overwhelmed to be greeted by resounding cries of: 'Vive l'Empereur! Vive Napoleon IV!'

"The Emperor is dead," Loulou murmured. "You should shout, 'Long live France,'" but Plon-Plon, much to Eugénie's annoyance, seized on the show of loyalty, and urged him to return to France to regain the throne.

When the ceremonies were completed, Eugénie asked Loulou directly what he wished to do, and she was relieved when he replied that he wanted to complete his education. Three weeks later, therefore, he returned to Woolwich, while Plon-Plon continued to make mischief for Eugénie at Chislehurst.

Plon-Plon had always detested the Empress and had once caused a scene by refusing to drink a toast to her health at an official banquet. Now, he showed no mercy to the grieving widow, as he insisted on reading Louis' medical records in the hope of proving that she had known that he was seriously ill when she callously urged him to lead his troops in the Franco-Prussian War. On discovering that one important document was missing, he falsely accused her of having taken it to conceal the true nature of the illness not only from the public but also from Louis himself. Eugénie angrily replied that everyone could see that her husband was unwell but, at the time, she had no idea of the exact nature of his illness or the full extent of his sufferings. Had she known how ill he was, she argued, she would never have entrusted the Prince Imperial to his protection. Dissatisfied, Plon-Plon went further, claiming that Louis' will, which left Eugénie in charge of all his affairs including their son's upbringing, was an out-of-date document, and he insisted on searching all the rooms in a vain attempt to uncover a more recent version.

The dispute was so acrimonious that trusted members of the household warned Eugénie that it was damaging to the Bonaparte family and to the monarchists' cause. Consequently, she attempted to effect a reconciliation by inviting Plon-Plon to return to Chislehurst but he curtly replied that he would see her when he had had time to formulate a plan. When he eventually appeared, he placed two conditions on their friendship: firstly, he must be named as the head of the Bonaparte family and the Imperial Party; and, secondly, he must be given sole charge of the Prince Imperial.

"Does the Prince, then, wish me to admit myself incapable and unworthy to bring up my son!" Eugénie cried. "What have I done to merit such an outrage?"[305]

Needless to say, she refused his demands, and Plon-Plon returned to Paris, where he wasted no time in spreading slanderous rumours about her. He told a French newspaper that, immediately before the war, she had prevented her husband from having surgery, which would have prolonged his life and possibly secured victory at Sedan; and, what was more, she had destroyed his will, to retain power over her son.

Eugénie's situation was made all the more uncomfortable by her immediate lack of funds. She might have once presided over one of the most glamorous courts in Europe, but neither she nor Louis had possessed a personal fortune, and she had been obliged to sell many of her jewels to pay for their upkeep in England. After her husband's death, she petitioned the French to return her private possessions but initially her requests were refused or ignored. When she attempted to regain possession of the property given to her and Louis by the people of Marseilles, the Municipality responded so aggressively that she decided to instigate a law suit. In court she was harshly referred to as 'the widow Bonaparte', which so offended her that, when the judge ruled in her favour, 'with quiet disdain she renounced her rights to keep possession of the palace.'[306]

In 1875, Patrice MacMahon was elected President of France. A veteran of the Italian campaign and the Franco-Prussian War, Louis had rewarded his service by creating him Duke of Magenta after the battle of the same name. Unlike his immediate predecessors, MacMahon felt genuine sympathy for Eugénie, and arranged to have her possessions sent to her in England. Grateful as she was, it was horrifying for her to discover that many of her priceless ornaments and paintings had been smashed or slashed by revolutionary bayonets.

Eugénie's financial limitations prevented her from granting her son more than a paltry allowance, and consequently he lacked the funds to entertain his fellow cadets or purchase suitable horses and necessary equipment. On several occasions, his friends secretly settled his bills to spare his pride, but, when his riding master offered to approach his mother to ask for an increase in his stipend, 'the Prince's countenance changed completely, and he forbade the Empress to be asked for anything.'[307]

Fortunately, in the midst of her woes, Eugénie could always rely on the support of the doyenne of widows, Queen Victoria A few weeks after Louis death, the Queen visited her at Chislehurst where she empathised with her grief and shared her abhorrence of Plon-Plon's behaviour. From then onwards their friendship deepened, much to the surprise of many outsiders, who could see only the great disparities in their characters. t

"The Queen," wrote the Prince Imperial's tutor, "was hard-working and methodical, desirous of housing facts in her brain and marshalling them in good order; the Empress was impulsive like all her race, but incapable of continuing any regular routine, quick to perceive a truth which might have escaped better-trained eyes, yet losing sight of it again after much reflection and discussion: the one woman was very reserved, the other was very imprudent, but both were incapable of deceit; they had reached the age when one esteems sincerity above everything."[308]

Queen Victoria had always taken an affectionate interest, too, in the Prince Imperial, and, after his father's death, she sent him regular invitations to Windsor, where he endeared himself to the entire Royal Family. The Queen never forgot his birthdays, and frequently sent him books to help him in his studies, as well as being kept informed of his progress by her cousin, the Governor of the college and Commander-in-Chief of the army, George, Duke of Cambridge. The Duke, who had been a good friend of the later Emperor and had known Loulou since his early childhood, was pleased to report that the young man acquitted himself well during manoeuvres and was proving himself to be an able soldier. The Queen replied that she was:

"...truly gratified and pleased at the success of the dear young Prince Imperial. I have written as well as telegraphed to the Empress about it...The Academy will, I am sure, always feel proud that he distinguished himself in their School, and that he should have acquitted himself so honourably, and above all, behaved so well!"[309]

On his eighteen birthday in March 1874, a contingent of over five thousand French people descended

213

on Chislehurst to participate in celebrations, and hail him as the Emperor Napoleon IV. Initially, he and his mother had discouraged such demonstrations, and when the Comte de Chapelle urged him to respond to the crowds, he replied that not everyone shared the Comte's enthusiasm for the monarchy. Nonetheless, under pressure from the imperialists, Loulou eventually agreed to welcome the crowds with a formal address. The speech, which he prepared himself, showed tact beyond his years, as, rather than accepting the homage for himself, he thanked the crowds for coming to show their respect for his late father. He could not, however, completely avoid the fact they were hailing him as their Emperor, and, therefore, having praised the French government, he added:

> "Will France, if she is openly consulted, cast her eyes upon the son of Napoleon III? This thought awakes in me distrust of my strength rather than pride. The Emperor taught me how heavy is the burden of sovereign authority, even upon manly shoulders, and how essential are faith in oneself and the sense of duty to carry out so high a mission."[310]

When the celebrations were over, he returned quietly to Woolwich to complete his studies, and, ten months later, he came first in his class in the final examinations.

His initial training was over, but he had become so enamoured of the military that, following a series of European tours with his mother, he requested permission to be attached to the Royal Artillery during their summer manoeuvres in 1875. Thanks partly to the Queen's intervention, his request was granted, which, according to the Duke of Cambridge, made him and Eugénie 'supremely happy.' Once again, he acquitted himself well, uncomplainingly accepting being soaked in mud, having his kit and tent swept away in a flood, and finding comfort in the fact that he and his comrades were provided with an excellent French cook.

Between further tours with his mother, he continued his service at Aldershot but, by 1876, he was frustrated by a lack of serious action. As Britain was almost constantly engaged in colonial wars, there were, he wrote, numerous opportunities for him to repay the Queen's kindness, by placing himself in the service of her army. Thought touched by his devotion, the Queen felt that his position made such a proposition untenable, and quietly asked the Duke of Cambridge to find him a safer role on his staff.

The Prince duly accepted his orders and, between his rather sedentary duties, had plenty of time to enjoy socialising with aristocrats at the races and the hunt, providing gossips with ample opportunities to speculate on his marriage prospects. When he visited Sweden and Denmark with his mother, it was widely reported that he was about to propose to a Scandinavian princess; and his regular visits to Windsor revived the story that he and the Queen's youngest daughter, Beatrice, were soon to be engaged.

Fond as she was of the Prince Imperial, Queen Victoria had no intention of permitting Beatrice to marry anyone, let alone a pretender to the French throne, whose future remained uncertain. Her youngest child, she believed, should remain beside her as her constant companion, and in order to prevent Beatrice from developing any other ideas, she insisted that marriage was not to be mentioned in her presence[hh].

For his part, Loulou was equally unenthusiastic about the prospect of marriage, which, he felt, was too great a commitment and would scotch his dreams of seeing active service. Already, he was frustrated by the

---

[hh] In 1885, Queen Victoria finally agreed to allow Beatrice to marry a Prince of Battenberg, on condition that the couple should live with her so that Beatrice would be able to continue as her companion.

lack of excitement in his life, and was tired of having to accommodate other people's expectations. Some, he complained, expected him to 'make himself conspicuous' by acquainting himself with journalists and politicians.

"Others want me to travel throughout Europe with a great retinue, going, like the fairy tale princes, to view all the princesses and boast of my political elixir that will heal all social evils. This comedy, think the authors, must end like every good play, with a marriage. I have turned a deaf ear; I have not cared to let my wings be clipped by marriage, and my dignity refused to stoop to the part of princely commercial traveller."[311]

For a few more months he restlessly continued as a staff officer with the Duke of Cambridge, but towards the end of 1878, a series of events occurred which provided him with the opportunity for excitement which he had been waiting.

Chapter 20 – My Heart Overflows & The Wound Bleeds Anew

In 1877, Sir Henry Bartle Frere was appointed Governor of Cape Colony with a mandate to organise a confederation of all the British colonies in South Africa. The greatest obstacle to his mission was a potential threat from the neighbouring Zulu Kingdom, ruled by King Cetawayo, who, suspecting an imminent British invasion, increased the size of his army and purchased large quantities of guns and ammunition.

Although neither the British Government nor Cetawayo wanted war, Bartle Frere believed that it would be impossible to guarantee the safety of the consolidated colonies with so powerful a nation at the border, and so he began a campaign to discredit the King in a series of pamphlets accusing the Zulus of all kinds of barbaric practices. Witchcraft, it was said, was commonplace, and 'disgusting ceremonies' were performed on pubescent girls, while 'full licence [was] given to wholesale debauchery' where 'both men and women glory in their shame.'[312] The British press described gruesome tortures, such as smearing a victim with honey and leaving him for ants and scorpions to devour; and, all in all, they concluded that:

> "The Zulu government is thoroughly despotic. The will of the tyrant is law, and he has unlimited power of life or death."[313]

Missionaries, who had spent many years working in Zululand rushed to Cetawayo's defence. The Anglican Bishop of Natal, John Colenso, complained that the British treated the King's emissaries as spies, and they were often manacled or imprisoned simply for bringing messages across the border. The accusation of witchcraft, he argued, had to be understood in the light of centuries of African culture; and the barbarism of the Zulus was often equalled or surpassed by the European invaders.

217

Cetawayo responded calmly to the accusations, stating that, since he did not interfere in Bartle Frere's running of the colonies, he expected the same courtesy in return. Nonetheless, Bartle Frere sent him a series of demands, including compensation for alleged border infringements, as well as the disbandment of his army, regardless of the fact that British troops were stationed along his border. When Cetawayo failed to comply with the demands, Bartle Frere sent him an ultimatum, and having received no satisfactory response, he ordered the British troops into Zululand where, on 22nd January 1879, they suffered a resounding and humiliating defeat at Isandlwana.

As Cetawayo's victory was reported in the British press, alongside graphic descriptions of the brutality of his regime, the Prince Imperial shared the public outrage, and wrote to the Duke of Cambridge for permission to participate in the campaign. After consulting the Queen, the Duke replied that, in view of the Prince's position, he could not grant his request, but he was touched, a few weeks later, when Loulou wrote to him again, stating that, while he did not flatter himself that he could be of any great use,

> "I nevertheless looked upon this war as an opportunity of showing my gratitude towards the Queen and the nation in a way that would be very much to my mind. When at Woolwich and, later, at Aldershot, I had the honour of wearing the English uniform, I hoped that it would be in the ranks of our allies that I should first take up arms. Losing this hope, I lose one of the consolations of my exile."[314]

Again, the Duke discussed the matter with Queen Victoria, and this time they agreed that the Prince would be allowed to go as a volunteer on the staff of Lord Chelmsford, the Commander-in-Chief of the British troops in the region.

When his distraught mother realised what he was doing, she pleaded with him to change his mind, as did several ardent French monarchists, who reminded him that, as the rightful French Emperor, it would be madness for him to risk his life in a foreign war. Loulou refused to be dissuaded, and, dismissing their arguments, told his mother that he was unafraid and was glad that at last he had a worthwhile career.

"I am glad I am not his Mother at this moment," Queen Victoria wrote to the Duke of Cambridge. "Still, I understand easily how in his peculiar position he must wish for active employment. But he must be careful not unnecessarily to expose himself, for we know he is very venturesome."[315]

In effort to ensure his safety, the Duke informed Lord Chelmsford that the Prince was 'a fine young fellow' but 'too go-ahead and plucky,' and, therefore, he must be given duties that would keep him out of harm's way. Even so, before he left, the Prince wrote his will, appointing his mother as his sole beneficiary and adding, ominously:

"I shall die with a sentiment of the deepest gratitude

to her Majesty the Queen of England, to all the royal family, and to the country where for eight years I have received such cordial hospitality."[316]

No sooner had he set sail aboard the *Danube* than reports appeared in the French press stating that he had contracted a serious illness and was probably dying. Although the articles were entirely false, they so distressed Eugénie that she decided to set out at once for Africa to bring him home. When Queen Victoria heard of her plan, she sent an urgent message to Lord Wolseley, who was about to replace Lord Chelmsford in the Cape, telling him to arrange for the Prince to return at once to Europe.

Loulou, though, was greatly enjoying the adventure, endearing himself to his fellow officers, most of whom were several years his senior, and making the acquaintance of a group of his countrymen, who had been dismissed from the French republican army and were now fighting for the British. Under the command of Colonel Harrison, he was appointed to assist in intelligence gathering around Rorke's Drift, but his eagerness to pursue the Zulus into unknown territory so disconcerted his senior officers that he was quickly recalled to a safer position as Deputy Quartermaster behind the British lines.

Since the defeat at Isandlwana, a steady stream of reinforcements had been sent into the region, and, by the end of May 1879, sufficient troops had arrived for Chelmsford to prepare a second invasion. As the army was put in readiness, the Prince Imperial was sent on a reconnaissance mission to look for a suitable place to set up camp. The assignment was not deemed dangerous, since he was familiar with the terrain, and would be accompanied by an escort under the command of the experienced Captain Bettington of the Natal Horse division. By the time, however, that Bettington was told of the plan, he had already been assigned to different duties, and consequently, at the last minute, he was replaced by Lieutenant Carey, who was given strict instructions to take good care of the Prince Imperial.

On the morning of 1st June, Loulou wrote a hurried note to his mother, before setting out with Carey and his companions, and, after riding for several hours with no sign of the enemy, they stopped to take coffee and assess their position. Having dismounted, they unsaddled their horses, allowing them to graze freely in a nearby field of maize, unaware that they were being watched by a group of between forty and fifty armed Zulus. At about four o'clock in the afternoon, as they began to re-saddle their horses, the Zulus suddenly sprang out from the long grass, instantly killing two members of the escort and causing Carey and the others to flee in a panic.

While Loulou was attempting to remount, the last of the escort flew past him calling, 'Make haste, sir, if you please!' but his horse suddenly bolted and he found himself alone at the mercy of the enemy. One member of the party, galloped on and warned Carey what had happened, but, without looking back, the Lieutenant ordered his men to continue back to flee to safety.

It was already dark when Carey and the survivors reached the British camp and, to the horror of Chelmsford, explained what had happened. Desperately hoping that the Prince had only been wounded, Chelmsford prepared a patrol to set out at once to find him but, on being told that it would impossible to locate the site in the darkness, he agreed to wait until morning when Sir Evelyn Wood would lead his company in the search.

The following day, Loulou's naked body was found, pierced with eighteen spears, beside the corpse of his faithful terrier, which had also been speared to death. Nearby, his watch was found, smashed into pieces, but the medals he wore around his neck remained untouched, and were taken back to the camp with his body so that they could be returned to his mother.

Due to the lack of a direct postal route between the Cape and Britain, two weeks passed before the news reached Queen Victoria, who was horrified that the 'good, exemplary, brave but alas! far too daring young man' had been abandoned by his companions. The Duke of Cambridge was equally distressed, writing in his journal:

> "This news is overpowering in its terribleness…No words can describe the dismay it has caused. How it could have happened that the Prince should have been allowed to get into so exposed a position is quite inexplicable…I feel quite broken-hearted."[317]

The Queen, desperate to ensure that Eugénie did not discover what had happened from the newspapers, asked the press to keep back the story until her Chamberlain, Lord Sydney, had had time to travel to Chislehurst to break the news to her directly. At Camden

Place, Sydney met Eugénie's old friend, the Duke of Bassano, who agreed that he would convey the dreadful tidings to the Empress.

Eugénie broke down completely, collapsing in such a state of shock that those around her feared that she was dying. For several days, she could neither eat nor sleep, and when, at last, she regained her strength, she declared that she wished to make a pilgrimage to the place where her son had died.

As telegrams of condolence poured in from Russia, Sweden, Austria and Germany, Queen Victoria sighed that she was haunted by the manner of his end, and could only hope that he had died quickly and had not greatly suffered. Within days, she wrote to Eugénie, offering to visit her at Chislehurst, only to receive a brief but polite reply stating that she was not yet ready to receive visitors. A few days later, the Queen wrote again, explaining that, if she did not visit, the public would assume that she was insensitive to the ex-Empress' sorrow, at which Eugénie reluctantly extended an invitation to her.

On 23rd June, Queen Victoria arrived at Camden House and found Eugénie 'uncomplaining in her grief' but clinging to the desperate hope that there had been a mistake, and that the Prince was still alive. The Queen gently explained that he had been positively identified and his body was, as they spoke, being transported back to England.

Following a service in the Cape, Loulou's corpse had been hastily embalmed – a process made more difficult by the extent of his wounds – and placed on HMS *Orontes,* bound for Britain. In early July, the coffin arrived at Woolwich where it was opened to allow for a formal identification, which proved to be such a fearful experience that Loulou's faithful valet fainted in shock. Decomposition and the embalming fluid had so disfigured and blackened his face that it was barely recognisable, and, only when his doctor and dentist explained that wounds he had incurred as a child, and certain peculiarities of his teeth left them in no doubt that this was the Prince Imperial, was the identification completed.

Much to the annoyance of Queen Victoria, Eugénie's grief was compounded when articles appeared in the press, describing in lurid detail the extent of the decomposition.

On 11th July, the sealed coffin was taken to Camden Place where Eugénie spent the night in prayer beside the bier; and, the following morning, Queen Victoria and Princess Beatrice arrived to place a laurel wreath on the casket, while over one-hundred-thousand Frenchmen gathered outside. The cortege wound through the silent streets to the church, where the Duke of Cambridge, the Duke of Bassano, the Prince of Sweden and three of the Queen's sons – the Prince of Wales and Princes Alfred and Leopold – carried the coffin to the altar where Cardinal Manning conducted the requiem service. As he had request, the Prince was laid to rest beside his father, but this was not to be a permanent arrangement as the church was too small to accommodate the shrine that Eugénie intended to build in his honour.

Already discussions were underway with a neighbouring landowner, in the hope that he might sell Eugénie his field so that she could construct a more ornate memorial. The neighbour, a German toy manufacturer, was, however, such a committed Protestant that he refused to sell his land to a Roman Catholic so Eugénie would have to look elsewhere for a suitable site for the tomb.

As the congregation departed, Queen Victoria returned to Camden House, but was told that Eugénie was not in a fit state to receive her. Undeterred, she walked past the attendants to Eugénie's bedroom, where she was met at the door by the Duke of Bassano. The Empress was in bed, he said, and did not wish to receive visitors, particularly as she had not even spoken yet to other members of the French Royal Family. Ignoring his protests, the Queen entered the room and uttered what words of comfort she could to the inconsolable Empress.

Queen Victoria's insistence on seeing Eugénie was, in part, an attempt to assuage her own sense of guilt. She was ashamed, she confessed, of the cowardice of her troops, who had left the young man to die unattended, and was still more disturbed when she discovered that the Duke of Cambridge ensured Cary's acquittal at a subsequent courts-martial. Worse was to follow when certain Members of Parliament spoke harshly of the Prince Imperial, claiming that 'irresponsible persons' caused only inconvenience by attaching themselves to the army, and, if they came to grief, they had only themselves to blame. The Liberal Member for Scarborough, William Caine, asked why the British Government had agreed to pay £572 8s.10d to cover the cost of transporting the body back to England, and when his fellow-Liberal, Lord Cavendish replied that 'it was thought right to incur these expenses inasmuch as the Prince died in the service of the country', Caine complained that, since the Prince had gone out as a volunteer, he was no in fact a member of the armed forces. It was left to a Mr Litton to explain that he:

> "...did not think any hon. Member of the House would object to the sum charged for the conveyance of The Prince Imperial's body to this country. That illustrious young gentleman occupied a very noble position, and he met an unfortunate death while engaged as a Volunteer in the late Zulu War. It would, indeed, be very ungracious to challenge the item."[318]

Still more irksome for the Queen was the 'distasteful' discussion which ensued in the House of Commons when, supported by the Dean of Westminster, she asked that a monument to the Prince should be erected in Westminster Abbey. Some Members objected on the grounds that, regardless of the young man's personal qualities, the Abbey was the resting place of Kings and heroes, whereas Loulou had taken himself off to Africa to draw attention to his claim to the French throne. Thomas Burt, the left-wing Liberal Member for Morpeth, stated that it would be unjust to build a memorial to the Prince unless similar monuments were created for each of the British soldiers who had died; and, moreover:

> "He saw nothing in the Prince going out to Africa to fight in a war of which Englishmen generally, would be proud...Prince Napoleon was not a Garibaldi going to fight for the independence of a people, or to emancipate an oppressed, nationality. He entered upon a war with which he had nothing to do. He took the side of the strong against the weak – he had almost said of the oppressor against the oppressed."[319]

Others objected on the grounds that the Prince was 'a foreigner' and a Roman Catholic, regardless of the fact the Abbey already housed a memorial to Louis Philippe's brother, the Duke of Montpensier.

"Where is chivalry and decency of feeling to be found in these days amongst many of the Members of Parliament?"[320] Queen Victoria gasped, before deciding that it would be safer to erect the monument, which would be 'one of the finest productions of modern art', in St George's Chapel at Windsor.

Politicians were not the only ones who failed to share the Queen's feelings about the 'heroic' Prince's death. Lord Wolseley, the new Commander-in-Chief of the forces in the Cape, could not understand the excessive outpouring of grief. He appreciated the effect that the loss of a son would have on his mother, but, as he wrote:

> "I have no wish to give the event undue importance. He was a plucky young man, and he died a soldier's death. What on earth could he have better? Many other brave men have also fallen during this war, and with the Prince's fate England as a nation had no concern. Perhaps I have insufficient sympathy with foreign nations; I

reserve all my deep feelings for Her Majesty's subjects."[321]

It annoyed him to receive Eugénie's request for the return of all that her son was wearing when he was killed; but he was even more put out when Queen Victoria asked him to make arrangements for the Empress to visit the site of his death. 'What a nuisance it will be!' he complained, adding that he had no idea how to relate to an Empress 'under such unusual conditions.'

Sir Evelyn Wood, who had been among the first to discover the Prince's body, was chosen to accompany Eugénie to Africa, and, unlike Wolseley, he behaved with such sensitivity that one member of the Empress' household commented that, although he had been successful in all his ventures, he never gained such a pinnacle of achievement as when he escorted the Empress on her sad pilgrimage.

Cetawayo, meanwhile, had been defeated and captured, and had shown himself more gracious in defeat than his enemies were in their victory. He had already arranged for the Prince's clothes and sword to be returned to the British but, while he was expressing sympathy for the Empress, his captors were cruelly digging up his father's bones from their ancestral burial ground.

As the war was over, Eugénie was able to travel freely, and, on arriving in the vicinity of her destination, she had a tent erected from which she made daily walks along the road that the Prince had taken on his last journey. There, she planted a willow and ivy, which she had brought from Camden Place, beside a cairn which had been constructed by the army.

> "If you were to see this spot," she wrote to a friend, "you would understand the surprise attack and the events which followed it...It fills my heart with bitterness to think that this precious life has been so wantonly sacrificed, and that this child, left alone, fell fighting like a brave soldier with no witnesses of his courage except a handful of

savages one degree removed from the brute!...But I cannot speak of him anymore; my heart overflows, and the wound bleeds anew and is powerless to heal."[322]

During the trip, she was introduced to a Zulu warrior who had been involved in her son's killing. He told her that they had not touched the medal that he wore around his neck as they feared it was a charm, but they had smashed his watch because, when they heard it ticking, they thought it was some kind of 'little beast' that needed to be stamped upon.

In June 1880, Eugénie returned to Chislehurst with various grasses and plants that she had gathered in Zululand with the intention of creating a garden dedicated to her son. All she had known and loved had been lost, and her sole purpose now was to find a suitable site on which to erect a fitting shrine for Loulou and Louis. That summer, her solicitor discovered that Farnborough Hill – the Hampshire home of the publisher, Thomas Longman – was for sale, and it did not take long to realise that this was her ideal home. The Swiss-style house was far grander than Camden Place, and, more importantly for Eugénie, it was surrounded by extensive gardens with ornamental lakes, wooded islands, greenhouses and graperies, providing plenty of space to build an abbey to house the tombs.

When the purchase was complete, Eugénie filled the place with furniture and paintings that were reminiscent of happier days: statues of the Bonapartes; cabinets belonging to Queen Hortense; portraits of various monarchs and historical figures; and the few souvenirs of French kings, which not been damaged by the revolution. One large room was dedicated entirely to the Prince Imperial, whose belongings, including unopened letters, were laid out exactly as they had been on the day he left for Natal. His books and paintings were put on display, and in pride of place was a gift from Queen Victoria: an album of sketches detailing all the events of Loulou's life in England.

> "Here also," recorded a visitor, "are two glass cases, containing all the little personal treasures and souvenirs of his father and of his childhood; his first little uniform; presents given him by sovereigns, among others a beautiful little diamond-sheathed scimitar, from the Sultan of Turkey; all of the personal effects he had with him at the Cape – his sketch-books, plans, maps, check books, and note-books, and also the sword (originally his father's) with which he so bravely defended himself on that fatal day against the Zulus, until overpowered by numbers."[323]

His medal and the bloody shirt that he had been wearing when he was killed, were kept in a small ebony cabinet in front of which was a small white cross inscribed with the words, '*Que votre volonte soit faite,*' beneath which Princess Beatrice had painted the word, 'Fiat', surrounded by violets.

Eugénie's overriding desire was to ensure that the tombs were worthy of a former Emperor and his son, and, to that end, she asked the renowned French architect Gabriel-Hippolyte Destailleur to design a chapel to contain the sepulchres. Queen Victoria paid for the red granite sarcophagi, which were surrounded by a tessellated pavement, identical to that of Les Invalides in Paris, where Napoleon I had been interred; and Eugénie was so delighted by Destailleur's designs that she invited him to return to England to discuss plans for creating an adjacent monastery for the Premonstratensian Canons, who would conduct a service each day by the tombs.

Early in the morning on the fifteenth anniversary of Louis' death – 9th January 1888 – Father Goddard celebrated Mass in the little church in Chislehurst, before closing the doors to the public to allow for the opening of the tombs. Apart from the handles, which were covered in Verdigris, the coffins were found to be in perfect

228

condition, and, once they had been draped in black palls and wreaths from the Empress, they were carried by officers of the Royal Artillery to the gun carriages that would take them to the local railway station.

"The coffins," reported a witness, "were placed in a baggage waggon, which the undertakers had arranged and decorated. Its walls were draped in black, spangled with silver stars, and displayed the Imperial crown and monogram. At one end was a large ivory crucifix, with a background of black velvet, in which was woven a Latin cross in white silk. The waggon was canopied with black drapery. Candles in silver sconces were lighted, and the waggon became a chapelle ardente, with the Monsignor [Goddard] as its only living occupant. In the Prince's coffin (the priest told me) was the scapula found on him when his mangled body was discovered; this was now in a cardboard box."[324]

At Farnborough a second service was held as the bodies were sealed in their ornate tombs, after which the widowed Empress returned home alone to contemplate all she had lost, and how to forge a meaningful future now that the project, which had carried her through her grief, was finally completed.

Epilogue

Following the creation of the shrine in Farnborough, Eugénie spent much of her time travelling throughout Europe, endearing herself to the Royal Families of Austria, Spain and Germany, and regularly returning to France, where she mingled incognito with the crowds. In spite of her white hair and the grief-stricken aspect of her face, she had retained the grace and charm of her youth, which made a memorable impact on all who met her. Following their first encounter, a neighbour at Farnborough recorded that she was:

> "Not more than 5 feet 5 inches, I fancy, the perfection of her proportions gave the idea of a far taller woman, and anyone interested in motion must at once have been struck by her walk. Less like walking than gliding, it was the easiest, most graceful style of progression imaginable. The face was very pale, and except as to the eyebrows not in the least made up (no powder, no rouge); and under the large hat you caught sight of her hair grey, inclining to white."[325]

In spite of all that she had endured, Eugénie's temper remained as fiery as ever, and her spirit of adventure increased rather than lessened with age. She embraced all the last innovations, learning to ride a bicycle, installing a wireless on her yacht, purchasing a motor car, and often expressing a desire to fly in a plane. Throughout her widowhood, she had also developed a shrewd business sense, which enabled her to buy properties in France and Spain.

In 1891, while staying at Cap Martin on the Côte d'Azur, she purchased some land on which to build a retreat from the cold British winters. The following year, her stunning Villa Cyranos was completed, which, with its beautiful gardens, balmy scents and view of the sea, soon became a holiday destination for various European royalties, including the beautiful Empress Elizabeth of Austria, and Eugénie's old friend, Queen Victoria.

With the passing of years, their friendship continued to deepen, as one of Queen Victoria's granddaughters, Princess Marie Louise, recalled. Eugénie, said Marie Louise, had arrived for luncheon at Windsor, and, on seeing her outside the dining room, Queen Victoria curtsied:

"The Queen: *Après vous, ma chère soeur!*

The Empress: *Mais non, ma chère soeur, après vous!*

They bowed and curtsied, and then, hand in hand, these two darling old ladies went into lunch together."[326]

Amusingly, Queen Victoria was always given a guard of honour during her visits to France, and, on one occasion, while she was expecting Eugénie to visit her in Nice, she stepped outside so that guards would stand to attention and, for a moment at least, the former Empress could enjoy a fitting reception from the republican soldiers.

All of the Queen's children felt a deep affection for Eugénie; the Prince of Wales frequently visited her, and Princess Beatrice, who, had the rumours been true, might have become her daughter-in-law, invited her to be godmother to her daughter, who was named Victoria Eugénie in her honour[ii].

Understandably, the Queen's death in January 1901 came as a great blow to her friend of more than fifty years. 'I feel even more than ever a foreigner, alone in this land,' she wrote, but her close contact with the late Queen's family continued. She received regular visits from King Edward VII and Queen Alexander, and in 1907 enjoyed a tour of the Norwegian fjords with Victoria's eldest grandson, the German Emperor, Wilhelm II. Seven

---

[ii] Interestingly, Victoria Eugénie later became Queen of her godmother's native Spain.

years later, as war erupted throughout Europe, Eugénie unashamedly stated that the Kaiser was not responsible for the conflict. Although she had little personal liking for him, she knew that he had done everything possible to maintain peace, and she saw him as a latter-day King Canute trying to hold back the tide of public feeling. 'When the river reaches the waterfall,' she sighed, 'no earthly power can stop it.'[327]

When war broke out, she donated her yacht to the Royal Navy; knitted garments for the troops; and turned her half of her home into a military hospital, equipped with every modern appliance to provide comfort and aid recovery. She took a personal interest in the patients, wept at their deaths, and rejoiced in their progress, and could not have been more delighted than when King George V came to inspect the wards. The officers, who came to know her, were so impressed by her grace and diligence that several believed her to be far younger than her years, and were amazed when they discovered that she was nearing ninety. 'She is thirty at most!' declared the writer, Maurice Baring, 'so brilliant, so amusing, such delicate exquisite tones in her voice...She is the marvel of the ages.'[328]

He was, though, undoubtedly flattering her, as a compatriot, who had met her over a decade earlier, commented that she looked older than her years:

> "...the woman of seventy-two might well be taken for eighty. Her hair is white, and her slender figure bent, without a trace of her former bewitching grace; dress has lost its charm; all about her bears the impress of sorrow; and the desire to please, which influenced her so strongly, is gone beyond recall. The pallid woman, with mournful eyes and lips compressed in bodily pain, or in a continual effort to restrain her tears, with tottering gait supported by a stick, has nothing to remind one of the magnificent Empress of the French."[329]

Concerned about the plight of wounded soldiers, she donated vast sums to hospitals in France and Belgium, but, while the French government accepted her money, ministers refused to allow the name of the donor to be published.

If she were hurt by the continued hostility of the French government towards her, she was even more distressed by the British Defence of the Realm Act, which, she said, made her feel as though she were 'a suspicious person.'

> "This used to be a free country where people were left alone," she complained, "but now you shower des petits papiers on one, just as military-mad Continental nations do, and ask for oaths, and dates, and signatures! It was because there was none of that over here that one loved England."[330]

She was so affronted at being viewed as a foreigner that she declared that she would leave England as soon as the war was over. In the event, she remained at Farnborough long after the armistice had been signed, insisting on maintaining her hospital until the government sent orders that her remaining patients were to be transferred to Aldershot.

After the war, she resumed the travels and, in the summer of 1920, visited her niece in Madrid, as she had heard of a Spanish surgeon who had discovered a method to cure her failing eyesight. Clinging to her relics, she willingly consented to 'formidable but painless' procedure, and was delighted by the outcome, which had completely restored her vision. A few days later, she prepared to return to Farnborough, but, on 11th July, she was suddenly taken ill and died just a few hours later. 'Her heart gradually ceased to beat,' wrote a witness to her passing, 'as it might be a little bird that dies in your hand.'[331]

Her coffin was transported back to England where, draped in a Union Jack, it was taken to the abbey which she had had built at Farnborough. There, a requiem was celebrated by the Benedictines, and, in the presence of King George V and Queen Mary, and King Alfonso XIII and Queen Victoria Eugenie of Spain, she was laid to rest in the tomb she had prepared beside her husband and son.

By the Same Author

Biography

Queen Victoria's Granddaughters 1960-1918
Queen Victoria's Grandsons 1859-1918
Queen Victoria's Cousins
Queen Victoria's Creatures – Royalty & Animals in the Victoria Era
Alice, the Enigma – A Biography of Queen Victoria's Daughter
Dear Papa, Beloved Mama – An intimate portrait of Queen Victoria & Prince Albert as parents
The Innocence of Kaiser Wilhelm II

Historical Fiction

Most Beautiful Princess – A Novel Based on the Life of Grand Duchess Elizabeth of Russia
Shattered Crowns: The Scapegoats
Shattered Crowns: The Sacrifice
Shattered Crowns: The Betrayal
The Fields Laid Waste

Novels

The Counting House
By Any Other Name
The Goose Girl

Children's Books

Wonderful Walter

Poetry

Child of the Moon
The Ragamuffin Sun

References

[1] Trollope, Anthony *Lord Palmerston* (W. Isbister, 1882)

[2] Lieven, Princess Dorothea (translated by Guy le Strange) *Correspondence of Princess Lieven & Earl Grey Vol 2* (Richard Bentley 1890)

[3] Oberkirch, Henriette *Memoirs of the Baroness d'Oberkirch, Countess de Montbrison Vol I* (Colburn & Co. 1852)

[4] Oberkirch, Henriette *Memoirs of the Baroness d'Oberkirch, Countess de Montbrison Vol II* (Colburn & Co. 1852)

[5] Genlis, Stephanie de *Memoirs of the Countess de Genlis Vol 2* (H. Colburn 1825)

[6] Dobson, Austin *Four Frenchwomen* (Chatto & Windus 1891)

[7] Abbott, Jacob *Louis Philippe* (Harper & Brothers 1901)

[8] Dumas, Alexander (translated by R. S. Garnett) *The Last King* (Stanley, Paul & Co. 1915)

[9] Dumas, Alexander (translated by R. S. Garnett) *The Last King* (Stanley, Paul & Co. 1915)

[10] Abbott, Jacob *Louis Philippe* (Harper & Brothers 1901)

[11] Oberkirch, Henriette *Memoirs of the Baroness d'Oberkirch, Countess de Montbrison Vol I* (Colburn & Co. 1852)

[12] Genlis, Stephanie de *Memoirs of the Countess de Genlis Vol 2* (H. Colburn 1825)

[13] Dumas, Alexander (translated by R. S. Garnett) *The Last King* (Stanley, Paul & Co. 1915)

[14] Genlis, Stephanie de *Memoirs of the Countess de Genlis Vol 2* (H. Colburn 1825)

[15] Montpensier, Antoine, Duke of *Memoirs of His Serene Highness, Antoine Philippe d'Orléans, Duke of Montpensier* (Treuttel & Wurtz 1824)

[16] Abbott, Jacob *Louis Philippe* (Harper & Brothers 1901)

[17] Montpensier, Antoine, Duke of *Memoirs of His Serene Highness, Antoine Philippe d'Orléans, Duke of Montpensier* (Treuttel & Wurtz 1824)

[18] Rush, Benjamin *Medical Inquiries & Observations* (Thomas Dobson 1798)

[19] Wright, Rev. G.N. *Life & Times of Louis Philippe, King of the French* (Fisher, Son & Co. 1842)

[20] Dyson, C.C. *The Life of Marie Amélie, the Last Queen of the French* (D. Appleton & Co. 1910)

[21] Dyson, C.C. *The Life of Marie Amélie, the Last Queen of the French* (D. Appleton & Co. 1910)

[22] Dyson, C.C. *The Life of Marie Amélie, the Last Queen of the French* (D. Appleton & Co. 1910)

[23] Berne, Catharine Mary *A Sister of Marie Antoinette; The Life Story of Maria Carolina, Queen of Naples* (E.P. Dutton & Co. 1907)

[24] Saint-Amand, Imbert de *The Duchess of Berry & The Court of Charles X* (Charles Scribner's Sons 1893)

[25] Sandars, Mary F. *Louis XVIII* (Hutchinson & Co. 1910)

[26] Saint-Amand, Arthur Imbert de *The Duchess of Berry and the Court of Charles X* (1892)

[27] Dyson, C.C. *The Life of Marie Amélie, the Last Queen of the French* (D. Appleton & Co. 1910)

[28] Saint-Amand, Arthur Imbert de *The Duchess of Berry and the Court of Charles X* (1892)

[29] Saint-Amand, Arthur Imbert de *The Duchess of Berry and the Court of Charles X* (1892)

[30] Abbott, Jacob *Louis Philippe* (Harper & Brothers 1901)

[31] Abbott, Jacob *Louis Philippe* (Harper & Brothers 1901)

[32] Abbott, Jacob *Louis Philippe* (Harper & Brothers 1901)

[33] Dyson, C.C. *The Life of Marie Amélie, the Last Queen of the French* (D. Appleton &

Co. 1910)

[34] Abbott, Jacob *Louis Philippe* (Harper & Brothers 1901)

[35] Genlis, Stéphanie Félicité *Memoirs de Mme Genlis Vol 8* (H. Colburn 1826)

[36] Genlis, Stéphanie Félicité *Memoirs de Mme Genlis Vol 8* (H. Colburn 1826)

[37] Dyson, C.C. *The Life of Marie Amélie, the Last Queen of the French* (D. Appleton & Co. 1910)

[38] Castille, Hippolyte *Les Princes de la Famille d'Orléans* (E. Dentu 1859)

[39] Vandam, Albert Dresden *An Englishman in Paris* (D. Appleton & Company 1893)

[40] Radziwill, Princess Catherine *France, From Behind the Veil* (Cassell & Co. 1914)

[41] Bush, Annie Forbes *Memoirs of the Queen of France* (Hart 1852)

[42] Juste, Theodore (translated by Robert Black) *Memoirs of Leopold I, King of the Belgians Vol 1* (Samson, Lowe and Marston 1868)

[43] Merode, Comte Felix de *Memoirs* (publisher unknown)

[44] Bazin, René *Le Duc de Nemours* (Emil Paul 1907)

[45] Sharpe T.B. *Sharpe's London Magazine Vol 1* (1846)

[46] Cox, William *His Royal Highness, the Comte de Paris* (Sabiston & Murray 1890)

[47] Harcourt, Jeanne Paule Baupoil *Memoir of the Duchesse d'Orleans* (C. Scribner 1862)

[48] Martin, Theodore *The Life of His Royal Highness, the Prince Consort Vol 1* (D. Appleton & Co. 1875)

[49] Dyson, C.C. *The Life of Marie Amélie, the Last Queen of the French* (D. Appleton & Co. 1910)

[50] Bazin, René *Le Duc de Nemours* (Emil Paul 1907)

[51] Motley, John Lothrop *The Correspondence of John Lothrop Motley Vol. 1* (John Murray 1889)

[52] Dyson, C.C. *The Life of Marie Amélie, the Last Queen of the French* (D. Appleton & Co. 1910)

[53] Daudet, Ernest *Le Duc D'Aumale 1822-1897* (E. Plon 1898)

[54] Metternich, Prince (translated by Gerard W. Smith) *Memoirs of Prince Metternich Vol. 5* (Richard Bentley & Son 1882)

[55] Lieven, Princess Dorothea (translated by Guy le Strange) *Correspondence of Princess Lieven & Earl Grey Vol 2* (Richard Bentley 1890)

[56] Dumas, Alexander (translated by R. S. Garnett) *The Last King* (Stanley, Paul & Co. 1915)

[57] Journal of the Statistical Society of London, Volume 2 1839 *An Account of Algeria, or the French Provinces in Africa*

[58] Metternich, Prince Richard (editor) translated by G.W. Smith *Memoirs of Prince Metternich Vol. 5* (Richard Bentley & Son 1880)

[59] Metternich, Prince Richard (editor) translated by G.W. Smith *Memoirs of Prince Metternich Vol. 5* (Richard Bentley & Son 1880)

[60] Greville, Charles C.F. *The Greville Memoirs Vol 1.* (Longmans, Green & Co. 1874)

[61] Trollope, Anthony *Lord Palmerston* (W. Isbister, 1882)

[62] Greville, Charles C.F. *The Greville Memoirs Vol II.* (Longmans, Green & Co. 1875)

[63] Lieven, Princess Dorothea (translated by Guy le Strange) *Correspondence of Princess Lieven & Earl Grey Vol 3* (Richard Bentley 1890)

[64] Benson, Arthur & Esher, Viscount *The Letters of Queen Victoria Vol 1* (John Murray 1907)

[65] Esher, Viscount *Queen Victoria In Her Girlhood & Womanhood Vol 1* (Longmans, Green & Co. 1912)

[66] Poore, Benjamin *The Rise & Fall of Louis-Philippe, ex-King of the French* (W.D. Ticknor & Company 1848)

[67] Benson, Arthur & Esher, Viscount *The Letters of Queen Victoria Vol 1* (John Murray 1907)

[68] Lieven, Princess Dorothea (translated by Guy le Strange) *Correspondence of Princess Lieven & Earl Grey Vol 3* (Richard Bentley 1890)

[69] Benson, Arthur & Esher, Viscount *The Letters of Queen Victoria Vol 1* (John Murray 1907)

[70] Benson, Arthur & Esher, Viscount *The Letters of Queen Victoria Vol 1* (John Murray 1907)

[71] Martin, Theodore *The Life of His Royal Highness, the Prince Consort Vol 1* (D. Appleton 1875)

[72] Martin, Theodore *The Life of His Royal Highness, the Prince Consort Vol 1* (D. Appleton 1875)

[73] Benson, Arthur & Esher, Viscount *The Letters of Queen Victoria Vol 1* (John Murray 1907)

[74] Weigall, Lady Rose *Correspondence Of Lady Burghersh With The Duke Of Wellington* (John Murray 1903)

[75] Benson, Arthur & Esher, Viscount *The Letters of Queen Victoria Vol 2* (John Murray 1911)

[76] Lovett, Richard *The History of the London Missionary Society, 1795-1895* (Henry Frowde 1899)

[77] Lyttelton, Lady Sarah *Correspondence of Sarah Spencer, Lady Lyttelton* (John Murray 1912)

[78] Punch Vol 4-7 (1844)

[79] Trollope, Anthony *Lord Palmerston* (W. Isbister, 1882)

[80] Martin, Theodore *The Life of His Royal Highness, the Prince Consort Vol 1* (D. Appleton 1875)

[81] Ernest II, Duke of Saxe-Coburg & Gotha *Memoirs of Ernest II, Duke of Saxe-Coburg & Gotha Vol II* (Remington & Co. 1888)

[82] Ernest II, Duke of Saxe-Coburg & Gotha *Memoirs of Ernest II, Duke of Saxe-Coburg & Gotha Vol II* (Remington & Co. 1888)

[83] Raikes, Thomas *The Private Correspondence of Thomas Raikes with the Duke of Wellington and other Distinguished Contemporaries* (Richard Bentley 1861)

[84] Stockmar, Ernest von *Memoirs of Baron Stockmar Vol 2* (Longmans 1873)

[85] Fontenoy, Marquise de *Within Royal Palaces* (Hubbard 1892)

[86] Benson, Arthur & Esher, Viscount *The Letters of Queen Victoria Vol II* (John Murray 1907)

[87] Martin, Theodore *The Life of His Royal Highness, the Prince Consort Vol 2* (Smith, Elder & Co. 1876)

[88] Brougham, Henry *The Life & Times of Henry Brougham Vol 3* (William Blackwood & Sons 1871)

[89] Poore, Benjamin *The Rise & Fall of Louis-Philippe, ex-King of the French* (W.D. Ticknor & Company 1848)

[90] Brougham, Henry *The Life & Times of Henry Brougham Vol 3* (William Blackwood & Sons 1871)

[91] Nassau, William Senior *Conversations with M. Thiers, M. Guizot, and Other Distinguished Persons, During the Second Empire* (Hurst & Blackett 1878)

[92] Fraser, Sir William *Napoleon III: My Recollections* (Sampson, Low, Marston & Company

[93] Benson, Arthur & Esher, Viscount *The Letters of Queen Victoria Vol II* (John Murray 1907)

[94] Stockmar, Ernest von *Memoirs of Baron Stockmar Vol 2* (Longmans 1873)

[95] Benson, Arthur & Esher, Viscount *The Letters of Queen Victoria Vol 2* (John Murray 1908)

[96] St. John, Percy Bolingbroke *The French Revolution 1848* (R. Bentley 1848)

[97] Martin, Theodore *The Life of His Royal Highness, the Prince Consort Vol 2* (Smith, Elder & Co. 1876)

[98] Benson, Arthur & Esher, Viscount *The Letters of Queen Victoria Vol II* (John Murray 1907)

[99] Lyttelton, Lady Sarah *Correspondence of Sarah Spencer, Lady Lyttelton* (John

Murray 1912)

[100] Martin, Theodore *The Life of the Prince Consort Vol 2* (D. Appelton & Co. 1876)

[101] Blanc, Louis, *1848 Historical Revelations Inscribed to Lord Normanby* (Chapman & Hall 1858)

[102] Greville, Charles C.F. *The Greville Memoirs Vol II.* (Longmans, Green & Co. 1875)

[103] Greville, Charles C.F. *The Greville Memoirs Vol II.* (Longmans, Green & Co. 1875)

[104] Dyson, C.C. *The Life of Marie Amélie, the Last Queen of the French* (D. Appleton & Co. 1910)

[105] Dumas, Alexander (translated by R. S. Garnett) *The Last King* (Stanley, Paul & Co. 1915)

[106] Trollope, Anthony *Lord Palmerston* (W. Isbister, 1882)

[107] Dumas, Alexander (translated by R. S. Garnett) *The Last King* (Stanley, Paul & Co. 1915)

[108] Martin, Theodore *The Life of His Royal Highness, the Prince Consort Vol 2* (Smith, Elder & Co. 1876)

[109] Flers, Marquis de (translated by Constance Majendie) *Le Comte de Paris* (W.H. Allen 1889)

[110] Martin, Theodore, *The Life of His Royal Highness, the Prince Consort Vol 4* (Smith, Elder & Co. 1879)

[111] Martin, Theodore, *The Life of His Royal Highness, the Prince Consort Vol 4* (Smith, Elder & Co. 1879)

[112] Benson, Arthur & Esher, Viscount *The Letters of Queen Victoria Vol 3* (John Murray 1908)

[113] Martin, Theodore, *The Life of His Royal Highness, the Prince Consort Vol 4* (Smith, Elder & Co. 1879)

[114] Fulford, Roger (editor) *Dearest Child, Letters Between Queen Victoria & the Princess Royal 1858-1861* (Evans Brothers 1964)

[115] Dyson, C.C. *The Life of Marie Amélie, the Last Queen of the French* (D. Appleton & Co. 1910)

[116] Helena Victoria, Princess (editor) *Alice Grand Duchess of Hesse, Biographical Sketch and Letters* (John Murray 1884)

[117] D'Abrantès, Duchesse *Memoirs of Napoleon, His Court and Family Vol 1* (Richard Bentley 1854)

[118] Derosne, Bernard *Hortense, Queen Consort of Louis Bonaparte, King of Holland, 1783-1837* (Hurst & Blackett 1900)

[119] Hill, Pascoe Grenfell *The Life of Napoleon III* (E. Moxon, Son & Co. 1869)

[120] Malmesbury, James Harris, Earl of *Memoirs of an Ex-Minister: An Autobiography* (Longmans, Green & Co. 1885)

[121] Vandam, Albert Dresden *An Englishman in Paris* (D. Appleton & Company 1893)

[122] Derosne, Bernard *Hortense, Queen Consort of Louis Bonaparte, King of Holland, 1783-1837* (Hurst & Blackett 1900)

[123] Hill, Pascoe Grenfell *The Life of Napoleon III* (E. Moxon, Son & Co. 1869)

[124] Greenwood, Grace, *Queen Victoria in her Girlhood and Womanhood* (Low, Marston, Searle & Rivington 1884)

[125] Malmesbury, James Harris, Earl of *Memoirs of an Ex-Minister: An Autobiography* (Longmans, Green & Co. 1885)

[126] Blanc, Louis, *1848 Historical Revelations Inscribed to Lord Normanby* (Chapman & Hall 1858)

[127] Walford, Edward *Louis Napoleon: Ex-Emperor of the French* (George Routledge & Sons 1873)

[128] Hill, Pascoe Grenfell *The Life of Napoleon III* (E. Moxon, Son & Co. 1869)

[129] Sheppard, Edgar (editor) *George, Duke of Cambridge – A Memoir of his Private Life Based on the Journals and Letters of His Royal Highness* (Longmans, Green & Co. 1906)

[130] Walford, Edward *Louis Napoleon: Ex-Emperor of the French* (George Routledge &

Sons 1873)

[131] Maxwell, Sir Herbert *The Life and Letters of George William Frederick, Fourth Earl of Clarendon, K.G., G.C.B. Vol 1.* (Edward Arnold 1913)

[132] Walford, Edward *Louis Napoleon: Ex-Emperor of the French* (George Routledge & Sons 1873)

[133] Blanc, Louis, *1848 Historical Revelations Inscribed to Lord Normanby* (Chapman & Hall 1858)

[134] De Puy, Henry W. *Louis Napoleon & His Times* (Buffalo, Phinney & Co. 1852)

[135] Trollope, Anthony *Lord Palmerston* (W. Isbister, 1882)

[136] Martin, Theodore *The Life of the Prince Consort Vol 2* (D. Appleton & Co. 1876)

[137] Martin, Theodore *The Life of the Prince Consort Vol 2* (D. Appleton & Co. 1876)

[138] Benson, Arthur & Esher, Viscount *The Letters of Queen Victoria Vol 2* (John Murray 1907)

[139] Benson, Arthur & Esher, Viscount *The Letters of Queen Victoria Vol 3* (John Murray 1908)

[140] Benson, Arthur & Esher, Viscount *The Letters of Queen Victoria Vol 3* (John Murray 1908)

[141] Sergeant, Philip Walsingham *The Princess Mathilde Bonaparte* (S. Paul & Co. 1915)

[142] Louée, Frederic (translated by Bryan O'Donnell) *The Life of an Empress* (E. Nash 1908)

[143] Soissons, Comte de *The True Story of the Empress Eugénie* (John Lane 1921)

[144] Walford, Edward *Louis Napoleon: Ex-Emperor of the French* (George Routledge & Sons 1873)

[145] Louée, Frederic (translated by Bryan O'Donnell) *The Life of an Empress* (E. Nash 1908)

[146] Greville, Charles, *The Greville Memoirs Vol VII* (Longmans, Green & Co. 1911)

[147] Vandam, Albert Dresden *An Englishman in Paris* (D. Appleton & Company 1893)

[148] Radziwill, Princess Catherine *France, From Behind the Veil* (Cassell & Co. 1914)

[149] Smythe, Ethel *Streaks of Life* (Longmans 1921)

[150] Hay, John *Castilian Days* (Houghton, Mifflin & Co. 1899)

[151] Smythe, Ethel *Streaks of Life* (Longmans 1921)

[152] Evans, Thomas Wiltberger (edited by Edward Crane) *Memoirs of Dr Thomas Evans: The Second Empire* (D. Appleton & Co. 1905)

[153] Paléologue, Maurice *The Tragic Empress; Intimate Conversations with the Empress Eugénie, 1901-1911* (Thornton Butterworth 1920)

[154] Smythe, Ethel *Streaks of Life* (Longmans 1921)

[155] Fraser, Sir William *Napoleon III: My Recollections* (Sampson, Low, Marston & Company

[156] Mayne, F. *The Life of Nicholas I, Emperor of Russia* (Longmans, Brown & Green 1855)

[157] Sheppard, George Edgar *George, Duke of Cambridge: A Memoir of His Private Life Based on his Journals and Correspondence* (Longmans, Green & Co. 1906)

[158] Longmore, Sir Thomas *The Sanitary Contrasts of the British and French Armies During the Crimean War* (C. Griffin 1883)

[159] Skene, James Henry *With Lord Stratford in the Crimean War* (R. Bentley 1883)

[160] Skene, James Henry *With Lord Stratford in the Crimean War* (R. Bentley 1883)

[161] Maxwell, Sir Herbert *The Life and Letters of George William Frederick, Fourth Earl of Clarendon, K.G., G.C.B. Vol 2.* (Edward Arnold 1913)

[162] Skene, James Henry *With Lord Stratford in the Crimean War* (R. Bentley 1883)

[163] Martin, Theodore *The Life of the Prince Consort Vol. 3* (D. Appleton 1875)

[164] Martin, Theodore *The Life of the Prince Consort Vol. 3* (D. Appleton 1875)

[165] Martin, Theodore *The Life of the Prince Consort Vol. 3* (D. Appleton 1875)

[166] Radziwill, Princess Catherine *France, From Behind the Veil* (Cassell & Co. 1914)

[167] Bolitho, Hector *Further Letters of Queen Victoria* (Thornton Butterworth 1938)

241

[168] Bolitho, Hector *Further Letters of Queen Victoria* (Thornton Butterworth 1938)

[169] Stanley, Lady Augusta *The Letters of Lady Augusta Stanley* – edited by the Dean of Windsor and Hector Bolitho (Gerald Howe Ltd. 1927)

[170] Greville, Charles, *The Greville Memoirs Vol VII* (Longmans, Green & Co. 1911)

[171] Fraser, Sir William *Napoleon III: My Recollections* (Sampson, Low, Marston & Company

[172] Saint-Amand, Arthur Imbert de *The Court of the Second Empire* (Charles Scribner's Son 1898)

[173] Greville, Charles, *The Greville Memoirs Vol VII* (Longmans, Green & Co. 1911)

[174] Benson, Arthur & Esher, Viscount *The Letters of Queen Victoria Vol III* (John Murray 1908)

[175] Benson, Arthur & Esher, Viscount *The Letters of Queen Victoria Vol III* (John Murray 1908)

[176] Stanley, Lady Augusta *The Letters of Lady Augusta Stanley* – edited by the Dean of Windsor and Hector Bolitho (Gerald Howe Ltd. 1927)

[177] Benson, Arthur & Esher, Viscount *The Letters of Queen Victoria Vol III* (John Murray 1908)

[178] Fleury, Comte Maurice *Memoirs of the Empress Eugénie* (D. Appleton & Co. 1920)

[179] Malmesbury, James, Earl of *Memoirs of an Ex-Minister, An Autobiography* (Longmans, Green & Co. 1885)

[180] Fleury, Comte Maurice *Memoirs of the Empress Eugénie* (D. Appleton & Co. 1920)

[181] Barthez, Doctor Ernest. *The Empress Eugénie and Her Circle* (Brentano's 1913)

[182] Smythe, Ethel *Streaks of Life* (Longmans 1921)

[183] Barthez, Doctor Ernest. *The Empress Eugénie and Her Circle* (Brentano's 1913)

[184] Radziwill, Princess Catherine *France, From Behind the Veil* (Cassell & Co. 1914)

[185] Lano, Pierre de (trans. by Helen Hunt Johnson) *Emperor Napoleon III* (Dodd. Meade & Co. 1895)

[186] Evans, Thomas Wiltberger (edited by Edward Crane) *Memoirs of Dr Thomas Evans: The Second Empire* (D. Appleton & Co. 1905)

[187] Lano, Pierre de (trans. by Helen Hunt Johnson) *Emperor Napoleon III* (Dodd. Meade & Co. 1895)

[188] Fleury, Comte Maurice *Memoirs of the Empress Eugénie* (D. Appleton & Co. 1920)

[189] Filon, Augustin *Recollections of the Prince Imperial* (Macmillan 1913)

[190] Barthez, Doctor Ernest. *The Empress Eugénie and Her Circle* (Brentano's 1913)

[191] Barthez, Doctor Ernest. *The Empress Eugénie and Her Circle* (Brentano's 1913)

[192] Filon, Augustin *Recollections of the Prince Imperial* (Macmillan 1913)

[193] Barlee, Ellen *The Life of the Prince Imperial* (Griffith 1880)

[194] Fulford, Roger (editor) *Your Dear Letter: Private Correspondence of Queen Victoria and the Crown Princess of Prussia 1865-1871* (Evans Bros. 1971)

[195] Soissons, Comte de *The True Story of the Empress Eugénie* (John Lane 1921)

[196] Fraser, Sir William *Napoleon III: My Recollections* (Sampson, Low, Marston & Company

[197] Paléologue, Maurice *The Tragic Empress; Intimate Conversations with the Empress Eugénie, 1901-1911* (Thornton Butterworth 1920)

[198] Viel Castel, Horace *Memoirs of Count Horace de Viel Castel* (Remington & Co. 1888)

[199] Walpole, Sir Spencer *The History of Twenty-Five Years Vol 1* (Longmans, Green & Co. 1904)

[200] Paléologue, Maurice *The Tragic Empress; Intimate Conversations with the Empress Eugénie, 1901-1911* (Thornton Butterworth 1920)

[201] Fleischmann, Hector *Napoleon III and the Women He Loved* (Holden & Hardingham 1915)

[202] Greville, Charles, *The Greville Memoirs Vol VII* (Longmans, Green & Co. 1911)

[203] Lano, Pierre de (translated by Ethelred Taylor) *The Empress Eugénie* (Dodd, Mead & Co. 1894)

[204] Trevelyan, George M. *Garibaldi & The Thousand* (Longmans, Green & Co. 1909)
[205] Dicey, Edward *Victor Emmanuel* (G.P. Putnam's 1882)
[206] Trollope, Anthony *Lord Palmerston* (W. Isbister, 1882)
[207] Greville, Charles, *The Greville Memoirs Vol VII* (Longmans, Green & Co. 1911)
[208] Martinengo-Cesaresco, Countess Evelyn *Cavour* (Macmillan 1904)
[209] Viel Castel, Horace *Memoirs of Count Horace de Viel Castel* (Remington & Co. 1888)
[210] Greville, Charles, *The Greville Memoirs Vol VII* (Longmans, Green & Co. 1911)
[211] Godkin, Georgina Sarah *The Life of Victor Emmanuel II Vol. 1* (Macmillan & Co. 1879)
[212] Taylor, John M. *Maximilian & Carlota; A Story of Imperialism* (G.P. Putnam's & Sons 1894)
[213] Benson, Arthur & Esher, Viscount *The Letters of Queen Victoria Vol III* (John Murray 1908)
[214] Viel Castel, Horace *Memoirs of Count Horace de Viel Castel* (Remington & Co. 1888)
[215] Louée, Frederic (translated by Bryan O'Donnell) *The Life of an Empress* (E. Nash 1908)
[216] Thompson, J.M. *Louis Napoleon & The Second Empire* (The Noonday Press 1955)
[217] Motley, John Lothrop *The Correspondence of John Lothrop Motley Vol. 2* (John Murray 1889)
[218] Alvensleben, Baron Maximilian *With Maximilian in Mexico* (Longmans 1867)
[219] Taylor, John M. *Maximilian & Carlota; A Story of Imperialism* (G.P. Putnam's & Sons 1894)
[220] Salm Salm, Prince Felix *My Diary in Mexico Vol 2* (Richard Bentley 1868)
[221] Fulford, Roger (Editor) *Your Dear Letter; Private Correspondence of Queen Victoria and the Crown Princess of Prussia, 1865-71* (Evans 1971)
[222] Salm Salm, Prince Felix *My Diary in Mexico Vol 2* (Richard Bentley 1868)
[223] Fulford, Roger (Editor) *Your Dear Letter; Private Correspondence of Queen Victoria and the Crown Princess of Prussia, 1865-71* (Evans 1971)
[224] Louée, Frederic (translated by Bryan O'Donnell) *The Life of an Empress* (E. Nash 1908)
[225] Paléologue, Maurice *The Tragic Empress; Intimate Conversations with the Empress Eugénie, 1901-1911* (Thornton Butterworth 1920)
[226] Walpole, Sir Spencer *History of Twenty-Five Years Vol. 2* (Longmans, Green & Co. 1904)
[227] Greville, Charles, *The Greville Memoirs Vol VII* (Longmans, Green & Co. 1911)
[228] Balfour, Lady Betty (editor) *Personal & Literary Letters of Robert, First Earl of Lytton Vol. I* (Longmans, Green & Co. 1906)
[229] Hansard *HC Deb 12 March 1860 vol 157 cc343-54*
[230] Martin, Theodore *The Life of the Prince Consort Vol. 5* (Smith, Elder & Co. 1880)
[231] Martinengo-Cesaresco, Countess Evelyn *Cavour* (Macmillan 1904)
[232] Walpole, Spencer *The Life of Lord John Russell* (Longmans, Green & Co. 1891)
[233] Arrivabene, Carlo *Italy Under Victor Emmanuel* (Hurst & Blackett 1862)
[234] Thompson, J.M. *Louis Napoleon & The Second Empire* (The Noonday Press 1955)
[235] Martin, Theodore *The Life of the Prince Consort Vol. 5* (Smith, Elder & Co. 1880)
[236] Martin, Theodore *The Life of the Prince Consort Vol. 5* (Smith, Elder & Co. 1880)
[237] Thompson, J.M. *Louis Napoleon & The Second Empire* (The Noonday Press 1955)
[238] Trollope, Anthony *Lord Palmerston* (W. Isbister, 1882)
[239] Walpole, Sir Spencer *History of Twenty-Five Years Vol. 2* (Longmans, Green & Co. 1904)
[240] Poschinger, Margarete (translated by Sidney Whitman) *Life of the Emperor Frederick* (Harper & Bros. 1901)
[241] Hohenlohe-Schillingsfürst, Chlodwig, Prince of *Memoirs of Prince Chlodwig of Hohenlohe-Schillingsfürst* (William Heinemann 1906)

[242] Paléologue, Maurice *The Tragic Empress; Intimate Conversations with the Empress Eugénie, 1901-1911* (Thornton Butterworth 1920)
[243] Paléologue, Maurice *The Tragic Empress; Intimate Conversations with the Empress Eugénie, 1901-1911* (Thornton Butterworth 1920)
[244] Ponsonby, Frederick (editor) *Letters of the Empress Frederick* (Macmillan 1928)
[245] Benedetti, Count Vincent *Studies in Diplomacy* (Macmillan 1896)
[246] Paléologue, Maurice *The Tragic Empress; Intimate Conversations with the Empress Eugénie, 1901-1911* (Thornton Butterworth 1920)
[247] Benedetti, Count Vincent *Studies in Diplomacy* (Macmillan 1896)
[248] Stoddart, Jane *The Life of Empress Eugénie* (E.P. Dutton & Co. 1906)
[249] Evans, Thomas Wiltberger (edited by Edward Crane) *Memoirs of Dr Thomas Evans: The Second Empire* (D. Appleton & Co. 1905)
[250] Paléologue, Maurice *The Tragic Empress; Intimate Conversations with the Empress Eugénie, 1901-1911* (Thornton Butterworth 1920)
[251] Graheme, F.R. *Life of Alexander II; Emperor of All the Russias* (W.H. Allen 1883)
[252] Jerrold, Blanchard *The Life of Napoleon III Vol 3* (Longmans, Green & Co. 1877)
[253] Radziwill, Princess Catherine *France, From Behind the Veil* (Cassell & Co. 1914)
[254] Sala, George Augustus *The Life & Adventures of George Augustus Sala Vol. II* (Charles Scribner's Sons 1895)
[255] Sala, George Augustus *The Life & Adventures of George Augustus Sala Vol. II* (Charles Scribner's Sons 1895)
[256] De Puy, Henry W. *Louis Napoleon & His Times* (Buffalo, Phinney & Co. 1852)
[257] Vandam, Albert *Personal History of the Second Empire, Vol VI – The Restoration of Paris* (North American Review 1895)
[258] Sala, George Augustus *The Life & Adventures of George Augustus Sala Vol. II* (Charles Scribner's Sons 1895)
[259] Fulford, Roger (Editor) *Your Dear Letter; Private Correspondence of Queen Victoria and the Crown Princess of Prussia, 1865-71* (Evans 1971)
[260] Graheme, F.R. *Life of Alexander II; Emperor of All the Russias* (W.H. Allen 1883)
[261] Cowdin, Elliot C. *The Paris Universal Exposition of 1867* (C. Van Benthuysen & Sons 1868)
[262] Paléologue, Maurice *The Tragic Empress; Intimate Conversations with the Empress Eugénie, 1901-1911* (Thornton Butterworth 1920)
[263] Fraser, Sir William *Napoleon III: My Recollections* (Sampson, Low, Marston & Company
[264] Paléologue, Maurice *The Tragic Empress; Intimate Conversations with the Empress Eugénie, 1901-1911* (Thornton Butterworth 1920)
[265] Malmesbury, James Harris, Earl of *Memoirs of an Ex-Minister: An Autobiography* (Longmans, Green & Co. 1885)
[266] Fleury, Comte Maurice *Memoirs of the Empress Eugénie* (D. Appleton & Co. 1920)
[267] Evans, Thomas Wiltberger (edited by Edward Crane) *Memoirs of Dr Thomas Evans: The Second Empire* (D. Appleton & Co. 1905)
[268] Fleury, Comte Maurice *Memoirs of the Empress Eugénie* (D. Appleton & Co. 1920)
[269] Fulford, Roger (Editor) *Your Dear Letter; Private Correspondence of Queen Victoria and the Crown Princess of Prussia, 1865-71* (Evans 1971)
[270] Fulford, Roger (Editor) *Your Dear Letter; Private Correspondence of Queen Victoria and the Crown Princess of Prussia, 1865-71* (Evans 1971)
[271] Benedetti, Count Vincent *Studies in Diplomacy* (Macmillan 1896)
[272] Ollivier, Emile (translated by George Burnham Ives) *The Franco-Prussian War* (Little Brown 1918)
[273] Paléologue, Maurice *The Tragic Empress; Intimate Conversations with the Empress Eugénie, 1901-1911* (Thornton Butterworth 1920)
[274] Fleury, Comte Maurice *Memoirs of the Empress Eugénie* (D. Appleton & Co. 1920)
[275] Ollivier, Emile (translated by George Burnham Ives) *The Franco-Prussian War* (Little Brown 1918)

[276] Ponsonby, Frederick (editor) *Letters of the Empress Frederick* (Macmillan 1928)
[277] Helena Victoria, Princess (editor) *Alice Grand Duchess of Hesse, Biographical Sketch and Letters* (John Murray 1884)
[278] Ponsonby, Frederick (editor) *Letters of the Empress Frederick* (Macmillan 1928)
[279] Barlee, Ellen *The Life of the Prince Imperial* (Griffith 1880)
[280] Fulford, Roger (Editor) *Your Dear Letter; Private Correspondence of Queen Victoria and the Crown Princess of Prussia, 1865-71* (Evans 1971)
[281] Balfour, Lady Betty (editor) *Personal & Literary Letters of Robert, First Earl of Lytton Vol. I* (Longmans, Green & Co. 1906)
[282] Raymond, Dora Neill *British Policy and Opinion During the Franco-Prussian War* (Longmans, Green & Co. 1921)
[283] Anonymous *The Empress Frederick; A Memoir* (Dodd, Mead & Co. 1913)
[284] Sergeant, Philip *The Last Empress of the French* (T.W. Laurie 1910)
[285] Lano, Pierre de (translated by Johnson, Helen Hunt) *The Emperor Napoleon III* (Dodd, Mead & Co. 1895)
[286] Jerrold, Blanchard *The Life of Napoleon III Vol IV* (Longmans 1874)
[287] Evans, Thomas Wiltberger (edited by Edward Crane) *Memoirs of Dr Thomas Evans: The Second Empire* (D. Appleton & Co. 1905)
[288] Evans, Thomas Wiltberger (edited by Edward Crane) *Memoirs of Dr Thomas Evans: The Second Empire* (D. Appleton & Co. 1905)
[289] Lano, Pierre de (translated by Ethelred Taylor) *Empress Eugenie* (Dodd, Mead & Co. 1894)
[290] Frederick III, German Emperor *The Suppressed Diary of Frederick III* (Pall Mall Gazette 1888)
[291] Frederick III, German Emperor *The Suppressed Diary of Frederick III* (Pall Mall Gazette 1888)
[292] Bolitho, Hector *Further Letters of Queen Victoria* (Thornton Butterworth 1938)
[293] Balfour, Lady Betty (editor) *Personal & Literary Letters of Robert, First Earl of Lytton Vol. I* (Longmans, Green & Co. 1906)
[294] Radziwill, Princess Catherine *France, From Behind the Veil* (Cassell & Co. 1914)
[295] Evans, Thomas Wiltberger (edited by Edward Crane) *Memoirs of Dr Thomas Evans: The Second Empire* (D. Appleton & Co. 1905)
[296] Evans, Thomas Wiltberger (edited by Edward Crane) *Memoirs of Dr Thomas Evans: The Second Empire* (D. Appleton & Co. 1905)
[297] Bolitho, Hector *Further Letters of Queen Victoria* (Thornton Butterworth 1938)
[298] Legge, Edward *The Empress Eugénie 1870-1910* (Harper & Brothers 1910)
[299] Filon, Augustin *Recollections of the Prince Imperial* (Macmillan 1913)
[300] Legge Edward *The Comedy & Tragedy of the Second Empire* (Harper & Brothers 1911)
[301] Barlee, Ellen *The Life of the Prince Imperial* (Griffith 1880)
[302] Fraser, Sir William *Napoleon III: My Recollections* (Sampson, Low, Marston & Company
[303] Filon, Augustin *Recollections of the Prince Imperial* (Macmillan 1913)
[304] Bolitho, Hector *Further Letters of Queen Victoria* (Thornton Butterworth 1938)
[305] Filon, Augustin *Recollections of the Empress Eugénie* (Funk & Wagnalls Company 1921)
[306] Sala, George Augustus *The Life & Adventures of George Augustus Sala Vol. II* (Charles Scribner's Sons 1895)
[307] Soissons, Comte de *The True Story of the Empress Eugénie* (John Lane 1921)
[308] Filon, Augustin *Recollections of the Empress Eugénie* (Funk & Wagnalls Company 1921)
[309] Sheppard, Edgar (editor) *George, Duke of Cambridge – A Memoir of his Private Life Based on the Journals and Letters of His Royal Highness* (Longmans, Green & Co. 1906)
[310] Filon, Augustin *Recollections of the Prince Imperial* (Macmillan 1913)

[311] Filon, Augustin *Recollections of the Prince Imperial* (Macmillan 1913)

[312] Wilmot, Alexander *History of the Zulu War* (Richardson & Best 1880)

[313] Wilmot, Alexander *History of the Zulu War* (Richardson & Best 1880)

[314] Filon, Augustin *Recollections of the Prince Imperial* (Macmillan 1913)

[315] Sheppard, Edgar (editor) *George, Duke of Cambridge – A Memoir of his Private Life Based on the Journals and Letters of His Royal Highness* (Longmans, Green & Co. 1906)

[316] Filon, Augustin *Recollections of the Prince Imperial* (Macmillan 1913)

[317] Sheppard, Edgar (editor) *George, Duke of Cambridge – A Memoir of his Private Life Based on the Journals and Letters of His Royal Highness* (Longmans, Green & Co. 1906)

[318] Hansard: HC Deb 14 March 1881 vol 259 cc994-1000

[319] Hansard: HC Deb 08 August 1879 vol 249 cc531-80

[320] Buckle, George Earle (editor*) Letters of Queen Victoria Vol. III* (John Murray 1928)

[321] Arthur, Sir George (editor) *The Letters of Lord and Lady Wolseley, 1870-1911* (William Heinemann 1922)

[322] Filon, Augustin *Recollections of the Empress Eugénie* (Funk & Wagnalls Company 1921)

[323] Carey, Agnes *Empress Eugénie in Exile* (The Century Co. 1920)

[324] Legge, Edward *The Empress Eugénie & Her Son* (Dodd, Mead & Co. 1916)

[325] Smythe, Ethel *Streaks of Life* (Longmans 1921)

[326] Marie Louise, Princess *My Memories of Six Reigns* (Evans 1961)

[327] Alice, Princess, Countess of Athlone *For My Grandchildren* (Evans Bros 1966)

[328] Smythe, Ethel *Streaks of Life* (Longmans 1921)

[329] Tschudi, Clara (translated by E. Cope) *Eugénie, Empress of the French* (Macmillan 1906)

[330] Smythe, Ethel *Streaks of Life* (Longmans 1921)

[331] Smythe, Ethel *Streaks of Life* (Longmans 1921)

25244116R00136

Printed in Great Britain
by Amazon